THE FIRST
CLAPHAM SAINTS

A London Village 1600–1720

by

Timothy Walker

ACKNOWLEGEMENTS

M any people have helped in the writing and production of this book, both in providing their own knowledge and improving the presentation; any errors are, of course, all mine.

My daughters read early drafts, as did Marie Christine Kerr and Ian Rodger, and I benefited from their encouragement. Perry Gauci, Patrick Wallis and Linda Peck kindly shared their knowledge of the seventeenth century, and Sandra Cruise, Giles Mandelbrote and Christopher Whittick helped me with some of the more difficult handwriting. It was a pleasure to share enthusiasm for Michael Mitford with Esther Sahle, and there is more scope for using Mitford's time in Clapham to shed light on the contents of his letterbook. Larry Kreitzer contributed information about William Kiffin, and Dorian Gerhold about villas in southwest London. Roger Knight often helped me to organize my thoughts, and his comments on a later draft were particularly helpful. I am very grateful to Rosie Lewis whose editing resulted in considerable improvement to the text.

As many others find, I am greatly indebted to those who maintain archives and are so helpful in enabling their use. The British Library, the National Archives, the Bodleian Library and the London Metropolitan Archives all provided more support than I had a right to expect, as did Dr Williams Library, Lambeth Archives, Wandsworth Heritage Services and the Norfolk Record Office.

I am also very grateful to copyright holders for permission to reproduce a number of images, as below.

The National Portrait Gallery for the portraits of William Bridge and Joseph Hussey

The Fairclough Portrait Collection, University of Leicester, for the portrait of Thomas Lye

Wandsworth Heritage Services for the picture of John Jackson's house, The Cedars

The Victoria and Albert Museum for the image of the maquette of Rebecca Atkins

The cartoon *A Common Councilman of Candlestick ward* ... is by courtesy of the Lewis Walpole Library, Yale University

The portrait of Richard Salwey by Gerard Soest is from a private collection, and I am very grateful to the owners for allowing me to reproduce it here.

For the other images, they are either from the author's own collection or it has not proved possible to trace the owner of any copyright.

Finally, I thank my wife, Anna, for putting up with yet another book and for supporting me in its research and writing.

INDEX TO IMAGES

INDEX TO ILLUSTRATIONS   PAGE

The portraits on the front cover are the coloured version of Illustrations 5 and 6, that is of William and Mary Daniel in the third quarter of the seventeenth century. The building is a print of an aquatint of Clapham Manor House drawn and engraved by John Hassell in 1804, six years after the Malcolm print in Illustration 1.

INTRODUCTION

L
ondon is even now a city of villages, each with its own character and history. Four hundred years ago they were real villages, distinct from the City and separated from it by fields and not very good roads. This book tells the story of one such village during the seventeenth and early eighteenth centuries. That village is Clapham, in Surrey, then four miles southwest of the City of London; the centre of the village moved a mile further away at the end of the eighteenth century as new houses were built around Clapham Common. The village was 100 feet above sea level, with pure air, clean water and good views across the river towards Hampstead. John Evelyn described it as 'Paradisian'.[1]

This book covers the period from 1600 to 1720, a turbulent period that includes the Civil War, Interregnum, Restoration and Glorious Revolution of 1688, and continues until the start of the Hanoverian period, when there is a gap in the source material. Puritans and, later, Nonconformists often found themselves in difficult positions; there were times when they were heavily involved in politics and times when they were excluded and suffered discrimination. All this is observed from the microcosm of the village of Clapham and its inhabitants during that period, including more than 300 of the better-off residents and their families. The vast majority of these were prosperous Puritan or, later, Nonconformist merchants, who continued to run successful businesses whatever the political situation; a very large number of Nonconformist ministers also lived there, sometimes preaching but also working as schoolmasters or doctors.

Clapham has the advantage of being smaller and geographically more isolated from other major villages around London than Hackney, the largest of all, which contained at least four distinct centres of population and had Stoke Newington nearby. This makes it easier to be sure that one is looking at a single village and that the relationships studied do indeed relate to that community. Much of the information available about Clapham in the seventeenth century is now available in searchable computer databases, allowing for the first time the identification and description of almost all the well-off who maintained a house there. The extent of the sources is set out in Appendix 1; it includes parish records and information about the houses and their contents, as well as other records from political, legal, business and family sources, including wills and deeds. Some diaries and letters survive, and there is extensive historical material on Nonconformists.

This detail goes much further than comparable analyses for seventeenth-century villages outside London such as Hampstead, Highgate or Kentish Town, which have little on their seventeenth-century communities.[2] It also allows systematic emphasis on social interaction, in contrast to more architectural studies concerned with the development of villas and landscape around London.[3] A remarkably full picture of the Clapham community emerges, confirming that a group of radical Puritan merchants had houses there during the Civil War and Interregnum and were followed by many other Nonconformist businessmen. Clapham material can be compared with statistical studies of businessmen drawn from a variety of sources, and with work on the characterisation of the rise of the middle classes.[4] This gives an insight into the development of the Nonconformist business class that is particularly important given the paucity of Nonconformist records for the City of London.[5] Detail on Clapham businessmen helps to fill this gap by showing the interaction among a particular group of Puritan or, later, Nonconformist merchants, complementing the studies of their political involvement.[6]

It is therefore possible to answer such questions as what kind of person had a house in Clapham and how much did they use it; what was their relation to London commerce and politics; was there a genuine local community, and if so, how did it manifest itself either socially or in religious belief? The answers show why these people chose Clapham for one of their homes, and changes over time demonstrate the development of the villages around London, the communities that used them, and so of the City of London itself.

Contemporaries recognised Clapham as a centre of Nonconformists after the Restoration. Sir Roger L'Estrange, the Stuart Licenser of the press and a staunch crusader against Nonconformity, had a first brush with Clapham in 1664, when he tried to execute an arrest warrant there for the Nonconformist agitator James Forbes. (He did eventually arrest Forbes, but not in Clapham.) Twenty years later L'Estrange wrote of 'Clapham which the Phanatiques (as Everybody knows) have turned into a kind of Whig-warren.'[7] In this it was comparable to Hackney and Stoke Newington; unlike Hampstead or Putney, it was close enough to Town to allow daily commuting. An analysis of villas just outside London identified it as one of the few villages in 1674 other than Hackney to have a high concentration of large houses;[8] Clapham was also one of the top four places for country residences of aldermen and Common Councilmen of the City of London between 1660 and 1689.[9] The sources for both these claims have their difficulties, and neither can be taken entirely at face value, but they are indicative of Clapham's character.

Clapham had become a centre for Puritan merchants well before the Civil War. They began to move in from 1630, replacing the court and church officials who had lived there earlier. The necessary increase in houses may have been facilitated by the absence of the Lords of the Manor, the Atkins family, who preferred their estate in Buckinghamshire and so were prepared to see their Clapham land developed. Even before the Restoration, almost thirty large houses were occupied by merchants (or their widows), constituting a third of the houses in the village and half its population.

This was a very different demographic structure from the typical country village, which would usually contain at most only three or four gentry families,[10] and Clapham had proportionally many fewer small houses than did most of the villages around London. The Hearth Tax returns of 1664 show that there were few comparable parishes. Chelsea, Kensington, and Brompton had a similar housing structure but were generally patronised by aristocracy and landed gentry rather than by merchants. At no stage did members of the aristocracy live in Clapham, perhaps because its distance from the River Thames meant that it did not have convenient river access to Westminster. Lady Jane Cheyne turned down a house south of the river on the grounds that her cousin Lady Devonshire, who lived at Roehampton, had told her that it cost an extra £100 to live on the wrong side of the river – presumably the cost of frequent crossings.[11] Hackney and Stoke Newington were the only direct comparators to Clapham; Highgate is harder to assess, since it lay on the boundary of two parishes and was a major transport hub.[12] Unlike Clapham, it began with aristocratic patrons, who were only gradually replaced by merchants.

It would have taken up to an hour by horse to travel the four miles from Clapham to the City of London in the 1640s, and possibly a little less, depending on traffic, when stagecoaches became available later in the century. Clapham was therefore different from the Thames-side parishes to the west of London, which were too far away for daily commuting and where many of the merchants' houses lay empty during the winter. There is ample evidence from the late 1640s onwards, drawn from presence at vestry meetings, rate books and entries in the parish register, that Clapham houses were used for at least some of the winter months. In some cases merchants lived most of the time in Clapham, and this was certainly true of those who moved there towards the end of their careers, those who had retired, or widows. By the late 1660s, some had already dropped their London residence and kept a coach to travel to and from the Exchange, or wherever they did business. Daily stagecoaches started in 1680, and by the turn of the eighteenth century at least four ran daily in each direction, going to and from the heart of the City's commercial district.

Access to Clapham from the City involved crossing London Bridge, and the vast majority of the early Clapham merchants with a London residence lived in parishes in the south of the City, near London Bridge, providing a high proportion of the elected Common Councilmen for Bridge Ward. Few if any moved to Clapham without already knowing one or more residents, a pattern continuing for the rest of the century. It was generally more than just an acquaintance:

they might have done business together, had common investments in North America, or served on the same Parliamentary and militia committees; many were related, whether directly or by marriage. They were active politically and in senior positions; some fought in the Civil War or supported it logistically, others were Commissioners of the Navy; they were heavily involved in affairs of finance, including decisions on the sale and taxation of ecclesiastical and Royalist estates, and regularly used their official positions to further their own interests or help their neighbours.

Many of the early residents were first-generation merchants, younger sons of provincial gentry or making their own way from scratch. While they did not all hold identical political views, they were avowedly Protestant. Some were Presbyterian, others favoured the Independents, but that did not prevent them from being business partners or working collectively to change the liturgical arrangements in the parish church, as they had done in their City parishes. They also made Clapham briefly a centre for secular marriage. Their interests in trade informed their politics. They had extensive interests in North America, providing two of the early financiers of the *Mayflower*, investing in many of the companies there, and providing crucial support to Edward Winslow in starting the first Protestant missionary society. Their North American interests made them keen to keep Ireland under Protestant control, and they supported the Adventures in Ireland, being rewarded with extensive land there. There were strong ties to Barbados, too, where many owned at least a share of plantations and were able to leave their sons, as one put it, 'my stock of negroes, utensils and all other appurtenances'.[13] A number participated actively in the start of the slave trade, either as suppliers or as customers.

By the end of the 1650s, Clapham was established as a centre for Puritans with an influential and sympathetic rector, John Arthur. This continued even when Puritan ministers were ejected from their posts in 1662 and forbidden to come within five miles of incorporated towns or the place of their former livings. Arthur was himself ejected, but died shortly afterwards, in 1663, without leaving the village. The next rector, John Gurgany, although Royalist and Anglican, made no effort to prevent Clapham from continuing as a centre of Nonconformity, even though it was well within the five-mile limit of London. It is not clear whether this was because he was in poor health or because he had been chosen for that purpose. His successor, John Savill, was similarly inclined, and for the next sixty years or more Nonconformity flourished in Clapham, with no fewer than fourteen ejected ministers preaching, teaching or practising medicine there, as well as a number of Dissenting schools. Most of the well-off residents can be identified as having Nonconformist interests by contemporary comments as well as by their contacts, membership of Nonconformist organisations or charities, and legacies.

After the Restoration, new businessmen gradually replaced the original merchants or their relations as they or their widows died. As before, many had their business in the southern parishes of the City, but the important links continued to be business or personal connections with existing residents. Shared Nonconformity was a natural consequence of those contacts. Their children intermarried, and neighbours were often asked to act as executors, trustees or guardians, confirming the picture of a real community. Although their political activity steadily declined, with fewer gaining elected posts, they were more active than merchants as a whole or than other Nonconformists. One in five merchants living in Clapham after 1660 was a Common Councilman or alderman, compared with one in seven for all London merchants.[14] One of these aldermen was Dennis Gauden, the Surveyor General of Victualling to the Navy, a businessman who was in close contact with Samuel Pepys; the diary of the latter records a number of visits to Gauden in Clapham. It was this connection that led Pepys to retire to Clapham for the last few years of his life.

In the thirty years following the Glorious Revolution of 1688, the number of larger houses in Clapham almost doubled, and the village began to provide a wider range of facilities. There were at least four inns, a coffee shop, a farrier and a livery stable as well as a blacksmith, shoemakers and apothecaries. Most of the better-off residents were still merchants (or their widows) and many were active as Assistants to the Court of the major trading companies, or what we would call directors. Michael Mitford was an Assistant in the Whig New East India Company, and his letters confirm the business interaction with his neighbours in Clapham, particularly those active in the Russia Company and the Baltic trade. There was a continuing, very substantial presence of Nonconformists active at a national level. Clapham Nonconformist post-holders amounted to a fifth of all London's Presbyterian and Independent office-holders between 1685 and 1715, a remarkable proportion for such a small village.[15] They played a prominent part in the two funds set up to provide for the education of Nonconformist ministers, and as governors of St Thomas' Hospital, long a pillar of the Nonconformist Whig community. Nevertheless, gradually a more diverse population emerged. Lawyers arrived, and bankers were represented by the founders of or very early partners in Hankey's and Martin's banks. There was also a group of rich Huguenot and Flemish merchants building on the business partners and extended relations of the Otgher and Lethieullier families.

The considerable majority of Nonconformists meant that there were few Anglicans and Tories in Clapham, but some Nonconformists were prepared to swear the oath and take Communion occasionally in order to achieve the positions they wanted, as Sir Dennis Gauden will have done to become Sheriff of London in 1669. Local yeomen and farmers provided less than half the parish office-holders, and Clapham merchants were well integrated into the governance of the local community. Thirty-one of the active Nonconformists served as churchwardens between 1660 and 1720, and forty-seven in other parish offices, even though many of them also held office in a City church. This included the Huguenots, of whom three were churchwardens and six held other parish offices, including while they were elders of the Huguenot or Dutch churches in the City. The Nonconformists still subscribed to the collections for the various (Anglican) parish lecturers and for the purchase of silver for the church. It is telling that virtually all legacies to priests or ministers from Clapham testators went to Nonconformist ministers. While John Arthur had been a frequent recipient, John Gurgany got none, and only three people left legacies to John Savill; even those three still left legacies either to the Clapham Nonconformist ministers or to 'ten ministers of the gospel'. Samuel Pepys is the only person to have left legacies solely to the Anglican rector and the lecturer of Clapham.

Many of those who came to Clapham stayed there for a long time, usually until the end of their lives. Twelve of the residents from the Interregnum were still there in 1673, while in 1688 nine houses had been occupied by the same family for more than twenty-five years, six of them since before the Restoration. This pattern continued, and in 1720 there were thirteen houses that had been occupied by the same family for more than twenty-five years; sixteen families had been there at least twenty years and thirty at least ten years. John Gould's widowed sister-in-law lived in the house into which he had moved seventy years earlier (we will hear more of him in later chapters). The houses themselves were clearly not viewed as special, since wills often directed that they be sold to provide a better investment, but it is noticeable how often the next generation continued to use them or found other Clapham houses. Five generations of both the Daniel and Hewer families lived in Clapham.

Given that many Clapham merchants had two homes for at least some part of their life, it is not surprising that they were better off than most merchants. They were wealthy but not extravagantly so until well into the eighteenth century, when people such as the brewer Josiah Nicholson and the merchant Richard Hopkins had homes there. No children married into the aristocracy until well into the eighteenth century. They did not flaunt their wealth, and their clothing appears to have been subdued, as was common for merchants. Only one man's will contains any mention of silk clothes. The avoidance of ostentation extended to keeping close control of the costs of funerals, and their wills often referred to their desire to be buried without pomp or with 'as much privacy as decency will admit'. On the other hand, inventories show the wealth of many of the merchants, with rooms furnished and decorated with current material and fashions; they were early adopters of new forms of furniture or fine china, but had few pictures. Laymen as well as ministers had extensive libraries, and two ministers and one layman had distinguished collections of religious books. They owned substantial property, in the City and elsewhere, but treated country estates as financial rather than emotional investments. They left legacies to charity, but usually of a relatively modest sort and not on a radically different scale from other merchants, although they gave both time and money during their lives.

None of the large seventeenth-century houses in Clapham survives, although a handful of smaller ones remain. There is substantial information about the two largest houses: the Manor

House, owned by the largely absentee Atkins family; and Clapham Place, rebuilt by Sir Dennis Gauden and later bought by William Hewer, who let Samuel Pepys retire there. Otherwise we know only the number of hearths and something of the amount of land associated with them. Eight of the houses were substantial, having fifteen or more hearths, but while some of them had tens of acres of land, others had very little. The lack of architectural information makes it hard to determine whether or not the houses were 'villas', and, apart from Clapham Place, there is no suggestion that they were built by the occupants but rather as a speculation by others. What seems most likely is that the houses were, or could be made, comfortable and relaxing places to avoid the City. Some of the early eighteenth-century terrace housing built for the better off, on what was then the western extremity of the village, near Clapham Common, still remains.

As well as yielding information about the lifestyles of Nonconformist merchants, the story of Clapham illuminates the evolution of the modern suburb. 'Suburb' was originally used to describe the buildings immediately outside the city walls.[16] While the original suburbs of London, such as Southwark and Clerkenwell, have been studied, they could not be regarded as countrified in the seventeenth century.[17] By 1630 Southwark was larger than any city outside London, while by 1664 the population of Clerkenwell had reached almost 10,000. Although an early meaning of the word suburb was 'a place of inferior, debased and especially licentious habits of life', by the middle of the seventeenth century it was also being applied to the superior neighbourhoods of Covent Garden, Bloomsbury and St James's Square. In the eighteenth century the word began to be used for residential areas separated geographically from the City, but whose residents had businesses there and were dependent on the city institutions for commercial, cultural and other activities. These were the first modern suburbs, far enough from the city to give some feel of the country but close enough for regular commuting. They were captured by William Cowper (1731–1800) in his poem 'Retirement' of 1782 as

> Suburban villas, highway-side retreats,
> That dread th'encroachment of our growing streets.

Some have argued that the move to suburbs was driven principally by religion, but the evidence points much more towards a desire for comfortable and available houses with clean water, pure air, attractive surroundings (ideally with a view) and congenial neighbours. In modern terms, it has been cast as an expression of the consumer society of the metropolitan middle class.[18]

The desire to move out of London was summed up in 1724 by Daniel Defoe, himself a Nonconformist:

> these fine houses ... are not, at least very few of them,
> the mansion houses of families, the antient residences of
> ancestors, the capital messuages of the estates, nor have
> the rich possessors any lands to a considerable value about
> them, but these are all houses of retreat, gentlemen's meer
> summer-houses, or citizens' country-houses, whither they
> retire from the hurries of business and from getting money,
> to draw their breath in a clear air, and to divert themselves
> and families, in the hot weather and who return to smoke
> and dirt, sin and seacoal as it was coarsely expressed in
> the busy city. So that in short all this variety, this beauty,
> this glorious show of wealth and plenty, is really a view of
> the luxuriant age which we live in, and of the overflowing
> riches of the citizens, who in their abundance make these
> gay excursions, and live thus deliciously all the summer,
> retiring within themselves in the winter, the better to lay
> up for the next summer's expense.[19]

Defoe wrote this after praising the view from 'the little rising hills around Clapham' and commenting on the 'innumerable number [of fine houses]' there. (An approximation of this view is shown in Illustration 19).

Many have tried to identify the first modern suburb, and a frequent choice is late eighteenth-century Clapham.[20] This work demonstrates that Clapham surely met the tests for being a suburb at least a hundred years earlier, if not by the 1660s. Indeed, given the strong religious views of the early Clapham merchants and their desire to put these into practice in government, it is reasonable to view them as the first Clapham Saints, 150 years before William Wilberforce and the Clapham Sect.

A note on structure

Chapter 1 gives further background on London and Clapham and introduces the concept of 'retiring houses' and the merchants who lived in them. Chapters 2 to 4 cover the period up to the Restoration and describe the Clapham merchants, their political involvement and the effects of Puritans on the parish. Chapters 5 and 6 cover the period after 1660, including the Plague and the Fire of London, and then show how Clapham became a haven for Nonconformists under Charles II. Chapters 7 and 8 continue the analysis until 1720, and show Nonconformists continuing to come to live there. Chapters 9, 10 and 11 are thematic chapters covering the parish community; possessions and expenditure; and marriage and the family. Chapter 12 summarises Clapham in 1720 and shows how it developed in the rest of the eighteenth century, also giving an insight into the extent to which the village as a whole shared the views of the Clapham Sect. Appendices include a description of the sources, a chronology and a list of Clapham residents with dates.

Dates are given with the start of the year at 1 January. Old money is expressed as pounds shillings and pence or £/s/d. The names of Clapham residents are given in **bold** at their first significant mention.

(Endnotes)

1. John Evelyn, letter to Samuel Pepys, 29 January 1703.

2. On Hampstead, see F.M.L. Thompson, *Hampstead: Building a Borough* (Routledge & Kegan Paul, 1974); on Highgate, John Richardson, *Highgate: Its History Since the Fifteenth Century* (Historical Publications, 1983); and on Kentish Town, Gillian Tindall, *The Fields Beneath: The History of One London Village* (Temple Smith, 1977).

3. Caroline Knight, *London's Country Houses* (Phillimore, 2009); John Archer, *Architecture and Suburbia* (University of Minnesota Press, 2005); Elizabeth McKellar, *Landscapes of London* (Yale University Press, 2013).

4. Richard Grassby, *Kinship and Capitalism* (Cambridge University Press, 2001); Richard Grassby, *The Business Community of Seventeenth Century England* (Cambridge University Press, 1995); Perry Gauci, *Emporium of the World* (Continuum Books, 2007). On the middle classes, see Peter Earle, *The Making of the English Middle Class* (Methuen, 1989).

5. Perry Gauci, *The Politics of Trade* (Oxford University Press, 2001), p. 42.

6. Robert Brenner, *Merchants and Revolution* (Verso, 2003); Gary S. De Krey, *London and the Restoration 1659–1683* (Cambridge University Press, 2005), p. 76; Gary S. De Krey, *A Fractured Society* (Oxford University Press, 1985).

7. Sir Roger L'Estrange in *The Observator*, no 163, 6 November 1684.

8. Dorian Gerhold, 'London's Suburban Villas and Mansions 1660–1830', *London Journal*, vol. 34, no. 3 (2009), p. 236.

9. McKellar, *Landscapes of London*, p. 149.

10. Peter Laslett, *The World We Have Lost* (Routledge, 2005), p. 53.

11. Lady Jane Cheyne, letter to her brother Charles Cavendish, Viscount Mansfield, 7 May 1656, Nottingham University Library, Pw 1/88.

12. Richardson, *Highgate*.

13. John Gould's will, 1679. PRO/PROB/11/360/490.

14. Gauci, *Politics of Trade*, p. 84.

15. De Krey, *Franctured Society*.

16. See entry for 'suburb' in the *Oxford English Dictionary*. Its first recorded use was 1380.

17. On Southwark, see Jeremy Boulton, *Neighbourhood and Society* (Cambridge University Press, 1987); on Clerkenwell, see the work of the People in Place Project, www.history.ac.uk/cmh/pip.

18. McKellar, *Landscapes of London*, p. xiv.

19. Daniel Defoe, *A Tour Through the Whole Island of Great Britain* (1724), pp. 125–26.

20. Robert Fishman, *Bourgeois Utopias* (Basic Books, 1987), pp. 51–62.

CHAPTER 1

RETIRING HOUSES AND NEW MERCHANTS

London

Big changes occurred during the early seventeenth century in London, which grew rapidly both in absolute terms and in relation to other cities in England and Europe. While there is still argument about the exact numbers, all agree on the scale of the change. In 1500 London's population was about 50,000; ten European cities were larger and six about the same size.[1] In 1550 it had reached 75,000; by 1600 London had 200,000 residents, and only Paris and Naples were larger, not by much. By 1700 London had reached 575,000 or more and become the largest city in Europe, all but about 70,000 of its inhabitants living outside the walls.[2] This growth continued even while the population of the rest of the country was stagnating. As a result, London's share of England and Wales's population increased from 1.5 per cent to 11.5 per cent. Norwich and Bristol, the two next largest cities, had grown only from about 10,000 in 1500 to 29,000 and 20,000 respectively by 1700.

Given that the death rate was higher in London than anywhere else in the country, and higher than the birth rate, sustaining this population growth required an enormous level of migration into the city. The influx was largely of young people looking for work or becoming apprentices. Many came because improvements in agricultural productivity had made rural jobs harder to find, while the apprentices were often younger sons of the landed classes, whose fathers had used their social networks to find a suitable master and who came to London hoping to make their fortune. There were also immigrants from abroad, estimated at about 10,000 at any one time at the middle of the seventeenth century and swollen later by up to 25,000 Huguenots. London was also a magnet for clergy, by 1640 overwhelmingly university graduates, who were attracted by the theological ferment there and the large number of jobs, including lectureships funded by rich Londoners. Many of them were Puritan, that is, they wanted to 'purify' the church of all Catholic thinking and ritual.

Such growth could not be accommodated within the confines of the city walls, and even by 1600 London had spread outside them into what were known as the suburbs. Most of these were north of the river, including the parishes immediately outside the walls and places such as Clerkenwell further north or Whitechapel to the east.

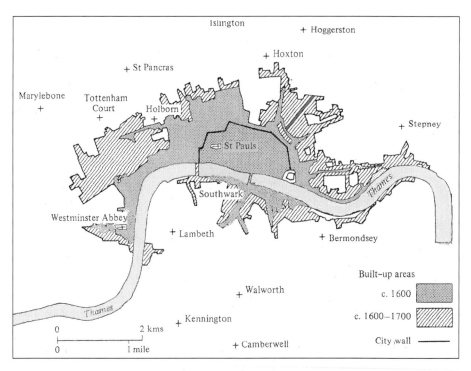

Map 1: Development of London, 1600–1700
Source: A.L. Beier and Roger A.P. Finlay (eds), *London 1500–1700: The Making of the Metropolis*[3]

This is illustrated in Map 1, which shows the extent of the building inside and immediately outside the wall in 1600 and 1700. By the start of the eighteenth century many of the parishes just outside the City walls had populations of over 10,000. South of the river, Southwark's population reached almost 26,000 by 1631 and over 31,000 by 1678, larger than any city in England except London.[4] The London Bills of Mortality, which recorded the weekly number of burials, were extended into outlying parishes. By 1636, as well as Westminster and Southwark, these covered Stepney, Hackney and Islington and, to the south, Lambeth and Newington as well as Rotherhithe and Bermondsey.

Living in the City of London had its disadvantages: seacoal from Newcastle (mineral coal brought by sea, as distinct from charcoal, which was brought by land) had been the fuel of choice since 1600,[5] and produced the 'hellish and dismal cloud ... an impure and thick mist ... corrupting the lungs' described by Evelyn in 1660 but obvious long before that.[6] London was noisy, smelly, dirty, cramped and above all dangerous. Disease was rampant, with plague and smallpox as well as tuberculosis and influenza; mortality rates were consequently high. Children in particular were at risk, and infant mortality stood at over 25 per cent, almost twice as high as in rural areas; only about half the children reached adulthood.[7] Even as late as 1693, Dr Henry Sampson recorded in his day book that people had been congratulating the king for safely passing the 'dangerous' month of September. He pointed out that July to September, 'which used to be our most fatal months' (providing between a third and half of annual deaths), had not even made up a quarter of the total, and that in the last three weeks of September the number of baptisms exceeded that of burials for the first time in forty or more years. In thanking God for preserving London from pestilence for about thirty years, he commented that 'He has not this year visited us with any epidemical sickness, smallpox, dysentery which would have counted their burials in thousands.'[8]

Retiring houses

As London grew larger and richer, there were more wealthy merchants ready and able to spend their money on consumption of one kind or another, including better housing and a healthier environment.

Their wealth came from trading or finance rather than land, the traditional source in the medieval world. They could not leave their business for long, since it was vital to keep in touch with world events and the progress of their shipping, and to maintain contact with their markets, often daily. Unlike traditional landowners, who could delegate the management of their estates, merchants needed to maintain a regular presence in the City. While many purchased estates outside London, often in the part of the country they came from, those represented an investment rather than a place to live.

That still left the question of how to acquire an improved environment, and some merchants looked for 'retiring houses', within easy reach of the City but away from it and the parishes immediately outside the walls. They expected the houses to have access to clean water and pure air, and many were in elevated positions that had the advantage of a good view. The family gained freedom and were removed from the cut and thrust of business and the presence of the apprentices who lived with them in the City. The houses might be used for much of the year, solely in the summer – the most dangerous time for disease – or at weekends, causing the eighteenth-century historian John Strype to give as one of the reasons the Fire of London spread so far and so fast that 'It was Saturday Night when many of the most eminent Citizens, Merchants, and others were retired into the Country, and none but Servants left to look to their City Houses.'[9]

Finding a retiring house in practice meant looking a range of up to four or five miles from the city centre, far enough to be definitely 'country'. Map 2 shows what this meant in practical terms, with the area within four miles of London Bridge shown in yellow and Clapham marked in red.

Many merchants had retiring houses, but the vast majority of those were in the villages north of the City walls, rather than south of the River Thames. A particular centre was Hackney; by 1602 over a hundred citizens of London (that is, members of livery companies and mostly merchants or tradesmen) already had houses there.[10] It was the most popular place for a country residence among the 140 aldermen elected in the first quarter of the seventeenth century, but that was only seven in total, with 'relatively few' south of the Thames.[11] Prominent merchants were so numerous in Hackney that from 1613 its parish government was carried out through a select vestry meeting, which, contrary to usual practice, found it necessary to consult a wider body of parishioners.[12] While some merchants had retired to Hackney, others merely retreated there when convenient, returning to London in years such as 1639 so as to avoid the Hackney element of national tax assessments.[13]

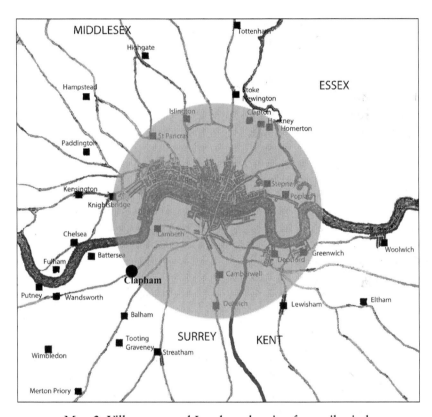

**Map 2: Villages around London, showing four-mile circle
from London Bridge**

Merchants also frequented other villages north of London. Highgate, which straddled the boundary of the parishes of St Pancras and Hornsey, started as an aristocratic retreat, but rich merchants began to move there; many of the larger houses were commandeered by senior Cromwellians, but a considerable aristocratic presence remained for some time after the Restoration. Neither it nor Hampstead was very attractive for a daily commute; Islington was a bit closer and on the main road to Smithfield. Stoke Newington, although small, was also a haven for merchants.

Retiring houses for merchants were different from the country houses of the aristocracy or landed gentry. They were often known as 'villas', but there is no accepted definition. By the end of the century a contemporary described the 'suburb villa' as 'quasy a lodge, for the sake of a garden, to retire to enjoy and sleep, without pretence of entertainment of many persons', while another stressed the need for them to be 'sequestered from the noise of a city, and the embarass or distraction of business'.[14] Lady Jane Cheyne was clear that even 'noble' houses such as that of the rich merchant Sir Nicholas Crisp in Fulham would not do to buy because it did not provide a 'seat' with substantial land, and would therefore be hard to sell.[15] She preferred to rent in Chelsea. The houses of the aristocracy were also in different places from those of merchants. The latter wanted easy access to the City, while the gentry and aristocracy were not interested in commuting to work; their journeys from Thames-side parishes, often by river, would take them to Westminster rather than the City, while those associated with the Court looked towards the Royal Palaces at Richmond, Hampton or Greenwich.

The parishes south of the river were not attractive to aristocrats. Transport was not yet good enough for City commuting from Putney, which was more than seven miles away, let alone from those parishes further upstream.[16] Putney was more a place for summer houses for those who did not have to be in the City for their business;[17] six of its large houses were either inns or schools, and even in the early 1660s only seven of the larger houses in Putney were occupied by merchants or their widows, compared to thirty in Clapham.[18] Nearer in, Dulwich was chiefly in the hands of the school supported by the Alleyn trust, and Camberwell had a resident lord of the manor, who kept a close eye on his tenants. Deptford, in the southeast, was already industrial. The only practical possibility for more than a few commuting merchants south of the river was Clapham.

The new merchants

Who were these merchants? In the usage of the times, 'merchant' meant wholesaler, especially one involved in overseas trade.

Traditionally, the major element of this trade had been the export of woollen cloth, subject to a commercial monopoly granted by Royal Charter to the Merchant Adventurers. By the seventeenth century the pattern of trade in England was changing; wool exports became subject to greater international competition, while improvements in agricultural productivity increased incomes and, with that, consumer demand.

The balance shifted to imports, particularly from the Levant, picking up trade from the East, and directly from India. A significant proportion of these imports were paid for by re-exporting imported products from England; 42 per cent of tobacco imports from Virginia in 1640 were shipped on to continental ports, and the East India Company re-exported a high proportion of its imported pepper.[19] There was also direct trade, so that tobacco and fish, particularly cod from Newfoundland, were shipped directly to European ports and the proceeds used to pay for imports. An important element of the Levant trade was the import of currants, especially from the Greek islands of Zakynthos and Cephalonia. These were consumed very widely, causing the Venetian ambassador to claim that 'the people consume a greater amount of currants than all the rest of the world.'[20] Others maintained that it was an 'inveterate habit' of the English, or claimed that they 'can hardly digest bread, pastries, broth and bag puddings without these currants'.[21] Sixty-two hundredweight of them were imported in 1638, and the associated customs duty was an important source of revenue to the king.

This trade was managed through monopolies under charters granted by the Crown, such as to the East India Company and the Levant Company. To participate in this trade it was necessary to be a member of the company, free to sons of members. An individual trader could try to circumvent the restrictions (called 'interloping'), but risked being fined or having his goods confiscated. Although it was possible to purchase membership of the companies, the trade required extensive knowledge and contacts that could realistically be gained only through family connections or from apprenticeship to a member, which was expensive. In return, prices and volumes were managed so as to maximise the return, and the number of members was restricted. A firm rule was that members could not have a shop in London, or be a small producer/artisan or ship captain.

This protected each member's position as middleman, which would have been undercut by someone with direct access to the retail market. Merchants of this kind were called 'mere merchants'. They tended to have close relations with the king because of their need for a Royal Charter and because customs duties on trade were a major source of income for the king, and not subject to parliamentary control.

Not all trade was subject to these monopolies. A charter for trade with Spain, rejuvenated at the end of the war in 1604, was overturned by Parliament, and hundreds of smaller businesses that were not 'mere merchants' entered the business. Most of the greater merchants withdrew once they could no longer benefit from their monopoly. Moreover, although risky, interloping could produce considerable benefits. One successful interloper was William Kiffin, who also became one of the most influential (and rich) Baptist ministers – and lived briefly in Clapham after the Restoration.

The success of the monopoly model for those benefiting from it made it the natural first choice for trade with North America, and the Virginia Company was created for this purpose. It failed at least in part because established merchants did not consider investment in plantations (requiring large-scale fixed capital and long-term investment) to be as attractive as the possibilities open to them in the Levant and India. The number of merchants involved in the Virginia tobacco trade doubled, from 175 to 350, in the period from 1634 to 1640, while the Levant Company maintained the number of its members dealing with currants at a constant sixty-one, ensuring good profits for all of them. As the established merchants lost interest, the Newfoundland Company and trade with the West Indies went the same way. By contrast, new entrepreneurial businessmen invested in the development of the plantations – often either living there or sending members of their family to do so – and became involved in all aspects of the business, production, supply of provisions, and marketing and sale of the product. They have been characterised as 'from unimpressive, often obscure socioeconomic backgrounds ... willing to accept profit margins ... take risks, and adopt methods of operation that neither the merchants nor the gentry would seriously consider.'[22]

While few started with money or an aristocratic or established merchant background, this comment seems something of an exaggeration, since many of them were younger sons of provincial gentry, albeit with very limited capital. A contemporary described them collectively as 'not merchants born, or versed in foreign ports, or any trade, but to those plantations, and that from either planters there or wholesale tobacconists and shopkeepers retailing in England.'[23]

As a result, trade with North America became open to all, involving the supply of provisions and people (from servants to ministers) on the way out and in return tobacco, furs, fish and later sugar. It required less capital or expertise to start up and fitted very nicely with retail activities in London; many new merchants started off as grocers or ironmongers or in other trades and had therefore been prevented from entering trade that was subject to monopolies. It is estimated that between sixty and one hundred merchants traded with New England in the middle of the seventeenth century.[24]

There was also a potential religious connection. Although colonists in both Virginia and the West Indies came from a variety of religious backgrounds, trade with North America involved dealing with the colonies, such as those in Bermuda, Providence Island and Massachusetts Bay, designed to provide a haven for godly people. Some new merchants were attracted to deal with North America because of the Puritan connections, and naturally wished to support North American colonies. Many went to North America themselves for a period of time, or sent relations to settle and act for them; others became committed to Puritan religious or political activities because of their commercial involvement with the Puritan colonies.

To sum up, trade with North America was a natural opportunity for those without prior connections or wealth, or who were prevented from operating in the monopoly trades by virtue of their retail or other activities, which they did not wish to give up. It gave them a good base for involvement in provisioning the colonies or selling the return trade and making money at the same time. This made them naturally antagonistic to the Spanish, who represented a potential threat to that trade, having captured (albeit temporarily) both St Kitts and Nevis in 1629 and the island of Association from the Providence Island Company in 1635. This reinforced any anti-Catholic feelings they might have had, and emphasised any tendencies to Puritanism. The need to put down the Catholic rebels in Ireland, who were seen as natural allies of the Royalist cause and probable supporters of Spain, was an integral part of reducing the Spanish (or French) threat to England's westerly trade. Many Puritan merchants were very active in Ireland's brutal colonisation, and financed their own 'Additional Sea Adventure' there to achieve this. These new merchants were also at the forefront of refusing to pay loans or taxes demanded by the king, both the Forced Loans in 1626 and Ship Money in 1636.

As the Civil War developed, Parliament needed to improvise an administration without the involvement of the king and his supporters, and its solution took the form of a range of committees, originally organized regionally, but later merged into a single or national committee.[25] At first the committees were partly or wholly comprised of MPs, but from 1644 many committees appointed and answerable to Parliament were composed entirely of non-MPs. Although new merchants had little administrative experience, and no university degrees or legal training,[26] their business background made them very suitable for anything to do with finance, shipping or trade of which they had knowledge and where their interests were affected. This included the various committees dealing with the Navy, or the Prize Committee, which allocated the rewards of seized ships between the State and the seizer, and they had no compunction in using their involvement to promote those interests.

New merchants were also represented on committees such as the Compounding Commission and its predecessors, which extracted money from Royalists or those who had not given loans to Parliament and in return allowed them to keep their lands. A related body was the Sequestration Committee, which dealt with the confiscated estates of those who were not allowed to compound (pay to regain their estates) or who were unable to do so. In 1650 these were finally combined into a single committee with a full-time professional commission of seven, paid £300 per annum each. Many of these estates, whether of Royalist or episcopal origin, ended up in merchant hands.

Finally, new merchants became more active in the governing structures of the City of London. These had previously been dominated by the rich mere merchants who filled the twenty-six places on the powerful Court of Aldermen, appointed for life and required to be worth at least £10,000. In the middle of the century about 300 or 1.5 per cent of London merchants had wealth of

£10,000–£20,000, and about a further 100 had wealth of over £20,000.[27] This balance necessarily changed only slowly, although the 240 members of the Common Council, elected annually by ward, were subject to greater and sometimes dramatic change. However, the Common Council, which met only at the request of the Lord Mayor, had comparatively little power, and that proved to be a bone of contention on many occasions.

Although there were strong connections between religious and political views, there was not a complete correlation. In political terms, Presbyterians were much more likely to accept or even want a state Church with clear lines of authority able to set out and, ideally, enforce lines of belief, particularly against the sectaries, such as Levellers and Diggers. They were not in favour of religious toleration; many wished to suppress religious dissent and saw the parochial structure as a good way of delivering the necessary discipline. A major division within the Presbyterians concerned the power to exclude members of a congregation from Communion if their views (or behaviour) were frowned upon. High Presbyterians wanted this to be left to the Church, either the minister or elected elders; others wanted it reserved for Parliament, whether directly or through those appointed by Parliament. Many would have been prepared to endorse a settlement with the king that made this possible and protected their commercial interests.

Independents had a different view of the Church, supporting individual congregations based on willing participants who met any doctrinal tests, rather than those from a specific geographical area. These 'gathered' churches drew their congregations from like-minded 'godly' people rather than those who lived in a particular parish. Sometimes they met in their own premises; sometimes they used specific parish churches, even running in parallel to the existing structure. There could be large arguments when the congregation and minister of a parish church viewed themselves as 'gathered' and then started to exclude existing members of the parish itself. In that respect, Independents were similar to the Separatists, who were more openly radical about their separation from the parochial structure. They were both much more likely to be against a deal with the king and to support rule by an unconstrained republican Parliament that reflected the views of the people, or at least of those entitled to vote.

They often allied themselves with those Presbyterians who wanted some Parliamentary control of the Church, if only to restrain those who opposed religious toleration. But, however radical they may have been at early stages of their careers, all were keen to see their economic and property rights protected; one of the Leveller leaders, William Walwyn, said of the political Independents' rapid rise to riches: 'It seems your congregation is of near relation to those that hold prosperity a mark of the true church.'[28]

Neither the politics nor the religion of the new merchants was homogeneous, and the differences were not clear-cut. Some Independents still valued the parish system, while some Presbyterians happily appointed Independent churchmen as their ministers. Generally, the Presbyterians wanted an ordered and structured state Church, ideally repressing at least the more radical sects, just not one run by bishops; others supported Independent or Separatist churches in the City, whether Congregational or Baptist. Both Presbyterians and Independents would come to live in Clapham.

(Endnotes)

1. Francis Sheppard, *London: A History* (Oxford University Press, 1998), p. 126.

2. Jeremy Boulton, 'London 1540–1700', in P. Clark (ed.), *Cambridge History of Britain* (Cambridge University Press, 2000), vol. 2, pp. 316–17.

3. Roger A.P. Finlay and Beatrice Robina Shearer, 'Population Growth and Suburban Expansion', in A.L. Beier and Roger A.P. Finlay (eds), *London 1500–1700: The Making of the Metropolis* (London, 1986), 37–59.

4. Jeremy Boulton, *Neighbourhood and Society* (Cambridge University Press, 1987), p. 19.

5. Derek Keene in Lena Cowen Orlin (ed.), *Materia London* (University of Pennsylvania Press, 2000), p. 68.

6. John Evelyn, *Fumifugium* (1661), p. 5.

7. C. Galley et al., *Infant Mortality: A Continuing Social Problem* (Ashgate, 2007), p. 65.

8. Dr Henry Sampson, day book, British Library, Add Ms 4460.

9. John Strype, *A Survey of the Cities of London and Westminster*, Book 1 (1720), p. 227.

10. T.F.T. Baker (ed.), *A History of the County of Middlesex*, vol. 10: Hackney Parish (Oxford University Press, 1995), p. 10.

11. R.G. Lang, 'The Greater Merchants of London in the Early Seventeenth Century' (D.Phil. diss., Oxford University, 1963), p. 295.

12. Baker, *Middlesex*, p. 110.

13. Ibid., p. 12.

14. Roger North, *Of Building* (1695); Timothy Nourse, *Campania foelix* (Thomas Bennett, 1700).

15. The estate around a 'seat' was supposed to provide sufficient funds for the running of the house. Lady Jane Cheyne, letter to her brother Charles Cavendish, Viscount Mansfield, 7 May 1656, Nottingham University Library, Pw 1/88.

16. Dorian Gerhold, *Putney and Roehampton in 1665* (Wandsworth Historical Society Occasional Paper 16, 2007), p. 25.

17. Ibid., p. 17.

18. Ibid., pp. 68–91.

19. Ben Coates, *The Impact of the English Civil War on the Economy of London 1642–50* (Ashgate, 2004), p. 12.

20. Calendar of State Papers, Ven. 1628–29, p. 553.

21. Calendar of State Papers. Ven. 1640–42, p. 234; Alfred Wood, *A History of the Levant Company* (Taylor and Francis, 1964), p. 67.

22. Robert Brenner, *Merchants and Revolution* (Verso, 2003), p. 113.

23. 'The Humble Remonstrance of John Bland of London Merchant', *Virginia Magazine of History and Biography*, 1 (1894), p. 144.

24. Richard Grassby, *The Business Community of Seventeenth-century England* (Cambridge University Press, 1995), p. 56.

25. G.E. Aylmer, *The State's Servants* (Routledge & Kegan Paul, 1973), p. 9.

26. In 1640–42 some 70 per cent of MPs had attended either Oxbridge or one of the Inns of Court, although this is likely to have been as much or more to gain social graces than for formal education. See Keith Wrightson, *English Society 1580–1680* (Routledge, 1982), p. 193.

27. Grassby, *Business Community*, p. 246.

28. William Walwyn, *Walwyn's Just Defence* (1649), p. 372.

CHAPTER 2

THE MERCHANTS COME TO CLAPHAM

Clapham's early history

In medieval times Clapham was a small village four miles from London Bridge, south of the River Thames. It sits about one hundred feet above sea level on gravel terraces above London clay, providing access to good water. The church, which is dedicated to the Holy Trinity, was first built towards the end of the twelfth century, and by 1195 was under the control of Merton Priory. The village was centred on the church, 400 yards east of the start of Clapham Common and about the same distance north of the old Roman road, Stane Street. This ran from London Bridge along the line now taken by the Northern Line, down what is now Clapham High Street and along the south side of Clapham Common, through Balham, Tooting and Epsom, eventually reaching Worthing and Chichester. It forms the basis of today's A24.

Another road, passing about 400 yards north of the church, linked the route to Kingston, Guildford and Portsmouth to the pilgrimage trail to Canterbury. At first this traffic would have missed the village, but it was rerouted at the end of the twelfth century to branch off what is now the A3 in Wandsworth and run along the north side of first Wandsworth Common (then called Battersea Common or Heath) and then Clapham Common, before passing the church at Clapham and going on northwards to Vauxhall.[1] A lease dating from 1501 called this stretch 'Canterbury Way', the name that was used into the eighteenth century. This is illustrated in Map 3.

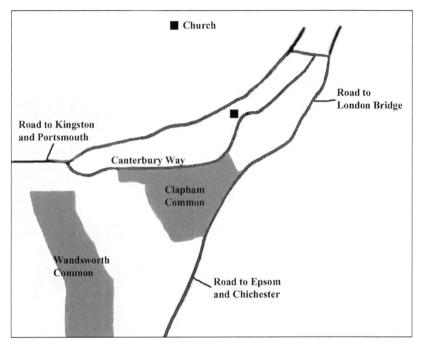

Map 3: Roads in Clapham

Both of these roads would have had plenty of traffic, and although the number of pilgrims was reduced radically after the Reformation, the development of Portsmouth as a centre of naval activity maintained the flow, while Epsom had become well-known for its medicinal waters and so stimulated visitors on the other road. John Ogilby produced maps of both roads in his series in 1675, and his written description of the routes demonstrates that they both went through the parish of Clapham.[2]

Being near two major routes out of London, Clapham was easily reached by road, at least by the standards of the time. The population remained small, however: it was estimated as 184 in 1326 and 285 in 1450, with only a handful of better-off households.[3] In the early sixteenth century the Manor House was owned by Robert Sherburne, the Bishop of Chichester, who stayed there during his visits to Westminster, and was later leased by one of his bailiffs. Bartholomew Clerke, a scholar, lawyer and diplomat, took up residence in 1580. He rebuilt the house, creating a large extension and leaving the older part still useable and sometimes let to other tenants.[4] In 1583 he acquired the whole Manor, which contained sixteen houses, gardens and orchards, eight cottages and two windmills, as well as a large amount of land, running in total to 1,200 acres.

Queen Elizabeth visited the Manor House in 1583, as indicated by an entry in the Lambeth churchwarden's accounts that year for three shillings and fourpence for 'ringing for ye Queen's majestie when she dined at Clapham and went to Greenwich'. Illustration 1 shows that the house was of brick with a six-storey octagonal tower, designed to register the movement of game in the adjacent fifteen-acre hunting park.

Illustration 1. James Peller Malcolm, *Manor House, Clapham, London,* 1798

Clerke died in 1590, leaving the manor of Clapham to his son Francis. Francis sold the manor house in 1611, having had a sale fall through in 1594 because the prospective purchaser, Henry Maynard, secretary to Lord Burleigh, had heard that the queen proposed to pay another visit, and was not inclined to bear the cost.[5] Shortly afterwards Maynard bought the manor of nearby Tooting Graveney.

The manor of Clapham passed through a number of hands, although it is not clear whether any of them ever lived there. Henry Atkins acquired a part share in 1616 and the remainder in 1630. He was president of the College of Physicians and doctor to James I, and supposedly saved the infant Prince Charles during a dangerous illness. His reward of £6,000 was spent on the manor of Clapham. Meanwhile, the house and eighteen acres of land were leased in 1624 by Sir Robert Heath (Attorney General and later Lord Chief Justice under Charles I). It is hard to know how much time Heath actually spent at Clapham, since he had a number of other large houses, but his grandson was baptised there in 1627.

The other substantial house in Clapham at the time was Brick Place, which had started life as a hunting lodge in the woods and in 1599 was inherited by Thomas Cockayne. He was the elder brother of Sir William Cockayne, one of the richest merchants of his time, and as an eldest son had enough inheritance to be able to live in Clapham without working. His family was, however, brought low by an outbreak of disease in Clapham, which killed Thomas, his wife, his daughter and his eldest son, William, all of whom were buried within a few months at the turn of the year 1618/19. William had been married only the year before and left a daughter, Jane.

Until the 1620s, those occupying the few larger houses in Clapham were mostly officials of one kind or another, whether Court, ecclesiastical or Parliamentary; only one London merchant, Thomas Reade (who died in 1620, leaving a legacy to the church), had land there. Such officials leave little or no trace in the parish register; apart from the members of the Cockayne family who died in 1618/9, the only such people to be buried in Clapham were the clergy and their children, and relations of the lord of the manor, Francis Clerke, using the family grave.

Brick Place was later occupied by Sir John Farwell, one of Charles I's gentlemen pensioners, who notionally formed the king's bodyguard but can perhaps be better thought of as attending Court part of the time. Farwell certainly spent time in Clapham, and by 1629 he had taken an eighteen-year lease on the house; he had two children baptised there and two others buried, and his daughter was married at the church.

There is little information about Clapham residents until a manorial extent giving the tenants of the manor of Clapham in 1628.[6] This shows fifteen houses in addition to the Manor House and Brick Place (including two that were newly built), of which only five occupiers are described as 'Mr', indicating those with some social status. Virtually all those not so identified appear in the parish register as 'father', being married or buried, showing that they did indeed live in Clapham. On the other hand, of the five called 'Mr' in the manorial extent, one is a local landowner, the other three are paying low rents, and only one appears in the parish register.

That one is Christopher Payce, who had a child baptised there as early as 1620 but clearly moved between London and Clapham, choosing in 1623 to be taxed in Surrey rather than in Middlesex. Two daughters were buried shortly afterwards in Clapham, but he then returned to the City before moving back permanently to Clapham in 1628. Payce was a merchant, being taxed on the basis of his goods rather than his land, and he signed the parish accounts rather than making his mark. He was attached to the village, since his will asked that he be buried in Clapham, next to the graves of his daughters.

The merchants move in

Demand for retiring houses was beginning to grow by the beginning of the 1630s, stimulating the development of a corresponding supply of appropriate houses. Some landowners were more prepared than others to allow this, no doubt reflecting the strength of their desire to enjoy their estates untrammelled by development, the value as farmland, and their relative need for money or access to capital. Although it did support agriculture, the parish of Clapham was not prime farmland, and the main Atkins family estate was in Buckinghamshire, as we have seen.[7] They were largely non-resident, and their main interest was to maximise the return from their Clapham estate, a fact that encouraged building. We shall see that Clapham did indeed have more large houses for its size than other villages south of the Thames.

Meanwhile, more merchants had moved to Clapham, bringing others with them. The first was **William Darrack**, a Grocer and seedsman, who moved in about 1630, although he kept his residence in London, where he was active in the church of St Pancras, Soper Lane.[8] His rent for about twelve acres and a house was £16 per annum plus 'one couple of sweete and fatt capons on the Twentieth Day of December in each year'. **Roger Hughes** from the same City church moved in shortly afterwards, and his daughter Hannah married his former apprentice and future Clapham resident **Anthony Stephens**.

Francis Bridges purchased a house with land in Clapham in 1631. Known as 'a man very eminent for Pietie', he was closely involved in Puritan activities and a vestryman of the Puritan City church St Antholin, where his cousin Charles Offspring was vicar.[9] Bridges had strong links to North America, both through being one of the investors in the Massachusetts Bay Company, which supported the first migration to that area, and because his brother Captain Robert Bridges emigrated to Massachusetts. Another member of St Antholin moved to Clapham, **Henry Colborne** or **Colbron**, a scrivener with a cousin in New England and an active promoter of Puritan causes.

When Farwell's wife died, in 1633, he sold the remaining years of the lease on Brick Place to two merchants, **John Beauchamp** and **James Sherley**. There were two other houses on that land, and although we do not know how they divided the properties between them, Brick Place itself became occupied by the husband of William Cockayne's daughter Jane, who may have brought the house as part of her dowry. This was **John Worfield**, who had a profitable office under the Exchequer as the Auditor for Imprest, responsible for checking that the large sums of money issued to officers such as the Treasurer of the Navy and the Paymaster of HM Forces were expended for the purposes intended.

Beauchamp and Sherley were two of the original Merchant Adventurers who financed the *Mayflower* (Sherley being one of the two Treasurers), and subsequently two of the four who took over the financing in 1626 in return for a six-year monopoly of the fur trade with the Native Americans and the responsibility for procuring the goods that the Settlers still needed from England. Such a task went well with their other trading activities. The fur trade provided the pelts necessary for beaver hats, an important fashion item of the early seventeenth century and one that gave ample opportunity for considerable profit. They may have been responsible for bringing two beaver makers and Haberdashers to Clapham, **William Daniel** of All Hallows Lombard Street and **William Hubbard**, one of the Presbyterian elders at St Mary Woolnoth.

Beauchamp had become one of the largest importers of consumer goods from the Netherlands, often working with James Sherley, who was a Goldsmith, a trade that often acted as a banker.[10] Both Beauchamp and, particularly, Sherley get a rather bad press from the historians of the *Mayflower*. They may well have been involved principally because they saw a business opportunity, rather than for any specific religious or political reason, but Sherley did share the Pilgrims' religious beliefs, and his letters are full of language to support this.[11] For example, in December 1627 he wrote to William Bradford, governor of the Plymouth Colony:

> *Assuredly, unless the Lord be merciful to us and the whole land in general, our estate and condition is far worse than yours. Wherefore if the Lord should send persecution or trouble here (which is much to be feared) and so should pit into our minds to fly for refuge, I know no place safer than to come to you, for all Europe is at variance one with another, but chiefly with us.*[12]

A desire to do business did not always go down well with the Settlers, who might have wanted to break up with Sherley and his associates, but were constrained by debt to them and the constant need for clothing, trading goods and other supplies from home. There were innumerable disagreements between those financing the exercise, who sometimes thought the Settlers were not doing enough to return goods for sale, and the Settlers, who thought the financiers were engaged in sharp practice, including sending goods for which they had not asked. Beauchamp also fell out with Sherley, whom he accused of not giving him a sufficient share of the income (or information) about incoming goods, and ended up taking Sherley to the Chancery Court. (Beauchamp lost, and left Clapham shortly afterwards.)

Already the residents were spending more time in Clapham. Francis Bridges had sold his London residence and was effectively retired when he came to Clapham. Three of Worfield's children, two less than a year old, were buried there. Sherley also spent time in Clapham; he paid his taxes there, and three of his children were baptised in Clapham, the earliest in 1635. He was certainly there during the serious outbreak of plague in London in 1636, when he wrote to the New Plymouth Colony:

> *You will and may expect I should write more and answer your letters, but I am not a day in the week at home in town, but carry all my books to Clapham. For here is the miserablest time that I think hath been known in many ages. I have known three great sicknesses, but none like*

this. And that which should be a means to pacify the
Lord and help us, that is taken away, preaching put down
in many places, not a sermon in Westminster on the
Sabbath, nor in many towns about us; the Lord in mercy
look upon us![13]

These men show common features that were reflected in all
those who came to Clapham. They were merchants, with strong
connections to North America; they were Puritan, and often active
in Puritan causes; and they already knew someone in Clapham or
with Clapham connections. (It was of course his wife who brought
Worfield there, even though he did not otherwise fit the pattern.)
These characteristics are reinforced by the names in the first surviving
rate assessment of 1638, which shows a substantially different picture
from that in 1628. There were forty-seven houses and sixteen men
given the title 'Mr' – more than three times the number ten years
earlier – demonstrating the extent of the new building. Clapham was
no longer a typical country village of its size, which would have no
more than three or four such families.[14] Most of the residents can be
identified as merchants, although Sir Henry Atkins (son of Dr Henry
Atkins) lived briefly in the Manor House until his death in 1638.

A number of the residents in 1638 had been there for some
time. Two were, like Bridges, subscribers to the Massachusetts Bay
Company: **Richard Tuffnell**, a brewer and MP from Southwark; and
George Foxcroft, a prominent member of St Stephen's, Coleman Street.
The latter owned land in Boston and elsewhere in Massachusetts, but
never lived there. He was described later as

a business man to his backbone. He was accustomed
to the desk and the counting-house. The man was an
uncompromising old Puritan and he took life with all the
Puritanical seriousness of the day.[15]

Richard Cranley lived in Clapham from before 1638 until 1645,
transferring his tax base there in 1641. He is a good example of a
new merchant, who had begun as no more than a shipmaster, started
trading with North America and became very successful. He was
part of a largely Presbyterian clique of ship-owning merchants and
Trinity House Elders who monopolised the naval administration
until they were removed by the radicals in December 1648 as part

of Pride's Purge.[16] He was involved in the slave trade from Guinea, through which he knew **John Brett**, a leading trader with the West Indies. Brett had been apprenticed to one of the leading North American traders and political activists, Randall Mainwaring, and married his daughter Martha. We shall find other Navy men in Clapham, one of them **Dennis Gauden**, well known as the chief victualler to the Royal Navy after the Restoration and as a friend and client of Samuel Pepys. Much of his activity in Clapham comes after the Restoration, but he moved there in the mid-1640s.

Three more merchants came from Daniel's church, All Hallows Lombard Street. Two of them, **Joshua Foote** and **Joshua Woolnough**, were leaders of the church, and the third, **Thomas Aymes**, was a parishioner. Foote had a house in Clapham from before 1638 until 1653, when he emigrated to Boston; he subsequently moved to Providence, Rhode Island. He was a leading exporter to Massachusetts and contributed to a fund to transport poor children to New England, intending thereby to secure them a godly upbringing. His shop at the Golden Cock in Gracechurch Street was a meeting point for settlers returning to London to pick up gossip and information.[17]

The merchants settle in

The pattern of occupation in Clapham changes further in the 1640s. The number of merchants and officials remained remarkably stable at between eighteen and twenty until the late 1650s, when it increased to twenty-six. These men also spent more of their time in Clapham. Until 1645 the only merchants attending the vestry meetings were Sherley and Payce, and the parish officers were chiefly local yeomen and farmers; after that date many of them attended the vestry meetings and the churchwardens and senor parish officials were almost all merchants, despite the fact that many were also active in their City churches.

Increasingly these men used Clapham rather than their City church for their rites of passage, as is shown in Table 1, which also gives the total number of baptisms and burials in the parish. Merchant families made up 15 per cent of these. The number of their children baptised there each decade increases from four in the 1620s to twelve in the 1640s and sixteen in the 1650s. More of them are buried there, both adults and children, and there is a remarkable increase in marriages in the 1650s, which is covered later in this chapter. (The totals for merchants and officials given in this table exclude the clergy; the three rectors between them had twenty children baptised from 1600 to 1660, and the same number buried. The marriage figures refer only to merchants etc.)

YEARS	BAPTISMS		BURIALS			MARRIAGES
	total	merchants etc.	total	adults	children	merchants etc.
1600–9	n/a	n/a	58	0	4	1
1610–19	53	0	56	4	3	0
1620–29	76	4	105	1	4	1
1630–39	79	7	79	1	2	0
1640–49	69	12	101	5	7	6
1650–59	91	16	112	12	11	22
1660–69	63	16	201	11	23	8
1670–79	n/a	n/a	197	13	18	n/a
1680–89	154	25	240	16	14	n/a

Table 1. Baptisms, burials and marriages in Clapham, 1600–89
Source: Parish register

Three merchants from the City parish of St Margaret, New Fish Street, moved to Clapham in the mid-1640s. Abraham Babington was one of the leading members of the congregation, and occupied one of the most highly rated houses in Clapham as well as two shops in Gracechurch Street in the City. William Molins, an elder of St Margaret's, emerged in 1644 as an active Parliamentarian supporter. He was Comptroller of the Ordnance for the City from 1645 to 1647, and had a large contract to supply the Navy with gunpowder.[18] He knew George Foxcroft, who was a member of the committee charged with procuring gunpowder. Yet another gunpowder supplier was the third St Margaret's parishioner to come to Clapham, Daniel Judd.[19] He and Molins had married sisters, and they were churchwardens in 1649. Their mother-in-law, Grace Crouch, lived in Clapham with the Molins.

John Gould was an active Presbyterian who lived in Clapham for a long time and will be discussed in later chapters. He was married three times, first to Elizabeth, the daughter of Thomas Thorold. Gould was a partner of Thorold's son Charles, himself a prominent Presbyterian. Both he and **Thomas Frere** owned shares of plantations in Barbados. Gould was a brother-in-law of the important radical **Samuel Moyer**, who leased the Manor House in Clapham for ten years and who married two daughters of Thorold (Margaret and, after her death, Rebecca).

Illustration 2. Gerard Soest, *Richard Salwey*, 1663
Source: Private collection

(Major) **Richard Salwey** (also Salway and Salloway) was an interloper in the Merchant Adventurers trade and a tobacconist, and is said to have been a radical spokesman for apprentices. A ballad speaks of him:

> *Salloway with tobacco*
> *Inspired, turn'd state quacko*
> *And got more by his feigned zeal.*
> *Than by his What d'ye lack-o!*[20]

He was a religious Independent and a major in the Army, taking part in the siege of Worcester in 1646; the gun in the portrait by Soest is perhaps a reference to his role there.

Two merchants held land and houses in Clapham from an early date but lived there only briefly themselves. **Lawrence Brinley** was a merchant trading with North America and one of the four elders of St Mary Magdalen, Milk Street. He acquired extensive land in Ireland and was also connected to Barbados, since his nephew Francis Brinley had emigrated there but – finding the climate not 'suited to his habits and constitution' – settled at Newport, Rhode Island. **Lawrence Bromfield** was a trading partner of Cranley. He was a leading Presbyterian at the strongly Puritan parish of St Dunstan in the East, and active on committees designed to suppress subversive pamphlets and to protect the tithe income. He sold a house to **Gabriel Carpenter**, the brother-in-law of Francis Bridges. Another of Bromfield's houses was occupied by his son-in-law **Thomas Corbett**, who named his eldest son Bromfield. Thomas was a younger brother of Miles Corbett, one of those who signed Charles I's death warrant, and another of his brothers, Edward, was a Puritan minister in Norfolk.

An important member of the Clapham community was **Gualter Frost**, Secretary of the Council of State, who had charge of the Council's books, papers and agenda. He leased one of the larger houses in Clapham from 1649 until he died, intestate, in 1652. His affairs were in such a mess after his death that Parliament set up a committee to sort them out, ending by granting £1,000 to help his estate meet its bills. His son, also **Gualter Frost**, who started as Manciple (in charge of buying and storing food) at Emmanuel College, Cambridge, did not succeed his father in the Council job but stayed on in the Clapham house until after the Restoration.

Another prominent merchant who was in Clapham for a short time in the early 1650s was **Thomas Hussey**, later described by a historian as 'obviously a new man on the make'.[21] He was an MP and nominated as alderman in 1645, but paid a fine of £800 to avoid the post. He had extensive holdings in Berkshire, and his daughter Margaret married **Lawrence Coles**, who came to live in what had been Hussey's house in Clapham since the latter's son, also Thomas, preferred a retiring house in Hampstead. Coles was also related by marriage to another Clapham resident, **Francis Polstead**. The alderman and sheriff **Thomas Chandler**, a Draper and silk dealer, was elected Master of the Drapers in 1658, so he would have known the other Clapham Drapers, Babington and Aymes.

Edward Winslow is well known to American historians, having crossed on the *Mayflower*. A prolific defender of the Settlers, he was governor of New Plymouth three times, and one of the people with whom Sherley corresponded on various subjects relating to the *Mayflower*.

Illustration 3. Print of Robert Walker, *Edward Winslow*, 1651

Winslow returned to England on a number of occasions, and for the last time in 1646. He was in Clapham around 1649 and, despite Sherley's bad reputation over his business with the Pilgrims, it is clear that Winslow regarded him as a friend. He would hardly have chosen to stay in Clapham if he really disliked Sherley, and his will appoints the latter as one of his 'four friends' (the rector, John Arthur, was another) to oversee the disposal of his personal estate in England – again indicating that he trusted Sherley. Winslow was also one of the two witnesses at Sherley's second marriage, which took place in Clapham in 1654. Finally, Winslow's daughter Elizabeth was married in Clapham a year after his death, with Sherley one of the witnesses. Winslow also had close connections with a number of other Clapham residents, so it is hardly surprising that he lived there for a time as well.

In the late 1650s other merchants came to Clapham, all of them closely connected with those already living there. **Thomas Rodbard** was a neighbour of Dennis Gauden in the City, a cheesemonger who also exported a range of goods to North America. He died in 1657, and the next year his son, also **Thomas Rodbard**, married Arthur's recently widowed daughter Sarah Wood and continued living in the house. Clapham provided a husband for another of its widows when **Thomas Powell** married his neighbour's widow, Winifred Burrows. Powell's brother Henry had married Winifred's sister Sarah Daniel.

John Corbett, who had a house in Clapham from the late 1650s, was on many committees from 1642 onwards, including the Committee for the Affairs of Ireland in 1647, the Council of State in 1651 and the Compounding Committee in 1659.[22] He met other Clapham residents on all these committees, and knew Richard Salwey well because their homes were only a few miles from each other in Shropshire.

One very well-known name who stayed in Clapham was **William Courten**, son of Sir William Courten, the fabulously rich merchant who finally went bankrupt. William junior leased the Manor House for a few years from 1640, during which time he fled his creditors to Italy. Both he and his father had been heavily dependent on King Charles for support for their various activities, but two of his sisters married in Clapham during his time there, both of them choosing active Puritans. His links with the Court continued, and he had business dealings with Charles' faithful courtier Endymion Porter, who was lord of the manor of Allfarthing in nearby Wandsworth. Just before Porter left to join the king at Windsor in 1642, he wrote to his wife:

> *I could wish you and your children in a safe place …:*
> *I could likewise wish my cabinets and all my other things*
> *were at Mr Courteen's but if a very discreet man be*
> *not there and take advice of the Joiner to convey them*
> *thither, they will be as much spoiled in the carriage as*
> *with the rabble.*[23]

His valuables were in fact moved to Courten's house in Clapham, and remained there until June 1643, when a servant revealed their location. Courten claimed that they had been given to him in payment of a debt, but that failed to keep them from the Parliamentary searchers.[24]

Two other residents, like William Courten, were not Puritan merchants. **Sir George Chute** was knighted in 1608 for his efforts in the Armed Forces in Ireland and inherited the nearby manor of Stockwell. His son, also George, remained in the house in Clapham and married Margaret, the widow of Lawrence Coles. The Royalist **Sir Robert Needham** (a member of the Welsh gentry with Shropshire connections) took over Brick Place in 1642 when he married John Worfield's widow, Jane (née Cockayne), a good friend of Sarah Bridges (Francis Bridges' wife), who had left her a gold bodkin as 'a token of her respect'.

Parish building

The vast majority of the large houses were on a 600-yard stretch of the Canterbury Way (see Map 3), which led from Brick Place to the Manor House and church; Map 6 (see Chapter 6) shows their location by the early 1660s. They were close together, and it is very unlikely that the occupants did not know one another. Most of the houses were developed by non-residents, but Gabriel Carpenter acquired his from Lawrence Bromfield, with complicated arrangements for giving Bromfield an option to buy or lease it back if Carpenter wished to dispose of it. Carpenter felt that he had had the worst of the deal 'in regard that I have laid out £100 on the house whereas I thought and tied myself to lay out but £30', and in his will advised his wife and children not to let or sell without 'good advice from some learned in the law'.[25]

How much time these merchants spent in Clapham is not clear, but the vestry minutes show that they were present for meetings in the middle of winter, an indication that, unlike those in Putney, these houses may have been in use all year round. There is no evidence of the arguments that occurred in Hammersmith, where 'divers citizens of the City of London who reside [there] only in summertime' petitioned to have their rating adjusted compared to 'divers others whose common residence is all the year in the same place'.[26]

Although some residents were transitory, a continued and increased presence over many years is clear despite gaps in the rate assessments. Payce, Hughes, Christopher Vivian, Tuffnell, Bridges and Carpenter were regulars for many years until their death. Babington, Thomas Corbett, Daniel, Darrack, Gauden, Gould, Molins, Sherley and Thomas Rodbard junior appear regularly in the rate assessments for up to twenty years. Cranley and Foote were there throughout the 1640s and possibly more. Moyer is a regular from 1648 to 1660, and one of his nephews was married in Clapham in 1658. Brinley and Bromfield both appear to have bought a house early on, but both leased it to someone else before returning after the Restoration or leaving it to a child. Salwey appears only twice in the rate assessment, in 1649 and 1650, but was a trustee of the school in 1648 and a Clapham subscriber to the Society for the Propagation of the Gospel in New England in 1649, and attended parish meetings at least until 1651, and two of his children were baptised in Clapham, in 1648 and 1650. Judd appears in the rate assessment for 1648 and 1649; one of his children was baptised there in 1647, and he was a churchwarden in 1649, when he was already well known there. Winslow appears only once in the rate assessment, but many other times in the minutes or for other fundraising. Woolnough, who similarly appears only once in the rate assessment, was also a trustee of the school and was described as an inhabitant of Clapham for his subscription to the Society for the Propagation of the Gospel in New England.

Further evidence of the closer involvement of the merchants in the parish comes in 1648, when the need to provide for a growing number of children was recognised. A school was started by voluntary contributions led by Dennis Gauden and the rector, John Arthur, who had begged the land as a gift from the current lord of the manor, Sir Richard Atkins. It cost £264 to build the schoolhouse, a sum that was raised easily by the parish. It was granted to eleven trustees, all but one being merchants who appear frequently in the parish records. There may have been continuing problems with the piece of wasteland because the school was described in a lawsuit fifty years later as being 'built on a boggy, mory piece of ground and in some sort a nuisance to the parish'.[27] The schoolhouse was enlarged a few years later, in 1651, when a turret was added; a few years later the parish voted to provide a further forty shillings per annum for the schoolmaster to keep the schoolhouse and surrounding rails in good repair.

The first teacher to be appointed was William Hughes, who was known to Bromfield as well as to Babington, who would have been party to his appointment as a lecturer at St Margaret, New Fish Street.[28] Hughes was a schoolmaster in Clapham after the Restoration, and we shall hear more of him later, but during the Civil War he was an Army chaplain and granted the rich living of Hinton Waldrist in Berkshire. His religious and political views can be judged from a sermon he preached in 1651 in which he asserted that regicide was 'not so uncouth as some do register it, having cured the wound' of monarchy.[29]

In 1650, owing to the population increase, the decision was made to extend the church. The vestry minutes record that the cost of £50 was guaranteed by nine merchant parishioners, although little seemed to happen for the time being. However, Gualter Frost senior died in 1652, and his son wanted to build a funerary chapel for him; permission was granted finally in 1653. This private chapel, for the use of the Frost family, had its own door from the east end of the churchyard. The chapel was well used, and no fewer than nine members of the Frost family were buried there in the decade 1650–60. The extension to the church the parish wanted was done at the same time as the chapel was built, providing a south aisle that ran the length of the church. The earliest picture we have of the church is from 1750, by which time there had been other changes (see Illustration 4).

Illustration 4. Clapham Parish Church, 1750

The growth in population also required better use of the public spaces available to the parish, and in 1660 it upgraded one of the rooms in the schoolhouse, ordering that 'the room at the end of the school should be waynscotted, with seat, and window shutte, and a table and chest to be fitted to the place, for a meeting place for the parishioners.'[30]

Table 1 showed the remarkable increase in merchant marriages in Clapham. This followed the Barebone's Parliament, which introduced secular marriage in 1653. Marriage notices had to be posted in the town or village, and the ceremony took place later in front of a Justice of the Peace and two witnesses. William Gurney, a retired waterman-turned-alehouse keeper, was appointed registrar by John Gould. Parishes were required to keep the date of births, but they continued to record the date of baptism as well. They recorded where the banns were published, usually 'in the market place at Southwark' but once 'at Wandsworth' and once 'in the church', as well as the name of the officiant and witnesses, and the parishes from which the couple came. In most parts of the country the traditional ceremony was strongly preferred, and there was a rush to be married before the change took place, so much so that across England there were 9,884 marriages in September 1653 and only 714 in October.[31] This did not occur in Clapham, although one local couple married three days before the change.

The cause of the increase in marriages in Clapham was the large number of merchants who chose to marry there rather than in London, a trend that had started in the late 1640s. Katherine, the daughter of Sir John Bourchier, a prominent member of the Rump Parliament who signed Charles' death warrant, married the Mercer John Eaton there in 1646; Colonel Fenwick married Katherine, daughter of the prominent republican Sir Arthur Haselrig, in 1652; neither of these has any obvious connection with Clapham, but Katherine Eaton did later invest in Joshua Foote's steelworks in Massachusetts. John Gould, James Sherley and Dennis Gauden all married their second wives in Clapham rather than the City; Prudence Thorold, the mother-in-law of Gould and Moyer, remarried there after her husband's death; Edward Winslow's daughter Elizabeth married there a year after her father's death, as did Moyer's nephew and Sherley's niece; and Nathaniel Pheasant married Dennis Gauden's sister-in-law Abigail Clarke.

With one exception, the officials administering the wedding ceremony were Samuel Moyer, Abraham Babington and John Gould, and the witnesses were drawn from the parish (including John Arthur, the rector) or the family of the couple. On one occasion an outsider officiated: Alderman Sir Robert Tichborne, an extreme republican and Independent who signed the death warrant of Charles I. He and Moyer were MPs for the City of London at the same time from 1653. The couple Tichborne married, Daniel Taylor (a wealthy haberdasher) and his second wife, Margaret Locke of Wimbledon, do not appear to have had any direct connection with Clapham. Taylor was a close associate of Salwey, Moyer and Babington, and served on many radical committees with them. The Marriage Act was extended for six months by the Second Protectorate Parliament, but came to an end in October 1657, after which there was some confusion about the proper way to be married.[32] By the end of 1659 the register was back to its previous form in all respects.

Why did merchants choose Clapham?

Clapham met the criteria for retiring houses with its clean air and good water, and was the only place south of the river with a substantial community of such houses, but even by 1660 only some sixty merchants or gentry were or had been living in Clapham, many of whom were dead or in North America. This can be compared with an estimated total of about 1,000 overseas merchants and four times that number of domestic traders in London itself.[33] Clapham was not necessarily widely known, and there would have been underlying reasons that brought these particular merchants to Clapham.

One possibility might have been an association with the Putney debates, which arose when the New Model Army under General Thomas Fairfax spent three months in Putney, only two miles from Clapham, while Charles I was kept prisoner at Hampton Court. However, there is no record of any Clapham resident being involved with the debates, and in any case twenty merchants were living there before they took place. More likely reasons are that those coming to Clapham found it relatively convenient, and that they had some connection with an existing or former resident.

Geography

The geographical constraint can be explored by looking at where Clapham residents had their City houses. Fifty-nine of the Clapham inhabitants (or their widows) appearing in more than one year's rate assessment between 1630 and 1660 can be identified as affluent, and of these only three cannot be identified further. Eight were either officials of some kind or in one of the professions, and no London residence can be identified for them. Of the forty-eight remaining merchants, City residences can be located for forty-five of them, giving a good basis for forming conclusions.

The natural route to Clapham would be to travel by road, crossing the river at London Bridge. Merchants with a retiring house in Clapham should therefore have their City house near the bridge and in the south and east of the city. Those living in the northern parts of the City, on the other hand, would find it more natural to have retiring houses in Hackney or the northern suburbs. This is borne out by the distribution shown in Map 4; Clapham residents were found in only 24 per cent of City parishes and, with only one shortlived exception, in the south and east.

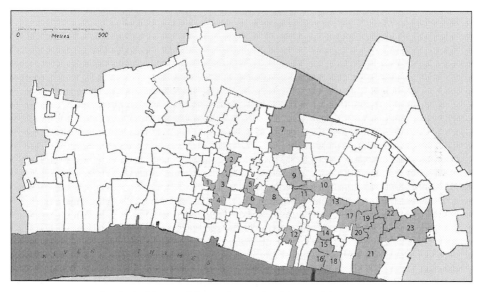

Map 4. City parishes where Clapham residents were active 1630–60

Key: Grey indicates parishes that are known to have Clapham residents, numbered as follows:

1. St John the Evangelist
2. St Mary Magdalen, Milk St
3. All Hallows, Bread St
4. St Mildred, Bread St
5. St Pancras, Soper Lane
6. St Antholin
7. St Stephen, Coleman St
8. St Stephen, Walbrook
9. St Christopher le Stocks
10. St Michael, Cornhill
11. St Mary Woolnoth
12. St Lawrence Pountney

13. All Hallows, Lombard St
14. St Leonard, Eastcheap
15. St Margaret, New Fish St
16. St Magnus the Martyr
17. St Dionis Backchurch
18. St Botolph, Billingsgate
19. St Gabriel, Fenchurch St
20. St Margaret Pattens
21. St Dunstan in the East
22. Allhallows Staining
23. St Olave, Hart Street

There is no simple relationship between wards and parishes, and many parishes were split between wards, but the pattern is even stronger if one looks at wards. No fewer than thirteen Clapham merchants lived in Bridge ward, and over 80 per cent of identified merchants lived in only six of the twenty-five City wards, as shown in Table 2.

Bridge	13	Cheap	2
Billingsgate	6	Walbrook	1
Tower	5	Aldgate	1
Cordwainer	5	Coleman St	1
Langbourn	4	Outside City	2
Bread	3	Not known	3
Cornhill	2		
TOTAL 48			

Table 2. Clapham residents by City ward

Only one resident lived in one of the northern wards: George Foxcroft, who lived in the Coleman Street ward. He did not stay long, but left in 1639, although he did return in the 1670s after eight years working for the East India Company at Madras.

This geographical distribution is illustrated further by Map 5, which also shows the five wards where sometime Clapham residents were councilmen.

Many radicals lived around St Paul's Cathedral, in the Cheapside region, or in the ward of Bridge Within, and this is exactly where we find the City base of most Clapham residents.[34] A number of them had shops in Cheapside (Brinley) or Gracechurch Street (Foote, Aymes, Stephens, Woolnough and Babington). Many residents came from strongly Puritan parishes, with four from All Hallows, Lombard Street, and three each from St Antholin, St Margaret, Fish Street, and St Magnus Martyr. These parishes claimed only fifty to sixty houses each, so those with houses in Clapham would have known one another before their move.[35]

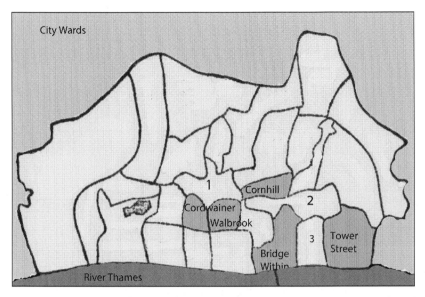

Map 5. Wards where Clapham residents were Common Councilmen 1640–60

Key: Grey indicates wards where Clapham residents were councilmen between 1640 and 1660.

The other numbered wards are: 1. Cheap;   2. Langbourn;   3. Billingsgate.

Family connections

There was also a multitude of family connections. John Gould and Samuel Moyer had married sisters, as had William Molins and Daniel Judd, who were also neighbours in the City. Thomas Corbett and Lawrence Coles moved into the houses occupied by their respective fathers-in-law, Lawrence Bromfield and the elder Thomas Hussey. The former Jane Cockayne brought both her husbands to Brick Place, and this is only one example of a widow remaining in Clapham. Two sons of residents married young Clapham widows. Richard Burrows had left his friend Thomas Powell £10 in his will, and Powell married his widow, who was also the sister of his brother's wife. Thomas Rodbard junior, having just taken over his father's house in Clapham, married the widowed daughter of the rector John Arthur. George Chute married Lawrence Coles' widow. Widows also remained in Clapham long after their husband's death. Sarah Bridges lived on for eight years after Francis died, bringing her mother and brother to the village. Ann Hughes and Ann Carpenter both stayed in Clapham as widows for fifteen years, while Mary Peers returned from Barbados after her husband's death.

Residents spent more time in Clapham and increasingly relied on one another for support in a wide range of personal financial activities; they were witnesses or executors for one another's wills, they were asked to oversee the education and marriage of orphans, their children intermarried extensively, and they left one another personal legacies. Corbett demonstrates the increased commitment to the village: his children born immediately after his move to Clapham are baptised by its rector, John Arthur, but in London, while the later ones are baptised in Clapham itself, and buried there.

Business connections

As 'new merchants' the business of these men was similar, and they naturally did business together, whether Corbett and Robert Whitlock jointly financing exports or imports, or Cranley and Bromfield trading together in wool as early as 1645. Other commercial links included Rodbard senior and Gauden making joint subscriptions to Irish Adventures, or arranging for their charities to purchase from one another, as did Babington, Woolnough and Arthur.

Most of them traded with North America and had close connections with the Puritan communities there. Foxcroft owned land in Massachusetts; Bridges, Brinley and Foote all had relations there to promote business; Sherley and Beauchamp had financed the *Mayflower*; four had invested in one or other of the New England Companies; and Bridges left a large legacy to Harvard. Joshua Foote was a part owner of an ironworks on the Saugus River in Massachusetts. Edward Winslow, Sherley's correspondent about the *Mayflower*, returned to England for the last time in 1646 and came to Clapham in the late 1640s.

There were also strong ties to Barbados. John Gould owned shares in plantations, and Christopher Payce's daughter married a prominent plantation owner. Thomas Frere left his son a 'stock of negroes'.[36] His brother Tobias became one of the larger landowners, and Thomas sent six of his sons and three of his daughters over to Barbados, providing a very substantial network. He obtained permission to trade in arms with Barbados in 1655. John Brett and Richard Cranley supplied Barbados with provisions and helped to start the slave trade there, while both Cranley and Salwey imported tobacco from the island. One of Brinley's nephews went there, but left when he found the climate too much for him.

Molins and Judd were connected through business as well as marriage. They were heavily involved, with Foxcroft, in contracts for the supply of gunpowder, and by 1645 Judd had substantial dealings with Molins. He was a supplier of English match, bullets and swords to Molins' Ordnance, and the two men collaborated over the siege of Basing House in 1645.[37] Judd had wanted sixty scaling ladders in a hurry for the Parliamentary armed forces, and Molins supplied them from the London Militia Stores.[38]

An important link among the merchants was Gualter Frost senior, who as Secretary of the Council of State was able to facilitate many deals. As a part owner of Foote's Saugus ironworks in Massachusetts, he helped to staff the plant with Scots soldiers captured at the Battle of Dunbar in 1650. Foote also applied to the Council of State to transport 900 of them, 'well and sound and free from wounds', to North America as indentured servants.[39] It was a good commercial deal for Foote, since it cost about £5 to ship the men over, but they could be sold for £20–30 as indentured servants for a period of seven years. Frost also helped John Gould and Charles Thorold (Thomas Thorold's son) to avoid taxation that became due when nine parcels of silk booked to travel on a Flemish ship at Antwerp were delayed until after the Act taxing goods transported on foreign ships came into force.[40]

The links with the Council continued after Frost's death, because both Salwey and Moyer were members from time to time. Thomas Rodbard senior was able to secure permission in 1654 to send eight ships to Virginia, loaded with 120 dozen shoes, six barrels of gunpowder and one tonne of shot.[41] Thomas Corbett, governor of the Merchant Adventurers in 1653, successfully petitioned the Council of State with **Robert Whitlock**, an assistant to the company and a neighbour of his in Clapham, to provide a convoy for Eastland merchants' ships to Hamburg.[42] Many of these connections existed before the merchants moved to Clapham, demonstrating that they knew one another well before moving there. It is hardly surprising that such bonds strengthened after they became neighbours.

Conclusion

Clapham was certainly a centre of Puritan merchants with strong mutual connections. This was no chance; the village was convenient geographically, and these men already had relations or colleagues there from business connections, City parish churches, City hierarchies and livery companies, as well as through politics. Their families spent more of their time in Clapham, with the result that it was increasingly common for their relatives to be baptised, married or buried there (even in winter) and for their children to intermarry, and they began to work together on parish affairs. Only one Clapham merchant does not clearly fit the complete picture: William Courten junior had close ties with the Court, and was no Puritan, but later was completely dependent on new merchants (including Moyer) for support of his operations in the East Indies.[43]

(Endnotes)

1. Michael Green, *Historic Clapham* (History Press, 2008), p. 106.
2. John Ogilby, *Britannia* (1675).
3. Green, *Historic Clapham*, p. 126.
4. Ibid., p. 137.
5. T.C. Dale, *Clapham and the Clapham Sect* (1927), p. 40.
6. Calendar of State Papers, Domestic Charles 1 154/93.
7. Green, *Historic Clapham*, p. 11.
8. Being a Freeman of a livery company entitled the man to operate in any other of the livery trades, and this was common. For that reason a capital letter is used when referring to membership of a livery company, and a small letter for the trade.
9. Samuel Eliot Morison, *The Founding of Harvard College* (Harvard University Press, 1935), p. 306.
10. Nick Bunker, *Making Haste from Babylon: The Mayflower Pilgrims and their World: A New History* (Alfred A. Knopf, 2011), p. 260–62.
11. William Bradford, *Of Plymouth Plantation*, ed. Samuel Morison (Alfred A. Knopf, 1952), p. 173.
12. Ibid., p. 382.
13. Ibid., p. 287.
14. Peter Laslett, *The World We Have Lost* (Routledge, 2005), p. 64.

15. Mrs Frank Penny, *Fort St George, Madras* (S. Sonnenschein, 1900), p. 24.

16. This is the name given to the exclusion or arrest in December 1648 of about 140 members of the Long Parliament likely to vote against a trial of the captive Charles I by soldiers under the command of Colonel Thomas Pride.

17. Susan Moore, *Pilgrims: New World Settlers and the Call of Home* (Yale University Press, 2007), p. 106.

18. G.E. Aylmer, *The State's Servants* (Routledge & Kegan Paul, 1973), p. 213.

19. Michael Wilks, Gunpowder Mills Study Letter, November 1990, pp. 10–11.

20. Percy Society, *Early English Poetry, Ballads and Popular Literature of the Middle Ages*, vol. 4 (1861), p. 158.

21. David Underdown, *Pride's Purge* (Oxford University Press, 1985), p. 250.

22. H.T. Weyman, *Shropshire Archaeological and Natural History Society*, vol. 10 (1898), p. 48.

23. Dorothy Townshend, *The Life and Times of Endymion Porter* (T. Fisher Unwin, 1897), pp. 198–201.

24. Ibid.

25. National Archives; 1657 PRO/PROB/11/268/86

26. Middlesex Sessions Book, December 1647.

27. Depositions from Chancery case 1700. Lambeth Archives IV/188/1/1.

28. Eric Smith, Clapham Antiquarian Society Occasional Note, October 1950.

29. Granshaw, Lindsay and Porter, Roy (eds.) *The Hospital in History* (London, 1989) p128.

30. Clapham vestry minutes, 23 April 1660.

31. Christopher Durston, *The Family in the English Revolution* (Oxford University Press, 1989), pp. 70–86.

32. Bernard Capp, *England's Culture Wars* (Oxford University Press, 2012), p. 31.

33. Richard Grassby, *The Business Community in Seventeenth-century England* (Cambridge University Press, 1995), p. 57.

34. Kenneth Lindley, *Popular Politics and Religion* (Scolar Press, 1997), p. 139.

35. Tai Liu, *Puritan London* (Associated University Presses, 1986), chapter 1.

36. Thomas Frere will, 1675, PRO/PROB/11/349/108.

37. This was the third – and successful – attempt by the Parliamentary forces to seize Basing House near Basingstoke. It finally fell to an attack commanded by Cromwell himself, and was stormed following extensive artillery fire.

38. Calendar of State Papers, Domestic 1645–47, p. 110.

39. Calendar of State Papers, Domestic 1650, p. 346.

40. *Journal of the House of Commons*, 5 January 1651.

41. Interregnum Entry Book, vol. 133, p. 46.

42. State Papers, 1653, vol. 38, p. 64.

43. Robert Brenner, *Merchants and Revolution* (Princeton University Press, 2003), p. 174.

CHAPTER 3

CLAPHAM AND POLITICS 1640–60

The role of Clapham residents in the politics of the time can be seen if we trace the history from 1640 through to the death of Oliver Cromwell and the Restoration, noting where they appear. This also shows how many of them worked together before they came to Clapham. Three of the merchants – Thomas Frere, Samuel Moyer and Lawrence Brinley – were signatories of a petition in 1640 in favour of Joseph Hawes, who had tried to seek reprisals in an English court against a Spanish ship, which seized one of his own tobacco ships from Virginia, worth £12,000. This was a campaign that it would have been natural for any new merchant trading with the Americas to support. The next important petition, that of 23 December 1641 against the appointment of Thomas Lunsford, a notorious Royalist, as lieutenant of the Tower, generated enough pressure to force the king to withdraw the nomination. It was signed by over eighty new merchants, including four from Clapham: Brinley, William Hubbard, William Darrack and George Foxcroft.

Clapham residents recognised the importance of securing Protestant control of Ireland and supported the raising of an armed force to subdue the country in return for being granted a share of the rebels' land. It took a contribution of £600 to secure a grant of 1,000 acres in the province of Leinster, around Dublin, but only £200 in Ulster; there were 180 subscribers in total. Table 3 lists the fourteen Clapham residents who subscribed, including a widow and a married woman.

Subscriber	February 1642	Seaforces July 1642
Richard Salwey		100
Samuel Moyer	300	300
Henry Colborne	75	
Abraham Babington	100	400
William Hubbard	100	
Joshua Woolnough	25	75
Elizabeth Tuffnell	100	
Thomas Hussey (senior)	223/6/8	200
William Molins	250	300
Lawrence Brinley		200
Sarah Brinley		50
Captain Richard Cranley		400
Thomas Rodbard (senior)	100	
Thomas Rodbard and		
Dennis Gauden		600

Table 3. Sometime Clapham residents subscribing to
Additional Sea Adventure to Ireland, in £
Source: J.P. Prendergast, *The Cromwellian Settlement of Ireland*, 1865

There are two points of interest. First, Abraham Babington was a large subscriber, despite being chiefly a retailer, a fact that perhaps reflects his staunchly Independent views. Second, while inclusion on a list of this size does not mean that the subscribers knew one another, the joint subscription by Gauden and Rodbard reflects their being neighbours in the City. Two other Clapham residents subscribed in a roundabout way, since a contribution of £250 made by Miles Corbett was really the property of his brother Thomas (£200) and Lawrence Bromfield (£50).[1] Many of the merchants retained an interest in Ireland, and Moyer, Brinley and Salwey were all appointed to the Parliamentary Irish Committee in 1647, Salwey being employed twice as a negotiator with the Irish.

Cranley, as a Commissioner of the Navy, was still entitled to have his ships hired for the Navy's use, and with others in 1644 he promoted a five-ship privateering squadron to intercept supplies to the Irish rebels. Since they were also Commissioners for the inventory and sale of prizes, they presumably thought they were on to a good thing. It cost about £1,500 to buy and set up a privateering ship, and, even though they took four prizes, they withdrew from the arrangement after a few months, 'finding the charge to exceed the benefit'.[2] The Navy Commissioners of the time were 'prompt, capable, honest and energetic, sparing themselves neither in purse nor person', but even at the time they were seen to enrich themselves further than was necessary.[3] A contemporary naval administrator wrote:

> At the first of the war it was accounted an high character of a well affected man to accommodate the service with ships for their money ... but I must tell the reader and them that their zeal burnt as hot in another chimney as the state's interest ... when the same man shall be as owner, a commissioner, a committee man, nay a chairman of that committee, and in these capacities hire to the state (as a signal service) his or their ships by order from themselves to a third man.[4]

Lawrence Brinley was active on a number of radical fronts in the winter of 1641–42. As well as signing the Hawes and Lunsford petitions mentioned above, he signed the petition of 24 December urging the House of Lords to stop delaying the bill to impress troops to put down the rebellion in Ireland, and on 9 March 1642 was one of the twenty-one signatories to a petition to the common council urging support of the militia ordinance (which gave Parliament, rather than the king, the power to appoint the militias' officers), and endeavouring to have those who had petitioned against it punished. He was involved in yet another petition, this time with William Walwyn, a future leader of the Levellers, asking the Common Council to take repressive action against those conservative Royalist citizens who had dared to petition Parliament against the City's revolutionary committee of safety. Both he and Thomas Frere were on the ward committees set up in 1642 to collect plate, money and horse to support the Parliamentary Army.

One of the arguments that divided the Puritans was the governance of the Church and the role in that, if any, of the state. This was given particular focus by the need to secure the assistance of the Scots against Charles I's army. The Scottish Parliament agreed to help, but only on condition that the Solemn League and Covenant should be accepted in England, as it had been in Scotland, thereby achieving a united religious approach. Apart from eschewing anything that could be regarded as popery, the Covenant also set out a very structured form of Church governance based on the parish system, with elected elders able to enforce discipline and appeals to higher bodies drawn from a wider group of elders. This was agreed by the English Parliament on 25 September 1643, and was followed in February by an ordinance requiring everyone over eighteen to swear support of it. Brinley's church, St Mary Magdalen, Milk Street, was one of the first to do so.

Progress was not smooth, however. There were many people in England, not least in London, who saw the Scottish regime as overly prescriptive. Others, particularly the Independents, feared that the disciplinary side was a means to eliminate diversity of religious views. They were correct: one Presbyterian divine wrote later, 'To let men serve God according to the persuasion of their own consciences was to cast out one devil that seven worse might enter.'[5] A meeting of London ministers declared: 'We detest and abhor the much endeavoured toleration.'[6] Finally, there were arguments about how discipline should be enforced. Some ministers wanted that to be confined to them, with no role for lay elders. Parliamentarian supporters believed in a role for the House of Commons, whether directly or through the power to appoint those hearing appeals. Further ordinances implementing the changes followed only slowly, and it was not until August 1645 that one was enacted providing for the setting up of Presbyterian government by organizing the parishes into groups called classes.

Whatever his original views, Brinley was established as a Presbyterian and played a leading part in organizing the petition of 20 September 1645 complaining about the delay in settling Presbyterian church governance.[7] Copies were circulated in every parish for signature by all taking the Covenant, and those signing were asked 'that their qualities should alsoe be sett downe' to emphasise their respectability. Brinley's house was the collection point for completed petitions, and George Thomason, a bookseller, was among the local canvassers. Learning of the petition, the House of Commons voted it to be scandalous and sent the Lord Mayor to call a meeting of the Common Council, which ordered its suppression. The detailed rules for the organization of elders were produced on 25 October and required more lay members than ministers to be appointed. This was naturally opposed by the ministers, who persuaded the Common Council to consider petitioning for its change. The debate was lost, however, when a number of Independents, including Samuel Moyer, argued successfully that the matter had been fully debated in Parliament by MPs, who had formed a considered view that ministers should not be given more power.

There were nevertheless still more contested points that required implementation, and the City continued to consider its position, which was becoming increasingly Presbyterian. Lawrence Bromfield was part of the Presbyterian leadership of the City and sat on four of the important Council committees, including the one that between October 1645 and 14 January 1646 consulted with those ministers and citizens who objected to a Parliamentary settlement of religion. Meanwhile, the Scots were worried that too little was being done too slowly, and were particularly concerned about the lack of control of Independents, separatists and sectaries. Many of their worries were shared by the Presbyterians. A pamphlet appeared at the end of 1645 entitled 'Truth its Manifest', eulogising the action of the Scots throughout the Civil War and violently attacking the English Parliament and its army. Its contents were sufficiently alarming to create a considerable stir, and the Parliamentary Committees of both kingdoms were ordered to discover the printer and publisher of the anonymous book. It turned out to have been written by David Buchanan, an ardent Presbyterian, and published by Brinley's colleague Thomason, two of whose daughters would come to live in Clapham in the 1670s. The book was voted false and scandalous by both Houses of Parliament, and ordered to be burned by the Hangman. Shortly afterwards a refutation appeared, and Abraham Babington published his own answer to the pamphlet two years later, in 1648.[8]

Bromfield's committee on the future of church governance had brought forth a clear demand for both strict Presbyterian discipline and the repression of both Independent and separatist congregations. It complained that

> Private meetings, especially on the Lord's day, of which
> they are at least eleven in one parish, are multiplied
> whereby the public congregations' ordinary and godly
> orthodox ministers are very much neglected and

condemned, as if they were like the primitive persecutions
or as if we were still under the tyranny of the prelatical
government; and by reason of such meetings and
the preaching of women and other ignorant persons,
superstitions, heresy, schism are much increased, families
divided, and such blasphemies as the petitioners tremble to
think on are uttered to the dishonour of Almighty God.[9]

Nothing could give a better picture of their views. Despite this, the ordinance requiring the choice of elders was passed unchanged on 14 March 1646. Brinley was elected one of the four elders in St Mary Magdalen, Milk Street, four months later, on 19 July, and their representative to London Provincial Centre. Like Bromfield, Brinley was a militant Parliamentary activist who had fought the war for a reformed state Church and City privileges, not for religious liberty and military domination.[10] He was one of those responsible for spreading a rumour that the Army was to be unleashed on those citizens planning a demonstration in favour of the City's Presbyterian petitions. The rumour was taken very seriously and investigated for three days in the Commons. Brinley's goal was to sow dissension between City and Parliament.[11]

Bromfield, meanwhile, was appointed to the committee to draw up the City's petition of 18 December 1646 calling for the Army's dissolution, and was also appointed to the 'Presbyterian' militia committee in May 1647. This was, however, short-lived. The king was captured in early June and the Army lost patience and began its march on London towards the end of July. One of its demands was the re-creation of the old city militia committee, full of Independents. Parliament agreed at once, but reversed its position in the face of a crowd of political Presbyterians besieging the House of Commons (causing Salwey to seek the protection of the Army). Bromfield was one of three staunch Presbyterians appointed to be treasurers of the loans raised in May and June 1647 for paying the Army's wage arrears, and it is possible that some of this money was used to support the Presbyterian cause.[12] Certainly Bromfield was one of the five organizers of this crowd, and they all paid for it by being impeached by the House of Commons in September 1647 for 'High Crimes and Misdemeanours', and committed to the Tower of London. They were eventually released in May the following year on a petition from the

Lord Mayor, Aldermen and Commons of the City. The anonymous Presbyterian author of 'A Pair of Spectacles for the City' (1647) describes Bromfield as

> *a gentleman of unquestionable faithfulness and integrity,*
> *upon God hath conferred extraordinary parts and*
> *abilities, and a heart to improve all to the service of*
> *his Country; a fit man to transact any military affair*
> *at that council of War where great Gustavus Adolphus*
> *sat President; a gentleman that at the famous Battle of*
> *Newbury proved himself a valiant soldier, and a discreet*
> *Commander; in the Committee for the Militia and Court*
> *of Common Council discreetly, faithfully and stoutly*
> *muted those apostates Fowke, Estwicke, Moyer and*
> *countermined their designs. This I believe was his great*
> *crime; but he is ousted.*[13]

On the other hand, a pamphlet published in response the following year, 'The Case for the City Spectacles', was much less supportive of those sent to the Tower:

> *I cannot condemn the Parliament for sending our Lord*
> *Mayor, Bunce, Langham and the rest into the Tower;*
> *who bid them be rich? Were they as poor as I am, their*
> *carcasses would never have paid the Tower Fees; but they*
> *have served the Parliamentary time; and Turkish Justice*
> *being now most in fashion, the best they can expect ...*
> *must be a bowspring or a mallet.*[14]

Clapham was well represented on the militia committees. Richard Salwey and Samuel Moyer were appointed to the replacement militia committee; Moyer doubled up on the Tower Hamlets militia committee. Gualter Frost was on the Westminster and John Corbett on the Southwark committees. Bromfield was by now a colonel and John Brett a major, and William Hubbard had been a captain before he died.

No Clapham resident was a Leveller, although a number had close ties to them. Moyer was one of the more radical of the Independents and one of the four men representing the City political Independents in their negotiations with the Levellers on the 'Second Agreement of the People', which was eventually ratified by the Army council in December 1648. This watered down the Levellers' demands, but still provided radical provisions on electoral redistribution, toleration and the protection of individual liberties. It received little if any support overall, but both Moyer and Babington agreed to serve on a committee to canvas signatures in support of it; they had little or no success.

A major change came in December 1648. Late in the night of 5 December the House of Commons finally passed a motion endorsing the partial agreement with the king at Newport as a basis for further negotiations, opening up the possibility of a restoration. The next day Colonel Thomas Pride conducted his purge of MPs; Robert Needham was excluded from Parliament, but Salwey survived and played an important part in the new administration.

Salwey was one of those who drafted the Commons resolution of 4 January 1649 proclaiming the legitimacy of the Commonwealth in terms of popular sovereignty while reserving to the Commons full authority with no appeal beyond it:

> *That the People are, under God, the Original of all just Power:*
>
> *And do also Declare, that the Commons of England, in Parliament assembled, being chosen by, and representing the People, have the Supreme Power in this Nation:*
>
> *And do also Declare, That whatsoever is enacted, or declared for Law, by the Commons, in Parliament assembled, hath the Force of Law; and all the People of this Nation are concluded thereby, although the Consent and Concurrence of King, or House of Peers, be not had thereunto.*

However fervently Independent Salwey's religious views, his chief concern was political reform and the primacy of Parliament.

Salwey remained active in Parliament only until the middle of January 1649, and played no part once the trial of the king was put in hand, even though he was appointed to the court to try Charles. His revolutionary zeal appears to have been dimmed, since it took him a further four months formally to record his dissent from the motion of 5 December. John Corbett was also appointed one of Charles' judges, but took no part, explaining that his absence was 'not for any disaffection to the proceedings of this court, but in regard of other especial employment that he hath in service of the state'.[15]

Following the wholesale change of personnel brought about by Pride's Purge, the radicals Salwey and Moyer played important parts. Richard Cranley was removed from his Navy post in 1649, at least in part because of his involvement in the peace proposals coming from Newport,[16] and in the same year Moyer, who was generally viewed as an efficient financial administrator, was put on the committee supervising both Army and Navy. Having been in various posts in Customs from 1643, he also became Head of Customs In from 1649, an interesting post for a merchant who was still very active in imports and exports. At one stage he was on seven different committees at the same time. Both Moyer and Salwey were appointed or elected to the Council of State on a number of occasions in the early 1650s, and Salwey came top of the poll in February 1651. Moyer also served on the Hale Commission, which reviewed legal practices and whose proposals for simplification were roundly rejected by the lawyers in Parliament. Table 4 shows those Clapham residents who served as MPs.

	Constituency	Year
Sir Robert Heath	City of London	1621–22
	East Grinstead	1624–25
Richard Tuffnell	Southwark	1640
Richard Salwey	Appleby	1645–53
Thomas Hussey	Whitchurch	1645–53
	Andover	1656–57
Sir Robert Needham	Haverford West	1645–48
John Corbett	Bishop's Castle	1648–53
Samuel Moyer	City of London	1653

Table 4. Clapham residents who were MPs 1620–60

Clapham residents continued to play an important part in various committees. Babington, Moyer and John Corbett were appointed to the High Court established in March 1650 to investigate and bring to judgment plotters against government mutineers and adherents of the king. Babington was a commissioner in Surrey in 1654 for dealing with 'divers scandalous and insufficient Ministers and

Schoolmasters in many Churches, Chappels and Publique Schools within this nation'.[17]

Salwey was appointed to the Council of Trade, which developed an aggressive overseas policy. In 1650, for instance, it ordered English government convoys for Levant Company shipping in the Mediterranean[18] and raised customs rates by 15 per cent to pay for them, an example of what the Venetian ambassador described as the protection resulting 'from Parliament, the government of the Commonwealth and that of its trade being exercised by the same individuals'.[19] In 1652 Salwey became one of the hardworking Commissioners for the regulation of the Navy, men who sent letters headed 'midnight – my bed' and were remarkably successful in transforming the operations of the Navy.[20] This was key to winning the Anglo-Dutch War, and of great interest to overseas merchants.

Three Clapham residents were on one very important committee, the Compounding Commission, which dealt with the lands of those deemed inimical to the regime. Moyer chaired it in 1650–51, and Molins and Winslow were among the other six members. This very busy committee met three or four times a week, both morning and afternoon; typically, Winslow attended meetings on fourteen or fifteen days in December 1650.[21] They heard the case involving a leader of the Levellers, John Lilburne, and Sir Arthur Haselrig. Lilburne had petitioned Parliament on behalf of his uncle and another about a colliery in Durham that had been sequestered by the Compounding Commission in favour of Haselrig (who, incidentally, was a cousin of Winslow's wife). The petition, which claimed among other things that Haselrig had unfairly influenced the committee, had been found by the Parliamentary committee considering it to be 'false malicious and scandalous'. Lilburne had been banished on pain of death, fined £3,000 and ordered to pay Haselrig a further £2,000, and £500 each to four of the Compounding Commissioners, including Molins and Winslow. Moyer, the chairman, was supportive of Lilburne, but was outvoted.[22]

The removal of the Rump Parliament in 1653 affected Clapham residents significantly. Salwey fell foul of the senior Army officers who dissolved it, although Cromwell viewed him as 'a man of great parts'.[23] He declined Cromwell's suggestion that he invite colleagues to 'draw up some instrument that might put power out of his hands'.[24] According to the memoirs of Edward Ludlow, Cromwell himself complained to Salwey how heavily affairs of state and their attendant worldly temptations weighed upon him.[25] Salwey gave a straightforward answer that echoed what he had helped to draft in 1649:

> *The way, sir, to free you from this temptation is for you not to look upon yourself to be under it, but to rest persuaded that the power of the nation is in the good people of England as it formerly was.*[26]

Salwey was asked to join the Council of State, but declined to attend even when re-elected on a number of occasions, and never took his seat in the Barebone's Parliament. He lost his posts. Molins and Winslow took a similar position and were among the thirty-six prominent Londoners who petitioned Cromwell on 20 May 1653 either to restore the Rump Parliament or to call another one. They too were dismissed from their posts, although Winslow was reappointed shortly afterwards.

Meanwhile Salwey had already been proposed for the post of ambassador in Constantinople in 1652, but everyone accepted that he would not take it up until the trade improved. He had been offered the post of ambassador to Sweden in 1653, but declined 'on account of his unfitness through want of freedom of spirit and bodily health'.[27] After the end of the Anglo-Dutch War and the anticipated improvement in trade, Cromwell wanted to get rid of the existing ambassador in Constantinople and approved Salwey's appointment in August 1654.[28] This followed a petition to that effect by the Levant Company, no doubt because of his involvement in securing the Council of Trade-sponsored convoys, and because he was himself a member of the company, as were two of his sons, one of whom was living in Aleppo.[29] However, the old ambassador, Sir Thomas Bendysh, wanted to stay, and by early 1655 Salwey had found another excuse not to go, saying that a friend had died and he had to sort out the estate.

Moyer supported the dissolution of the Rump and was nominated to the subsequent Barebone's Parliament, being one of its leading radical members, often leading the prayers, and on seven or more of its committees.[30] He was appointed to the Council of State and became its president in October 1653, but was not re-elected in November when the radical group, of which he was a leader, began to offend the moderate majority. When the moderate majority asked Cromwell to dissolve the Parliament, in December, Moyer was asked by the thirty or so radicals remaining in the chamber to take the Speaker's Chair. He agreed, but did not resist when the troops finally came to close it down. Although reappointed to the Compounding Council he stepped down shortly afterwards, lost his Customs post in January 1654, and left his administrative work. He did, however, serve as both Elder Brother and Master of Trinity House.

Clapham merchants were also directly active in City politics by being elected or appointed to a range of posts, as identified in Tables 5–7. They provided no fewer than six of the Common Councilmen for the ward of Bridge Within up to 1660, and five between 1649 and 1654. It is inconceivable that they did not know one another well, and they worked together in the politics of the ward and the City as a whole.

	Ward	Year
Henry Colborne	Cordwainer	1643–44
William Molins	Bridge Within	1643–44
Lawrence Bromfield	Tower Street	1647; 1660
Richard Salwey	Bridge Within	1649–50
Abraham Babington	Bridge Within	1649–51
William Daniel	Bridge Within	1649–54; 1658–59
John Doggett	Walbrook	1649–50; 1652–62
Joshua Woolnough	Bridge Within	1649–52; 1654–60
Richard Burrows	Bridge Within	1651–53; 1655–56
John Brett	Cornhill	1655–57
Thomas Frere	Tower Street	1660

Table 5. Clapham residents who were City
Common Councilmen 1630–60

	Ward	Year	Sheriff
Thomas Hussey senior	Vintry	1645*	
John Beauchamp	Billingsgate	1651	
Richard Cranley	Candlewick	1652–53	
Samuel Moyer	Cheap	1653	
Thomas Chandler	Bishopsgate	1657–58	1658
William Love	Portsoken	1658–62	1659

Table 6. Clapham residents who were aldermen 1630–60

* A fine was paid to avoid the position

Their livery companies would also have provided a source of contact, since there are a number of Fishmongers (six), Merchant Taylor (five), Grocers (five) and Clothworkers (four), and nine of them became Masters of their livery in due course. Table 7 gives the details for 1630–60.

	Company	Post	Year
Lawrence Brinley	Haberdashers	Warden	1648; 1647
		Master	1657
William Darrack	Grocers	Warden	1649
Lawrence Bromfield	Cutlers	Master	1650*
Samuel Moyer	Mercers	Master	1653
Thomas Chandler	Drapers	Master	1658
William Love	Drapers	Master	1659

Table 7. Clapham residents holding posts in their
livery companies 1630–60

* A fine was paid to avoid the position

Many of these men were politically active, if not leaders, in support of Parliament, and many signed the key petitions. At least three had close family ties to people who signed King Charles' death warrant, and a number were invited to join the trial but declined to do so. Three were important enough to be imprisoned in the Tower of London under one or other of the administrations. At one time or other five were MPs, twelve Common Councillors, ten aldermen and nine Master of their livery company.

They were also closely involved in military matters. Salwey, a major, had fought in the Battle of Worcester in 1651 and reported to Parliament on the outcome. His neighbour, **Nicholas Kempson**, was a lieutenant colonel. A number were officers of the London militia or served on the various militia committees. Molins was Comptroller of Ordnance for London and, with his brother-in-law Daniel Judd, supplied gunpowder to the militia and New Army. Two prominent Cromwellian soldiers, William Sydenham and John Desborough, stayed in Clapham just after the Restoration, near their friends and colleagues Moyer, Salwey and William Kiffin.

As might be expected of overseas merchants, the Clapham men were heavily connected with a range of naval, customs and tax business that was of the first significance to their own commercial activity. Cranley and Salwey were both Commissioners of the Navy, and Salwey was offered two ambassadorial posts; Cranley and Moyer were high up in Trinity House; Salwey was on the Council of Trade, which approved the escorts for merchant convoys and was able to give quick endorsement of Thomas Corbett's request for a convoy to support his ships to Hamburg; Moyer and Foxcroft both held senior positions in Customs. Dennis Gauden was already a supplier to the Navy, although he did not become Surveyor General of Victualling to the Navy until 1660. They all used their positions to further their own interests and those of their friends, including other Clapham residents. Both Moyer and Salwey were members of the Levant Company, and they and many other residents owned stock in the East India Company and some in the Companies dealing with Africa.

They were also important players in financial administration, not least because the Navy was a major expense of the government. Moyer, Molins and Winslow were all on the Compounding Committee, meeting two or three times a week, and Henry Colborne was the Registrar for all Crown lands. Many Clapham residents were purchasers of Crown and ecclesiastical land, no doubt benefiting from their contacts; Gabriel Carpenter, Daniel Judd, William Molins and the Society for Propagating the Gospel in New England all gained in this way. Gualter Frost used his position as secretary of the Council to promote – and participate in – commercial schemes run by other Clapham residents.

Cromwell's death and the Restoration

Much changed when Oliver Cromwell died. Once installed, Richard Cromwell secured a new elected parliament. In February 1659 Samuel Moyer presented a petition that had been tried before and was generally regarded as an application for the creation of a republic.[31] Moyer spoke for over an hour in support of it, but the House rejected it by a majority of over one hundred, and refused even to thank the petitioners. Not downhearted, Moyer appeared two days later with an address expressing the hope that the opportunity of pursuing the Lord's work would not be neglected, and that the government might be so settled. The elected parliament was closed down by the Army in May 1659 and the Rump Parliament recalled. Moyer again appeared before it to urge that the government

> *may not be too long trusted in any man's hands: that it may not be perpetuated to men: For we have found by woeful experience, that the best of men, be they what they will, if they have power long in their hands, they may too much exalt themselves; and so forget that they ought to know what it is to obey, as well as to rule.*[32]

A Council of State was created and Salwey appointed to it. It took prompt action to ensure that the militias were controlled by the like-minded, and many of the Clapham connections took up positions they had held previously:

City militia	Abraham Babington, Samuel Moyer, Richard Salwey
Westminster militia	George Foxcroft
Surrey militia	Babington, John Gould, Moyer

Moyer and Molins were reappointed as Commissioners for Sequestration and Moyer as a probate judge, but he had withdrawn from his posts by the end of the year. Meanwhile Salwey took part in the negotiations between the Army and the members of the Rump, and was appointed to both the Council of State, being chairman in September, and the Council of Safety. A popular ballad went:

At first he was a Grocer, who now we Major call:

*Although you would think no Sir, if you saw him
in White-hall.*

*Where he has great Command, and looks for
cap in hand,*

*And if our eggs be not addle, shall be of the next
new Model.*

Sing hi ho Mr Salloway, the Lord in Heaven doth know.

*When that from hence you shall away where to the
Devil you'll go.*[33]

Although the Rump Parliament had returned, many felt uneasy at the removal of an elected parliament and a regime essentially maintained by the Army. There was great and growing fear of the sectaries, including Levellers and Quakers, not least because of their influence on the Army. The whole edifice created by Oliver Cromwell, whereby there was a clear Church structure but independents were tolerated, began to crumble. None of the organizations involved could find a satisfactory method for electing a new parliament, if only because of their concerns that it would prove insufficiently radical. Colonel John Lambert finally dissolved the Rump on 13 October 1659.

This was opposed by many, not least the members of the Rump, and attempts by the Army to create a Committee of Safety to act as a provisional government ran into trouble. Many prominent Parliamentarians refused to join it, and the Army had difficulty securing enough members. Salwey wrote on the Army's request to join, 'I utterly refuse to act as a member of that Committee.'[34]

His Army connections were still important, however, and when the Navy under Vice Admiral Lawson came out in favour of the restoration of Parliament, he was one of two Army representatives sent on 17 December with Sir Henry Vane from Parliament to try and persuade them to change their minds. A contemporary commentator, the diarist Thomas Rugg, said that 'all their faire speeches made by them could not prevail.'[35]

The Navy stuck to its position – that the Army must be subservient to Parliament – and by then Salwey was completely out of favour. Rugg wrote that whereas Salwey and Vane were 'so very active under

To The
RIGHT WORSHIPFUL
The Master, Wardens and Assistants of the Company of
GROCERS
The Humble Petition of Major Salloway

SHEWETH

That being Smok't out of the Parliament, and sent to their Ware-house, the *Tower*, he hath looked about him, and bethought himself, how if in Lieu of his being their Tenant at will and pleasure, they had made him Lieutenant of the place; he might like *Baxter* to the Goldsmiths been a great Honour and Ornament to your company: He well remembreth himself, to have once been one of your Cunning Profession, but that it is no more than a Puny Craft to the Grand Mistery of a Senator, and that the Divel ought not to be longer baited with a GROCER. He applies himself therefore to your worships, Beseeching your brotherly Intercession for him to the Parliament, and presumes to advise you of the words wherewith he stands charged, and which he Humbly Requests you to Extenuate: First that he cared not a FIG for the Parliament; That they were sweetly Dissolved in the *Armies* Tears like any Sugar; That a *Retail* Safety Committee Man, was better than a *Tail* Parliament Member; That he your Petitioner was too *Sweet-scented* for such as House; besides this he conjectures also that the Parliament have taken *Pepper* in their Nose at being *Spiced* with Sir *Harry Vane's* principles, by whom, he was Garbled and made *Net* for the interest of *John Lambert*, when he threw out the Refuse and the Tare.

He therefore beseecheth you to mind the Parliament that he is a *Frail*-Man, & in such a year & such inconstant weather, they must not expect reasons for what he did. & that if he is not *Currant* 'tis General *Moncks* fault, that engrost all and spoilt the Market, and hath also traded into *Spain* for better things than *Plums*. And furthermore to hint to the Parliament his Submissive demeanour at his charge in the House; how *Gingerly* he sate, and how *Tongue-bitten*, how he reverenced the *Mace*, so that he has great hopes he shall not be *Bank-rumpt* or Diffeated, though for a while he may be superseded, and in good time suspended. But if the worst comes to the worst he hath a small stock to set up with at *Queen-Hithe*, which with your helping hand to a beginner may prove better than the stock he had from Sir *Harry*, and if all trades fail him (as he never doubted of that last) he is sure to have a Licence to sell *Stued Prunes* Excise Free.

In tender consideration of these Premises, May it please this worshipful Society, effectually to Address themselves to, and Mediate with the Parliament that they would be pleased to put into the Scale his present Heaviness, and Balance *their Anger with his former Merits, and rebate pro Parliament rato. That's 60 for 500. Considering what a bad bargain he hath made, and how bad the Times are, that have more need of a* Committee of Insurance *than* Safety: *always remembering that good City* Adage, To do as they would be done by; no man knowing whose Turn may be next, according as your learned Clerk Mr Bunbury hath it in his Suburb Exercises upon Ganymede.*

And your Petitioner, &

the Council of Safety against the Parliament in the defection, [they are] now in no esteem but very much slighted by Parliament.'[36]

The Rump Parliament was restored on 26 December and regarded Salwey as a traitor, ordering him to be sent to the Tower on 16 January 1660 (with Sydenham). This was a significant enough event to be recorded by Samuel Pepys in his diary,[37] but Salwey was allowed to retire to his house at Wychwood in Oxfordshire ten days later on grounds of ill health, prompting yet another satirical pamphlet, full of wordplay.[38]

A tug of war followed whereby both the Army and friendly MPs on one side and the City of London on the other sought to get General George Monck to support them. Clapham resident Lawrence Bromfield played a prominent part in the denouement. He was one of three Commissioners sent by the Common Council to bid for Monck's support for the City against the republican MPs. As a result, he was one of eleven members of the Common Council whom Parliament charged Monck to imprison in the Tower on 10 February 1660. Monck finally decided in favour of the City and its demands for a 'free parliament' elected without restrictions, and recalled the secluded members of the Long Parliament, which on its third day of business resolved that its elected successor should meet on 25 April. Meanwhile Bromfield and his colleagues were released after ten days in prison.

Conclusion

In this chapter we have seen both the important roles played by Clapham residents in the politics and administration under Cromwell and the extent of the ties between them. They worked closely together on a range of issues of political significance but also allied to their own particular interest. The fact that they had retiring houses in the same village outside London cemented these contacts and helped the merchants to make the most of them.

(Endnotes)

1. Calendar State Papers, Ireland, 1641, p. 66.

2. Kenneth Andrews, *Ships, Money, and Politics* (Cambridge University Press, 1991), p. 198.

3. M.A. Oppenheim, *A History of the Administration of the Royal Navy* (1896), p. 306.

4. John Hollond, *Two Discourses of the Navy* (1638 and 1659), pp. 265–66.

5. Quoted in John Brown, *The English Puritans* (Cambridge University Press, 1910), p. 133.

6. Quoted in ibid.

7. Keith Lindley and David Scott (eds), *The Journal of Thomas Juxon, 1644–1647,* (Royal Historical Society, 1999), p. 85.

8. Abraham Babington, *An Answer to a Discourse Intituled, Truth it's Manifest, &C.* (1648).

9. Robert Brenner, *Merchants and Revolution* (Verso, 2003), p. 472.

10. Ann Hughes, *Gangraena and the Struggle for the English Revolution* (Oxford University Press, 2004), p. 350.

11. Keith Lindley, *Popular Politics and Religion* (Scolar Press, 1997), p. 371.

12. Ian Gentles, 'The Sale of Bishops' Lands in the English Revolution, 1646–1660', *English Historical Review*, vol. 95, no. 376 (July 1980), pp. 573–96.

13. *A Pair of Spectacles for the City* (4 December 1647), BL E.419/9.

14. *A Case for the City Spectacles* (6 January 1648), BL E.422/7.

15. *Journal of the House of Commons*, 10 January 1649.

16. Bernard Capp, *Cromwell's Navy* (Clarendon Press, 1992), p. 49.

17. *Acts and Ordinances of the Interregnum, 1642–1660* (28 August 1654), HMSO 1911.

18. Brenner, *Merchants and Revolution*, p. 631.

19. Calendar State Papers, Ven. 1647–52, pp. 187–88.

20. Stephen K. Roberts, 'Protecting the Rump', *History Today*, vol. 53, no. 5 (May 2003), p. 92.

21. Jeremy Bangs, *Pilgrim Edward Winslow: New England's First International Diplomat: A Documentary Biography* (New England Historical and Genealogical Society, 2004), p. 268.

22. G.E. Aylmer, *The State's Servants* (Routledge & Kegan Paul, 1973), p. 214.

23. Henry Glass, *The Barbone Parliament* (1899), p. 118.

24. François Guizot, *History of Cromwell and the English Commonwealth* (Bentley, 1854), vol. 2, pp. 5–6; Roberts, 'Protecting the Rump', p. 92.

25. Edward Ludlow, *Memoirs* (1698), p. 176.

26. Quoted in Roberts, 'Protecting the Rump'.

27. Sean Kelsey, 'Richard Salwey', in *Oxford Dictionary of National Biography*.

28. Alfred Wood, *A History of the Levant Company* (Taylor and Francis, 1964), pp. 93–94.

29 Ibid., p. 24.

30. The Independents and Separatists were much more open to lay members leading prayers and put much less emphasis on the need for formal theological education; they were therefore less enthusiastic about the need for universities.

31. It called for a restoration of commonwealth forms of government, with Parliament enjoying untrammelled legislative power and control of revenues, freedom for tender consciences, and no soldiers cashiered without court martial.

32. *Journal of the House of Commons*, 12 May 1659.

33. Percy Society, *Early English Poetry, Ballads and Popular Literature of the Middle Ages*, vol. 4 (1861), p. 158.

34. Thomas Salwey, *Occasional Poems: With a Memoir of the Author, and a Selection from Old Family Letters* (1882).

35. W.L. Sachse (ed.), *The Diurnal of Thomas Rugg: 1659–61* (1961), p. 18.

36. Ibid., p. 24.

37. Samuel Pepys, diary, 17 January 1660.

38. British Library, 1660, General Reference Collection, 669.f23.(16).

CHAPTER 4

CLAPHAM UNDER THE PURITANS

The demands of the Civil War made claims on the parish of Clapham, and the vestry accounts show the variety of contributions it made. It contributed thirty shillings for horses that pulled an artillery train, and £3 for equipping two soldiers at Kingston; it paid one Goodwife Hattonby thirty-five shillings when her husband went off as a Parliamentary soldier and lent her a further £2 to set up a shop. When five horses owned by a number of the yeomen of the parish were commandeered by the Parliamentary army, it was agreed that the cost should be borne by the whole parish, not just those who had lost their horses, a decision that was no doubt helped by the fact that two of those concerned were churchwardens at the time.

Clapham church had already undergone several liturgical changes and consequent reordering following the Reformation. Most, if not all, the silver plate had been sold in 1553, but the next stage took place in the 1640s. In 1644 Parliament passed an Ordinance 'for the further demolishing of Monuments of Idolatry and Superstition'. It required the removal or defacement of statues, pictures and fonts, the levelling of any raised altar, the removal of organs, the destruction of surplices and 'superstitious vestments' and the removal of decoration from silverware. This was naturally enforced in Clapham, and the parish accounts for 1645 include the costs of doing so:

Paid John Payne for taking down ye Crosse	1s 6d
For taking away the font and mending the ground where it stood	4s 0d
For a new marble font	16s
To Goodman Blacklock for taking out ye rubbish	1s 0d

Joshua Foote, himself an active Puritan, was an ironmonger by trade and an obvious choice to deal with the iron communion rails. He removed and sold them for ten shillings, putting the money towards buying an apprenticeship for the son of a poor Clapham widow.

It might be thought that these changes were of little importance except to those with very strong theological views, but that was not so. Moving the Communion table from the nave to the chancel and surrounding it with rails has been described as the liturgical equivalent of enclosing the common fields, since it meant that only the more prosperous parishioners, who sat in the front pews, had unrestricted sight and sound of the celebration of Communion.[1] It may therefore have been significant that the churchwardens at the time the rails and altar were removed were local people rather than London merchants. Surplices, which were regarded by Puritans as examples of popish practice, were not finally abolished until 1644, but in many places were disposed of before then. There are entries in the Clapham parish accounts every year until 1640 for washing, and sometimes mending, the surplice used by the rector in services, but no such reference was made after John Arthur became rector in 1642.

While at first sight this appears to have been speedy implementation, that is not necessarily the case. There had been a number of Ordinances from Parliament from 1641 on, and they had been implemented much more quickly in many City churches, including those with which the Clapham merchants were associated.[2] Foote had been a member of the parish since before 1638, but his City church, All Hallows Lombard Street, had levelled its chancel in response to the order of 1641. William Darrack, resident since 1631, had been a churchwarden at St Pancras, Soper Lane, where radical action against crosses and a variety of images had also been taken in 1641; Lawrence Brinley, resident since 1642, had seen similar changes in his church of St Mary Magdalen, Milk

Street; St Margaret, New Fish Street, Lawrence Bromfield's church, had made the changes in 1641; and finally John Brett, resident since 1642, had seen his church, St Christopher le Stocks, acting in 1643. This may reflect the fact that merchants played an important part in local parish affairs only from 1645.

In 1644 the parish was also required to have the Covenant (the agreement with the Scots to create a Presbyterian Church in England in return for their joining the civil war against Charles I) read out, and each member to swear to it and either sign or make his mark. (The parish had already paid five shillings to have it framed and hung up.) Among other things, this included the commitment 'to adopt the example of the best reformed churches' and to achieve 'the extirpation of Popery Prelacy superstition heresy schism profaneness and whatsoever is contrary to sound doctrine'. Another of the strictures of the new regime was to prohibit the ringing of church bells, but this meant that there was no way to announce the time. As a result, in 1651 a new tower was built near the schoolhouse for the watchmen to stand in, warmed by a stock of seacoal. The two church bells were sold for £6, and £22 was spent on a new 'greate bell' for the tower, weighing five hundredweight.[3]

This shows that the parish of Clapham was now taking its responsibilities very seriously. It is hardly surprising, given that a number of its members were on the committees to deal with 'Scandalous clergy' both nationally and specifically for Surrey. This can be contrasted with what happened at Battersea, where the vicar, the Parliamentary supporter Rev. Dr Thomas Temple, lived happily in the same village as his Royalist cousin and lord of the manor Sir John St John. Battersea's Communion rails, which were installed in 1636 following Archbishop William Laud's enforcing of his requirement for them, were not removed until 1649, four years later than Clapham's, and although a list of those signing the Covenant was taken to the committee in Croydon, they did not pay for it to be framed so as to be readily available to the congregation.[4]

There are further examples of Clapham's Puritan zeal. The new provisions for the Presbyterian governance of the Church of England put Clapham in the fifth classis (a group of churches governed by the same elders) of Surrey, with Camberwell, Battersea, Wandsworth, Streatham, Croydon, Morden and a number of parishes around

Croydon and Sutton. Not many of the churches were very interested, and only Clapham, Battersea, Camberwell, Coulsdon and Morden nominated either ministers (John Arthur for Clapham) or lay elders, of which three were chosen from Clapham: James Sherley; Christopher Vivian, an active Puritan who had invested in the Virginia Company in 1623; and the farmer Edward Meade, whose brother Robert was the only representative at all from Wandsworth.

In 1649, following promotion of the scheme by Edward Winslow, the Rump Parliament passed an Act shortly after the execution of Charles I creating a Corporation (or Society) to Propagate the Gospel in New England. Four of its eighteen members lived in Clapham – Abraham Babington, William Molins, Sherley and Winslow, and Joshua Woolnough later became a member.[5] Given that only half of the eighteen ever turned up, the Clapham members (who did) clearly played an important part. Members had been chosen for their wealth and influence and were 'entirely Puritan, mostly independent, and mostly merchants'.[6] Bromfield and Brinley joined after the Restoration, and over its lifetime no fewer than sixteen Clapham residents were members. Ministers were required to read the Act to their parishioners and make a collection in support. By six weeks after the Act, the parish of Clapham had raised the large sum of some £90 for the cause, almost 10 per cent of the total raised in London. Dennis Gauden was appointed 'to carry [the money] into Mr Floyd the Treasurer living at the Maremaide in Cheapside'.[7] The Corporation invested the money and transmitted the income to New England. At first it passed the money directly, but later goods were transferred instead, often purchased from those members of the Corporation who traded with North America. Babington sold £100 worth of cloth to the society in 1651 and £180 worth in 1652, jointly with Joshua Woolnough; the latter also sold goods himself in this way, as did Daniel Judd.[8] John Arthur sold a horse to the Corporation in 1656. At one stage its members thought of paying Winslow a salary directly from its funds, but they realised that this might not look good and found an alternative way of paying him for the work he did in support of the Corporation. Winslow and Molins made use of their position on the Commission for Sequestered Estates to sell the Corporation a number of lands under its remit, including some fee farm rents in Northumberland. The Clapham members of the Corporation continued to work together, and as late as 1659 Babington, Molins and two others were sent to get help from Sion College for 'the printing of the Bible in the Indian tongue.'[9]

Being godly did not mean that the merchants were a soft touch for the poor, and a principal problem of the parish was how to reduce the financial consequences of the Poor Law, presumably because appearing rich attracted many who hoped for support. The parish kept a constant watch on those for whom it might be required to provide maintenance, and was on its guard to avoid poor strangers coming to them for help. One of the farmers was forced to undertake 'to save harmless this parish' from any costs arising from 'a poor woman with child' who worked for him. In another case, in 1648, a widow, having admitted that she did 'harbour in one of my outhouses a vagrant woman with her child for several days and nights without the permission of the parishioners of the said parish and afterwards the said woman went away and left the said child in the said outhouse,' promised to indemnify the parish from all cost, while 'humbly entreating' the parish to assist her with such a 'great charge'. In response, and stressing the voluntary nature of their action, the parish officials granted her two shillings and sixpence a week for the child's upkeep while she was put to nurse, and an offer to look at a continuation if that became necessary.

Not long afterwards the parish strengthened its defences by building a cage at the cost of £12 to secure vagrants and others worthy of imprisonment, and gave the Constable a staff to help him assert his authority, but it continued to look for other means of reducing the poor bill. Goodman Humphrey was granted a pension of two shillings a week 'so long as he is able to keep beggars and vagrants out of the town', and a little later he was awarded a pension of twelvepence a week and a further twelvepence a week as a warder, presumably of the cage, both depending on his good behaviour. The cage was later moved to a more convenient place for watching, and a chimney attached to it to keep the watchman warm.

Churchwardens were abolished during the Commonwealth, and, unlike in many places, this was implemented in Clapham, at least in form. After 1649 the vestry records show that nominees were appointed simultaneously to the offices of churchwarden and overseer and collector of the poor. There was obviously some worry about this restriction, because they were sometimes given a wider responsibility: in 1656, for example, they were appointed to be 'Overseers for the poore and other affairs for the parish', while in 1657 they were 'Overseer and Collector for the poore who shall do in place of churchwardens under that name'. There were other vestry posts, two 'surveyors of roads' who had the responsibility of ensuring that the roads in the parish were maintained, and a Constable/Headborough, who organized the minor policing and delivered any miscreants to a Justice of the Peace. The merchants played their full part in filling these posts – and of course they could be fined if they declined to do so. James Sherley was a churchwarden in 1639 and 1643 and held other offices; Abraham Babington was churchwarden from 1652 to 1655; Colonel (later Sir) Lawrence Bromfield in 1651 and his son-in-law Thomas Corbett in 1653–54; and William Molins together with Daniel Judd in 1649. Dennis Gauden was surveyor or churchwarden for a long period, and John Gould, William Daniel and Thomas Rodbard senior all held posts.

The better-off locals, including Thomas Crencher, an innkeeper in the village and the lessee of the windmill, were also elected to parish office, but apart from Edward Meade they were not churchwardens after the late 1640s until 1663. Another important post was that of Ale Conner; appointed for the first time in 1657, charged with ensuring that beer was served in proper measures, and in 1657 and 1658 the vestry officials were told to buy the necessary 'weights, drafts and measures' for his work. There was also a tightening of parish control over documents and money. The law required all parish documents, including the register, to be kept in a chest with three locks, one for each churchwarden and one for the rector. But at the beginning of 1656 the parish took steps to enforce this by recovering documents held by Gauden and moving the chest from the rector's house to a small room in the schoolhouse.

There must have been pressure to observe the Sabbath and prevent any activity that might be viewed as inappropriate. However, there is only one report of such enforcement, when John King, a farmer and churchwarden, imposed a twenty-five-shilling fine on William Wonnals in 1658 for 'breaking the Sabbath'. There is no evidence that Wonnals lived in Clapham, so it may well have been that it was easier to enforce the law on strangers.

All this demonstrates that the merchants living in Clapham were clearly Puritan, but exactly what their religious views were is not always easy to determine, nor were they necessarily constant in time. We have already seen something of Sherley's views, and these are confirmed by part of a letter he wrote to William Bradford in May 1641:

> *Now blessed be God, the times be much changed here.*
> *I hope to see many of you return to your native country*
> *again and have such freedom and liberty as the Word of*
> *God prescribes. Our bishops were never so near downfall*
> *as now. God hath miraculously confounded them and*
> *turned all their popish and Machiavellian plots and*
> *projects on their own heads.*[10]

There were certainly a number of Clapham merchants of more radical beliefs, and who supported separatist and Independent churches. Moyer and Salwey were two, and a ballad about Salwey reveals his views very clearly:

> *The tobacco-man Salway, with a heart full of gall,*
> *Puffs down bells, steeples, priests, churches and all,*
> *As old superstitious relicks of Baal.*[11]

Salwey himself saw the hand of God supporting the action of a government run by the godly. He described English victories in the naval war against the Dutch as 'miraculous works' of God's power, which pointed to 'the more spiritual appearance of our Lord Jesus in his kingdom'.[12] His religious views were such that no less a person than the radical minister Hugh Peter wrote that he 'deserves well of his Countrey and the Kingdom for his wisedom and faithfulness in many ways'.[13]

But probably more of these Clapham men were Presbyterians who wanted a structured national Church with clear leadership – as long as it was not Episcopal. Certainly, Richard Cranley requested in his will that 'some godly Presbyterian minister' should be arranged to preach a sermon at his funeral.[14] Bromfield was fiercely Presbyterian, and as vestryman of St Dunstan in the East was involved in that church's decision to overrule the order to its minister, Henry Wilkinson, to refuse the sacrament to those who were thought unworthy. Wilkinson ended up running a school in Clapham after the Restoration, and it is natural to suppose that Bromfield had a hand in his appointment.

For others, the position is more complicated. George Foxcroft was a prominent member of St Stephen, Coleman Street, and one of those nominated by the Independent minister John Goodwin to identify those parishioners whose views were sufficiently orthodox to receive Communion (their names recorded in a ledger), and correspondingly to withhold the rite from others. Clapham residents were still being appointed in 1654 to the oversight of the removal of 'scandalous ministers', and William Sydenham, John Corbett, William Molins, James Sherley and Abraham Babington all played this role.

A good way to judge religious views is to look at the pastors who were left money in the merchants' wills. Francis Bridges left £10 to his cousin Charles Offspring at St Antholin; his wife, Sarah, left money to a large number of clergy, including Thomas Temple of Battersea, Matthew Haviland of the Presbyterian parish of Holy Trinity the Less, Mr Norton of St Michael le Querne, Simeon Ashe the strong Presbyterian and opponent of Independents, and Edmund Staunton, vicar of Kingston upon Thames, who was active in moves to establish a classical Presbyterian system in Surrey. (Staunton was appointed President of Corpus Christi Oxford in 1648, but ejected after the Restoration.) She also left a legacy to Henry Burton, an extreme separatist minister who had been imprisoned under Laud and had his ears cut off for claiming in a sermon that the innovations being introduced by the bishops amounted to a popish plot. However, Burton died shortly after she wrote her will, and in a codicil she transferred the legacy to the Puritan vicar of Lambeth, John Rawlinson. Lawrence Brinley left a legacy to 'my dearly beloved pastor and faithful minister of Jesus Christ Edmund Calamy', one of the leading Presbyterian clerics and vicar of St Mary, Aldermanbury.

Another way to understand the religious views might be to look at the introduction to wills, which usually contained religious language relating to the beliefs of the testator. However, these were usually relatively standard texts, corresponding to what is now called 'boilerplate', and the same words appear frequently, possibly because the detailed wording of the wills was written by lawyers or scriveners. The preamble to Sir Henry Atkins' will went further than the standard rubrics used by many Clapham residents, however:

First I give to my soul to Almighty God, my Creator,
Redeemer and Preserver, trusting through His mercy
that the same shall be presented to His Divine Majesty,
without spot or wrinkle, being first washed with the most
precious blood of My Saviour Jesus Christ, Who is able
to make my sins, though they were as red as scarlet, to be
as white as snow. And for my body, the coffin of my soul,
I commit the same to the mother earth from whence it
came, to be buried without pomp or vain glory.

A minor variation is found in the will of Ann Carpenter, Sarah Bridges' sister-in-law, in which she expressed the hope that 'I shall have eternal life in his most glorious Kingdom prepared for the elect.' Francis Polstead, meanwhile, hoped for 'eternal happiness with the Saints in heaven'.

Whatever their religious views, they were all fiercely opposed to the changes proposed and enforced by Archbishop Laud. Francis Bridges was one of the Feoffees of Impropriations who bought up advowsons, giving the right to appoint to those parishes Puritan ministers whom they trained at St Antholin. Henry Colborne endowed schools in his home of Kirkham, Lancashire, and ensured that they would be run by Puritan ministers, provoking continued litigation with the aggrieved parish council.[15] Clapham parish itself played its part in implementing the reversal of Laud's changes. The parish eagerly accepted the change to civil marriage and became a centre for Radicals to marry. Instead of a rush to marry before the changes, in Clapham there was an increase afterwards. A school was also built, and continued to appoint Puritan schoolmasters for fifty years. Clapham merchants also played a full part in the affairs of the county of Surrey. As well as being on the militia committee from time to time, John Corbett, William Molins, Abraham Babington and James Sherley were all on the Surrey Committee dealing with scandalous ministers, and Babington was on the committee appointed to investigate Dulwich College, which was accused of failing to appoint suitable (meaning Puritan) ministers as schoolmasters.

The clergy in Clapham during this period would normally have been appointed by the lord of the manor, although as it happens neither was put in place by the Atkins family. There were only two of them, both scholars. **Francis Taylor** was rector from 1615 until 1642 and was known as a scholar of Hebrew, maintaining an extensive correspondence (in Latin) with Boethius and Archbishop James Ussher. Taylor was distinguished by his 'great learning and moderation' and was 'a learned linguist and worthy divine'; he managed to be both nominated to the Assembly of Divines and presented by Archbishop Laud to the living of Yalding in Kent.[16] He had two blind sons, whom he still managed to send to university. He asked his friend the master of Sidney Sussex College, Cambridge, to suggest a tutor for one of them, saying that he had Latin, Greek and 'perfect' Hebrew grammar.[17]

In another letter Taylor asked the same man to intercede to help another son get a scholarship to Oxford, 'so my charge will be eased ... for I have another blind son ... besides seven other children'.[18] The sons had been blinded as a result of smallpox, so it may be that they had already been well into studies while still sighted, but it must have been a great effort to continue to learn three languages while not being able to read them. The eldest son, also Francis, took his degree, was ordained and began by preaching at Canterbury Cathedral. He became a Presbyterian, was excommunicated and finished up a Congregationalist minister.

The father held the parish of Yalding for three years at the same time as residing at Clapham, provoking a petition in 1640 from the residents of Yalding to the House of Commons. After explaining that the living was worth some £250 a year and that Taylor was very rarely present, it catalogued a list of Puritan concerns:

> Wee have had noe preaching Pastor that hath been conscionable to performe his office faithfully amongst us by the space of thirty years and upwards, whereby honest hearts are sadded, and others are ignorant and lewd.
>
> Our Communion table is sett upp close to the wall at the east end of the chancel alterwise; the east end of the said chancel (to which the said table is joined) is new winscotted, with Cherubyms carved in the said wainscot, and a rayle with two ascents thereto lately made. Mr Thomas Tourney, who was our late Vicar, ... did usually bowe to the said Table, and adore it; soe wee not knowing what the end and meaning of such things are, are thereat much troubled, and our consciences offended.

*Wherefore, wee doe earnestly and humbly desire
this honourable house to take consideracion of our
condicions, and to remove our grievances; and so to
provide that we may have faithful pastors. We humbly
make bold to mencion Mr Francis Cornewell, a painfull
preacher of good report, which wee nevertheless
recommend to your godly wisdom.*[19]

This petition seems to have left Taylor unmoved, but he finally left
for Yalding in 1642, probably because of Francis Bridges' will, which
left him £50 if he took up the post and left Clapham within five
months of Bridges' death. (Taylor must have known what was going
to be in the will, because his successor was in fact instituted the day
before the will was signed.) His stay in Yalding does not seem to
have been a happy one, since he was deprived of the parish in 1648
following further complaints to Parliament from the parishioners.
He subsequently moved to be a preacher at Canterbury Cathedral
until his death in 1656.

Taylor was succeeded by **John Arthur,** who was presented by the
king since Richard Atkins, the lord of the manor, was a minor at the
time. Arthur came from a family of landed gentry in Essex and was
at Emmanuel College, Cambridge, at the same time as Gualter Frost.
His wife, Susan, died in Clapham in 1642 and he quickly married
Dorothy Hall. She had eight children in thirteen years, of whom only
one, John, survived to adulthood, marrying Anne, the daughter of
Thomas Corbett.

John Arthur was well connected both politically and theologically,
and was one of the clerics appointed by the Common Council
to preach at one of the feasts or special occasions. This suggests
that, in common with the majority of the others so appointed, he
was a Presbyterian rather than Independent by inclination.[20] His
contemporary Edmund Calamy said of him that 'he lived and died
a moderate Nonconformist.'[21] He is credited with having drafted a
petition to Parliament that was enough of a submissive recantation to
prevent the impassioned Presbyterian William Jenkyn from execution
in 1651, following his involvement in the City Presbyterian plot to
restore Charles II. Arthur had had some trouble extracting the £250
dowry of his second wife, Dorothy, from her father, Sir John Hall,
and appointed Sherley and two others to act for him to secure its

return. He petitioned Parliament not long after the marriage, accusing his father-in-law of fraud, and was successful in getting his dowry. Relations were clearly mended, because Sir John died in Clapham and was buried there. Arthur's will demonstrates that he was well-off, with substantial property to leave.

Arthur had been a lecturer in the parish for a year or so before taking over from Taylor, and was relaxed about more radical ministers preaching in Clapham. We have already seen that William Hughes may have preached there, and other radicals included William Bridge and Jeremiah Burroughs. Anthony Wood, the strong Royalist chronicler of Puritans and so hardly an unbiased observer, describes Bridge as

> A frequent preacher before the Long Parliament, a
> notorious independent, and a keeper up of factions by
> continual preaching during the time of the usurpation,
> silenced upon his Majesty's return, carried on his cause
> with the said Jeremiah Burroughes in conventicles in
> Clapham in Surrey.[22]

Burroughs, another product of Emmanuel College, was one of the first Congregationalists. His views are summed up well by the following:

> If their congregations might not be exempted from that
> coercive power of the classes, if they might not have
> liberty to govern themselves in their own way, as long
> as they behaved peaceably towards the civil magistrate,
> they were resolved to suffer, or go to some other place of
> the world where they might enjoy their liberty. But while
> men think there is no way of peace but by forcing all to
> be of the same mind; while they think the civil sword
> is an ordnance of God to determine all controversies
> of Divinity, and that it must needs be attended with
> fines and imprisonment to the disobedient; while
> they apprehend there is no medium between a strict
> uniformity and a general confusion of all things; while
> these sentiments prevail, there must be a base subjection
> of men's consciences to slavery, a suppression of much
> truth, and great disturbances in the Christian world.[23]

These words describe very well the desire of the Independents to protect their 'tender conscience', and, although written in the context of the Presbyterians wishing to control the Church, apply just as well to the subsequent arguments between Anglicans and Dissenters after the Restoration.

While there is information about the merchants and gentry who lived in the parish, there is almost nothing about the other residents. Their names appear regularly in the parish register as they were baptised, married or buried, and there was intermarriage between the families, often where it made sense for landholdings to be preserved or confirmed in a single ownership. The only two sources are material in the vestry accounts and wills, the latter of which are necessarily associated with those who had something worth writing a will for. This did not have to be very much, and there are wills existing for the less well-off, often given orally but in front of witnesses, specifying particular legacies to children or grandchildren before the rest of their belongings went to the main legatee, normally their wife or eldest son.

One example of a will of this type is that of **Edward Meade**. He was a local farmer, not a merchant, but was clearly a man of parts. He was one of the Clapham delegates to the Surrey Presbyterian classis, a churchwarden with Dennis Gauden and the only 'local' who was a trustee of the school. He could read and write, since he left a coffer of books to his son and he signed the parish accounts rather than making his mark, but his will, although probated under Canterbury, contains almost no legacies, the largest being forty shillings and a gilt bowl to his eldest daughter.

On the other hand, **Bartholomew Cottingham** was shown as having a house and nineteen acres in the manorial extent of 1628, and paid £8 a year rent for it. He was a man of some substance, churchwarden twice in the early 1640s and a regular scrutineer of the parish accounts, making his mark rather than signing his name. Although his estate was large enough to be probated under Canterbury, it was dealt with by the Winchester diocese, and he carefully divided it between his two surviving sons. When he died in 1645 he left £40 to his younger son, Humphrey, and a further £20 to Humphrey's three-year-old daughter for when she came of age, or married if that were earlier. His will went on:

> I do give unto my son John my best feather bed, two
> blankets and four pairs of sheets, beside those he hath,
> a bolster and a pillow, 8 napkins, and the middle brass

*kettle, an iron kettle and a great joine chest. All the rest
of my moveables I do give unto my son Humphrey to
whom also I do give the benefit of both my leases which I
have of Balaam house and land, and wood fields for two
full years and a half.*

Everything remaining went 'solely' to his elder son, John.

But even smaller landholders made wills. In 1640 **Robert
Shasberry**, who rented a house and one acre, left £3 each to his two
sons and three grandchildren; **John Wells**, who jointly leased two
large plots of twelve and twenty-two acres, left £10 to his son in
1639 and the rest to

*my loving wife Elizabeth Wells for her maintenance and
the breeding and providing for all those children which
I have by her not doubting but that she will perform the
part of a loving mother to them and discharge the trust
that I have in her, when I shall be dead and gone.*

John Sole, a yeoman and three times churchwarden who died in
1650, wrote: 'It is my will that my well beloved wife Mary Sole
shall continue and live with my sonne John Sole so long as they can
lovingly agree together'; 'in case they shall think fit to depart one
from another', he made provision to divide the estate, including
leaving fifteen acres to his wife.

At the lowest end, we have an inventory for a Clapham
husbandman, Blacklock, who died insolvent in 1650. The inventory
of his goods, which were sold by auction to pay his bills, has very
little that is worth more than one shilling.[24] The most valuable pieces
were two flock beds and bolsters that sold for ten shillings between
them, more than the two beds, which sold for three shillings. There
was one coverlet, but no sheets or rugs. The whole of his possessions
sold for £2 5s, which only just covered the rent he owed.

Conclusion

This chapter has shown that despite heavy commitments in the
City for both business and their parishes, the merchants played an
important part in the administration and activities of Clapham itself.
They managed to do this successfully even though they held a range

of religious views, albeit within the Puritan framework. They may well have been helped in this by the presence of two heavyweight rectors who themselves were active in the discussions in London about the structure and beliefs appropriate for the national Church.

(Endnotes)

1. Steve Hindle, in Alexandra Shepard and Philip Withington (eds), *Communities in Early Modern England: Networks, Place, Rhetoric* (Manchester University Press, 2000), p. 213.

2. Julie Spraggon, *Puritan Iconoclasm during the English Civil War* (Woodbridge, 2004), passim.

3. Robert de Montjoie Rudolf, *Clapham before 1700* (1904), p. 46.

4. J.G. Taylor, *Our Lady of Battersey* (George White, 1925), p. 73.

5. Society for the Propagation of the Gospel to New England, *The New England Company of 1649 and John Eliot …* (The Prince Society, 1920).

6. William Kellaway, *The New England Company* (Longmans, 1961), p. 12.

7. Clapham vestry minutes, 23 September 1649.

8. Kellaway, *The New England Company*, pp. 65–66.

9. Ibid., p. 129.

10. William Bradford, *Of Plymouth Plantation*, ed. Samuel Morison (Knopf, 1952), p. 399.

11. Percy Society, *Early English Poetry, Ballads and Popular Literature of the Middle Ages*, vol. 4 (1861), p. 159.

12. Quoted in Stephen Pincus, *Protestantism and Patriotism* (Cambridge University Press, 2002), p. 49.

13. Hugh Peter, *Last Reports of English Wars* (1646).

14. Kenneth Andrews, *Ships, Money, and Politics* (Cambridge University Press, 1991), p. 47.

15. Joseph P. Ward, *Culture, Faith and Philanthropy* (Palgrave Macmillan, 2013), p. 1.

16. Daniel Neal, *The History of the Puritans*, vol. 4 (1738), p. 230.

17. Rev. Francis Taylor, letter to Dr Samuel Ward, 9 March 1637, Bodley Tanner Ms 70 f92.

18. Ibid., 14 June 1636, Bodley Tanner Ms 90 f123.

19. See http://yaldinghistory.webplus.net/page142.html.

20. Robert Brenner, *Merchants and Revolution* (Verso, 2003), p. 568.

21. Quoted in A.G. Matthews, *Calamy Revised* (Oxford University Press, 1934), p. 16.

22. Anthony Wood, *Athenae Oxonienses*, vol. 3 (1691), Col. 714.

23. F. Reynolds Levett, *History of Clapham Congregational Church* (1912), p. n13.

24. Rudolf, *Clapham before 1700*, p. 33.

CHAPTER 5

THE RESTORATION: CONTINUITY AND ADJUSTMENT

T
here is a gap in the annual rate assessments for Clapham from
1658 to 1663 which the records for a new tax help to fill. The
Hearth Tax was levied on the number of hearths in a house,
a direct measure of size, as well as the name of the occupier. Returns
survive for Clapham for 1662, 1664 and 1674, and comparable
data is available for the City of London, Middlesex and Surrey.
Combining information from the Hearth Tax and rate assessments
shows that the number of merchants increased only a little, from
twenty-five in 1657 to thirty-two in 1662, and the number of larger
houses then remained approximately constant until the early 1680s,
although there was a slight increase in smaller dwellings. There is a
considerable degree of continuity; while four of the merchants present
in Clapham in 1657 had died by 1662, the remaining twenty-one (or
their widows) were still there – fourteen since the late 1640s – and
very few moved house. Seven large houses were added between 1657
and 1664, but three quarters of the merchant houses had been built
before the Restoration and all of them before the Plague and Great
Fire, events that are sometimes assumed to have been the driver of
Clapham's growth. Moreover, apart from one substantial rebuilding,
the declared hearths for the houses hardly change during this period.
We can assume that the Hearth Tax returns in 1664 describe the
Clapham houses from the 1650s up to the early 1680s.

The gentry and better-off merchants in London and the immediate
suburbs had houses with seven or more hearths, and this is also true

in Clapham; in 1662 only four merchant families were in houses with fewer than seven hearths, and those four were are all headed by widows and had five hearths.[1] None of the yeomen farmers or 'locals' had seven hearths, although three of them had six. The overall distribution of houses by hearths is shown in Table 8.

hearths	1–2	3–6	7+	10+	15+	20+	total
houses	30	34	28	17	8	4	92

Table 8. Clapham houses by number of hearths, 1664
Source: Hearth Tax Online

Only a third of the houses had one or two hearths, compared with the average proportion over the whole of Surrey and Middlesex of 64 per cent and 54 per cent respectively.[2] On the other hand, 30 per cent of the houses have seven or more hearths, and the average number per house is just over six. This is very unlike an ordinary rural village, which might have had at most two or three large houses,[3] and is much more typical of an urban environment.[4] It is also different from other Surrey parishes near London: Putney and Mortlake, both twice the area of Clapham, have roughly the same number of houses with more than seven hearths, but about 120 houses each with only one or two hearths (compared with thirty for Clapham); the average number of hearths per house is under four.

The boundary between 'middling' houses in metropolitan London, lived in by merchants and professionals, and 'great' houses for the very rich and the aristocracy is usually put at fifteen hearths.[5] On this basis, there were eight 'great' houses in Clapham. Dennis Gauden's house, with thirty-nine hearths and more than 400 acres, was certainly substantial and notable enough to appear on maps;[6] the Manor House had thirty hearths with a 200-acre park, but by 1670 it had been split into two parts and the park was usually let to a farmer. Next were two houses with twenty to twenty-two hearths; one was lived in by Hugh Forth and the other by Gualter Frost. John Gould's house had eighteen hearths; John Arthur's seventeen, although his successor lived in a smaller house; the house lived in variously by Thomas Corbett and Lawrence Bromfield had fifteen hearths, as did that of Thomas Langham, who had moved into the house of his fellow silkman Alderman Thomas Chandler.

As well as these eight houses, there were a further nine with between ten and fifteen hearths, and eleven with between seven and nine. This indicates a remarkable concentration of wealthy merchants, and there are only five parishes around London with a comparable distribution of house sizes at the time. They fall into two groups: the first comprises three parishes west of the City of Westminster – Chelsea, Brompton and Kensington – frequented by the aristocracy and landed gentry rather than merchants. The second group is Hackney and Stoke Newington, both of which were well-known as Nonconformist centres after the Restoration; Hackney had, at 109, by far the largest number of houses of seven or more hearths. This is partly because it was one of the largest parishes, four times the size of Chelsea, three times that of Clapham, and half as large again as Hampstead. In practice it consisted of a number of distinct clusters of dwellings, all but one of which clusters individually shows the same housing distribution. Hampstead and Islington both had larger properties, but almost half their houses had only one or two hearths.[7] This analysis confirms that Clapham was indeed unusual in having such a large concentration of merchant houses, and a similar conclusion was reached in a study using the Hearth Tax returns of 1674.[8]

Although these merchants' retiring houses were substantial, they were not like those built by the aristocracy or substantial landed gentry on their estates, designed for entertaining the locals as much as for living in. Nor were they 'villas', such as those built in the eighteenth century by Alexander Pope and Henry Walpole. They were rarely built by the merchant himself, who usually took a lease or even rented for a short term only. Merchants had no great emotional attachment to their houses, and their wills often directed that the lease and contents be sold and the money invested in property elsewhere to provide an income. All the houses from this period have been demolished, but a careful study of the rate assessment and various deeds allows most of the early 1660s merchants' houses in Clapham to be located (see Map 6).

Almost 80 per cent of them were concentrated along what had been called 'Canterbury Way' and so avoided the two main roads from London to Kingston and Portsmouth on the one hand and Epsom and Worthing on the other. The six remaining merchant's houses were along the road to London Bridge but it has not been possible to locate them exactly. In any case there were very few houses round Clapham Common which was very different from the present park like environment[9]. Its soil was poorly drained, acid and infertile, and the commonest flora were thorn bushes and brambles; it constituted what we could call a heath. Indeed its name was Clapham Heath until the eighteenth century.

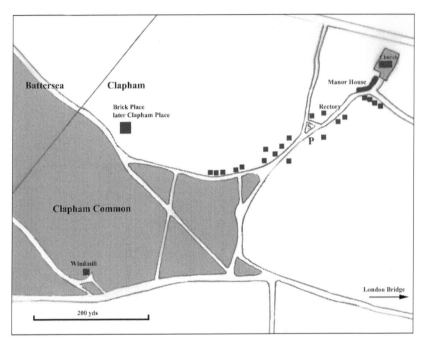

Map 6. Merchant houses in Clapham, early 1660s

The stability of the population meant that new people could move in only when existing houses became available, and it is not surprising that incomers already had some connection with Clapham, whether through family, politics, business or religion. This helped to maintain the homogeneity of the residents.

Although there are no rate assessments for the early 1660s, Clapham's vestry records show that three radicals attended meetings in 1661, all of them friends or colleagues of existing residents. Two were Oliver Cromwell's major generals **William Sydenham** and **John Desborough**, both part of the group who forced Richard Cromwell to dissolve Parliament. Sydenham was expelled from Parliament in 1660, at the same time as Richard Salwey, but took the oath of allegiance, putting up a bond of £1,000 that he would not act against the government. He certainly lived in Clapham. He left a house there; he and his wife were buried there in 1661; his will describes him as 'of Clapham', and two of his neighbours, Robert Whitlock and John Corbett, were his executors; and he also deposited a large sum of money with John Gould, asking him to support his children rather than buy land for them. The third radical was **Captain William Kiffin**, who was also described as 'of Clapham' on a security bond issued around the same time.[10] He was a prominent merchant, a leading Particular Baptist preacher, a captain in the militia and a close associate of Samuel Moyer. All three were well-known personally to Salwey and Moyer, who were on the Council of State in 1653 and 1659 with both Sydenham and Desborough. Kiffin had been on the City militia committee with Abraham Babington, Salwey and Moyer when the Rump was recalled in May 1659, and Sydenham on the Surrey militia committee with Babington, Gould and Moyer.

None of these three stayed long in Clapham, and the changes following the death of Oliver Cromwell had very significant effects on the Puritans in Clapham and elsewhere. Gradually the return of Charles began to seem more attractive, even if it meant a return to an episcopally governed Church. This was reinforced in April 1660 by Charles issuing the Declaration of Breda, which offered religious liberty to 'those of tender consciences' and agreed to pardon many of his father's enemies. There was continued worry that the sects would take over, and Samuel Pepys commented that 'either the Fanatiques must now be undone or the Gentry and citizens throughout England and clergy must fall.'[11] The new so-called Convention Parliament, dominated by Royalist and Anglican MPs, assembled on 25 April 1660 resolved to proclaim Charles king and invite him to return.[12] Bromfield was chosen by the City to be one of the members of the committee sent to meet Charles in The Hague and to prepare for his return to England; he was knighted as a result. Charles sailed from his exile to Dover and arrived in London on 29 May, his thirtieth birthday.

At first, all appeared to try to work together to settle the future of the Church. Moderate Presbyterian ministers looked for possible compromises, wanting not just to be tolerated but to be comprehended (that is, included) in the national Church, and Charles pressed Anglicans to accept some deal. However, the supposed commitment to toleration did not last long, despite the thought expressed in a ballad of 1661:

> Come, come, Independent, and cast off thy hate,
> Consider the workings of God here of late,
> How miraculously he hath brought it about,
> To bring in the king whom they thought to keep out.
> The Presbyter and the Episcopal man
> May safely rejoyce now, because that they can
> Freely enjoy what is duly their own,
> That's to have their estates and the king have his crown.[13]

The more rigid Presbyterians rejected the compromises, as did the bishops, and the House of Commons failed, albeit by a small majority, to proceed with a bill in November 1660 for Protestant accommodation. This was followed by the millennialist Fifth Monarchist uprising in London, which, although insignificant in the support it received, revived the worries about sectaries. Anglican fears were confirmed when London's reformed Protestants turned the election of City MPs for the new parliament in 1661 into a plebiscite against an unequivocal Anglican restoration of the Church. The MPs elected were strong Presbyterians and one Independent, **William Love**, who owned land in Clapham.

All compromise was rejected. The new 'Cavalier' Parliament repudiated the Solemn League and Covenant, and one of its first pieces of legislation, the Corporation Act of November 1661, required holders of office to have taken Holy Communion according to the rites of the Church of England and to renounce the Covenant. This effectively excluded those who did not conform from office in the City, and the Uniformity Act, which received Charles' support in May 1662, went further. It required the deprivation from their posts of all parish clergy who failed to conform to the entire Book of Common Prayer, to accept episcopal ordination, to repudiate the Covenant and to renounce the legitimacy of political resistance under all circumstances. It was coupled with a statute directed against separatist worship.

The Uniformity Act was brought into operation on 24 August, St Bartholomew's Day, which was subsequently known by those affected as Black Bartholomew's Day. This was the day on which clergy were due their tithes, in arrears, so failure to conform meant losing the money owing to them. In an irony that will not have been missed at the time, it was the ninetieth anniversary of the massacre of Protestants in France on St Bartholomew's Eve in 1572. On 17 August 1662, the last Sunday on which the Dissenting ministers could preach legally, Thomas Lye told his flock that he knew of many hundreds, if not thousands, of congregations who were at that moment 'mingling tears with us'.[14] Some 936 clergy refused to take the oath and were ejected from their parishes; a further 1,000 had already been ejected for one reason or another.[15] This refusal to conform created the first 'Nonconformists'. The vast majority of these ejected clergy lost their income as a consequence and had to look elsewhere for work; 101 became schoolteachers, 47 became chaplains in sympathetic aristocratic or gentry households, and 59 became doctors, usually by qualifying in European universities, particularly that of Leiden in the Netherlands.[16] Clapham provided a sympathetic home for at least fourteen ejected ministers in a variety of roles, both immediately after their ejection in 1662 and later, resulting in a continuing history of Nonconformist preaching and teaching in Clapham into the eighteenth century.

John Arthur was also ejected, even though he had not been prevented from receiving an Oxford degree of Doctor of Divinity under Charles II (supposedly obtained for him by his friends, without his involvement). He was too old to travel to Oxford to receive it in person; his ejection did not result in his moving, and he died in Clapham the next year, 1663. Unusually, his father's ejection does not seem to have affected the son (also John), who was allowed to proceed to his degree of Doctor of Medicine at Oxford a few years later.

The Uniformity Act was succeeded in 1664 by the Conventicle Act, which was designed to prevent private worship outside the revived episcopal order, and still further controls were soon introduced. During the Plague, Dissenting ministers returned to the City to preach and support their parishioners, in signal contrast to the Anglican priests who had replaced them. The Five Mile Act, passed at the height of the Plague in October 1665, prevented Nonconformist ministers from coming within five miles of incorporated towns or the place of their former living, thus formally preventing them from working in Clapham.

The rectors of Clapham after John Arthur show no Nonconformist tendency. The new rector was John Gurgany, who had a long-standing connection with the Atkins family. As a Royalist, he had been removed from his Oxford positions in 1648, but, following the Restoration, he accumulated a number of honours and rich livings before finally becoming rector of Clapham. Curates in Clapham in this period were also Royalist, and one of them was **William Sherlock**, who came in 1667 as curate for two years. It is possible that his stay in Clapham gave rise to the later charges that he had been a Dissenting preacher, but he rapidly became known as a strong Anglican controversialist, taking on both Nonconformists and Roman Catholics.

At the same time, there was a lessening of the Puritan restrictions on entertainment in Clapham. Molins created a 'bowling alley' on the part of the Common next to his house; 'he had [it] fenced in and planted with trees', and managed to get it excluded from any rate assessment during his ownership. The merchant **Edward Munns** organized frequent archery matches on the Common, including with William Hughes, the Nonconformist clergyman. Social pressure against drinking may also have declined, but only temporarily; the parish minutes show several complaints in 1665 of 'the great abuse … by the increase of such Alehouses as are not according to law'. The Justices were asked to suppress all such houses except the White Hart (kept by William Gurney, a former parish officer) and 'one that Thomas Crencher either do or shall keep'. The Surrey Quarter sessions record the prosecutions of two women and one man for keeping an unlicensed alehouse or a common tippling house.

Discrimination against Clapham residents

The number of Dissenters on the City Common Council fell from 110 in 1660 to 21 in 1665.[17] In keeping with this change, the Independents and Presbyterians in Clapham withdrew or were rejected from their prominent positions in City and national politics, and returned to business or retired. John Corbett was obliged to surrender his seals as a judge after the Restoration. Joshua Woolnough was appointed briefly as an alderman in 1664 but paid a fine to be excused, not being able to swear the oath. Sir Lawrence Bromfield, despite being one of the pillars of the Presbyterian establishment, was voted off the City Common Council in 1663.

Clapham radicals also lost their positions on other bodies. Neither Molins nor Babington were put forward for the board of the reincorporated and renamed Society for Propagating the Gospel in New England and parts adjacent in America; Lawrence Brinley died in 1662, and Love, Bromfield and Woolnough were members for 1662 only. The ousted members kept up their contacts with the society, and Molins was one of those who initiated successful litigation in 1662 to regain for it one of the sequestered lands that he had sold it when on the Committee for Sequestered Estates.[18] Bromfield returned to Clapham and was buried there in 1668 with two of his grandchildren. Babington and Molins returned to their business and were not heard of again in wider political affairs.

The radicals Salwey and Moyer were the Clapham residents to have suffered most after the Restoration. The former was arrested on a number of occasions and committed to the Tower for three months in 1663–64, writing from there to his wife that he 'rejoices in his spiritual consolation and will suck honey out of every flower of Providence'. He was eventually released in early February 1664 after taking the Oaths of Allegiance and Supremacy, giving security for good conduct and paying the prison dues. Later, in 1678, Charles II ordered Salwey to absent himself beyond the sea, and he was again under suspicion at the time of Monmouth's rising. It is hardly surprising that Salwey's grandson's memorial in Ludlow church says of his grandfather that 'he sacrificed all and everything in his power in support of public liberty and in opposition to arbitrary power.' He survived long enough to return briefly to Clapham in the early 1680s.

Moyer was removed from his posts at the Restoration and, even though given a royal pardon, was imprisoned for treason in 1662, when he still leased the Manor House in Clapham. He remained in prison for five years, first in the Tower of London and then in Tynemouth, until his elder brother, Lawrence, paid £500 for his release. He was known as a bluff, outspoken mariner and had been a Parliamentary supporter. The story Pepys tells about that release illustrates the difficulties arising when money oiled the wheels of such transactions:

> *Mr. Moore ... did tell me how Mr. Moyer, the merchant,*
> *having procured an order from the King and Duke of York*
> *and Council, with the consent of my Lord Chancellor, and by*
> *assistance of Lord Arlington, for the releasing out of prison*
> *his brother, Samuel Moyer, who was a great man in the late*
> *times in Haberdashers' Hall, and was engaged under hand*
> *and seal to give the man that obtained it so much in behalf*
> *of my Lord Chancellor; but it seems my Lady Duchess of*
> *Albemarle had before undertaken it for so much money,*
> *but hath not done it. The Duke of Albemarle did the next*
> *day send for this Moyer, to tell him, that notwithstanding*
> *this order of the King and Council's being passed for release*
> *of his brother, yet, if he did not consider the pains of some*
> *friends of his, he would stop that order. This Moyer being an*
> *honest, bold man, told him that he was engaged to the hand*
> *that had done the thing to give him a reward; and more he*
> *would not give, nor could own any kindness done by his*
> *Grace's interest; and so parted. The next day Sir Edward*
> *Savage did take the said Moyer in tax about it, giving ill*
> *words of this Moyer and his brother; which he not being*
> *able to bear, told him he would give to the person that had*
> *engaged him what he promised, and not any thing to any*
> *body else; and that both he and his brother were as honest*
> *men as himself, or any man else; and so sent him going, and*
> *bid him do his worst. It is one of the most extraordinary*
> *cases that ever I saw or understood; but it is true.*[19]

Samuel Moyer returned to business, serving again on the court of
the Levant, Royal African and East India companies, and remained
a rich man. He did not forget his past, however, and his will left
£5 to Richard Goodgrome, a fellow prisoner in the Tower and a
radical Fifth Monarchist who was regularly sent there for seditious
preaching. Moyer's mother, Lydia, was living in Clapham when she
died in 1675, but was buried elsewhere.

Many of those in Clapham before the Restoration stayed on
afterwards, but two are of particular interest. **William Daniel** had
moved to Clapham in 1641, but played only a minor role in parish
affairs, subscribing to various collections but only once filling
a parish office. His property was extensive, including 'orchards,
gardens, and lands thereto belonging and several tenements thereto
adjoining', and he must have been a rich man since he was nominated

for alderman in 1670 (although paying a fine to avoid having to take the oath). There are good portraits of both him and his second wife, Mary, showing them soberly dressed (see Illustrations 5 and 6); he had one son and two daughters by her. The only son, Peter, we shall hear more of later, while one daughter came to live in Clapham with her husband, Richard Steele, and the other married an apprentice of Joshua Woolnough. Daniel's two daughters by his first wife both married and lived in Clapham. He died in Clapham in 1678 and his wife Mary in 1681.

Illustration 5. William Daniel,
date unknown

Illustration 6. Mary Daniel,
date unknown

The second important figure who remained was **Dennis Gauden**, who is first recorded in the rate book in 1649 and married his second wife, Elizabeth Clarke, in Clapham in 1653. He had been one of the contractors to the Navy Victualling Board in the early 1650s (so would have known Salwey, Moyer and Richard Cranley), and became Surveyor General of Victualling to the Navy in 1660. He makes frequent appearances in Pepys' diaries and gave him regular gifts, although Pepys claimed that he never accepted any gift before a contract had been signed. The first recorded is around Christmas 1660, when Gauden sent Pepys 'a great chine of beef and three dozen tongues', a gift that was repeated in 1662.[20] For Christmas 1663, Gauden contrived another way to give Pepys a present, losing an after-dinner wager of 'a payre of gloves of a crowne … upon some words in his contract for victualling'.[21] More gifts followed:

> This morning to the office comes Nicholas Osborne, Mr. Gauden's clerke, to desire of me what piece of plate I would choose to have a 100l., or thereabouts, bestowed upon me in, he having order to lay out so much; and, out of his freedom with me, do of himself come to make this question. I a great while urged my unwillingnesse to take any, not knowing how I could serve Mr. Gauden, but left it wholly to himself; so at noon I find brought home in fine leather cases, a pair of the noblest flaggons that ever I saw all the days of my life; whether I shall keepe them or no I cannot tell; for it is to oblige me to him in the business of the Tangier victualling, wherein I doubt I shall not; but glad I am to see that I shall be sure to get something on one side or other, have it which will so, with a merry heart, I looked upon them, and locked them up.[22]

Pepys did decide to keep them after Gauden assured him that the gift was for past services rather than to secure the Tangier contract, worth £40,000 a year. He also received £300 a year after Gauden had secured the contract. Pepys took care to protect himself, however, and when he later had to appear before a hostile Parliamentary committee investigating the Navy Board, his diary recorded:

> I did prepare Mr Warren and, by and by Sir D. Gawden, about what presents I have had from them, that they may not publish them; or, if they do, that in truth I received none on the account of the Navy, but Tanger. And this is true to the former, and, in both, that I never asked anything of them.[23]

The one time Pepys did have second thoughts was after proposing a deal to offer his sister as a wife for Gauden's son Benjamin. He recorded his change of heart, concluding: 'I was convinced that it would be for neither of our interests to make this alliance, and so am quite off of it again.'[24]

By 1664 Gauden had completed the extension and rebuilding of Brick Place to produce a very large house of thirty-nine hearths, a third larger again than the Manor House. It was renamed Clapham Place, and its 430-acre estate was a source of food for his victualling of the Navy. It was described by Pepys as Gauden's victualling office, and Gauden's clerk, **Nicholas Osborne**, also maintained a house in Clapham until 1666 so as to be able to give more administrative support. Clapham Place is referred to in the diaries of both Pepys and John Evelyn, and recent research into its history has identified a possible painting of it, which gives some idea of its size as well as showing the formal gardens (see Illustration 7).[25]

Illustration 7. Possible picture of Clapham Place, Robert
Streeter 1662-4

Pepys visited in July 1663, when the house was almost completed, and in his diary also comments on Gauden's family and their musical skill:

> I resolved to go to Clapham, to Mr. Gauden's, who had
> sent his coach to their place for me ... When I came to
> Mr. Gauden's one first thing was to show me his house,
> which is almost built, wherein he and his family live. I find
> it very regular and finely contrived, and the gardens and
> offices about it as convenient and as full of good variety

> *as ever I saw in my life. It is true he hath been censured*
> *for laying out so much money; but he tells me that he built*
> *it for his brother ... Besides, with the good husbandry in*
> *making his bricks and other things I do not think it costs*
> *him so much money as people think and discourse.*
>
> *... After dinner by Mr. Gauden's motion we got Mrs.*
> *Gauden and her sister to sing to a viall, on which Mr.*
> *Gauden's eldest son (a pretty man, but a simple one*
> *methinks) played but very poorly, and the musique bad,*
> *but yet I commended it. Only I do find that the ladies*
> *have been taught to sing and do sing well now, but that*
> *the viall puts them out. I took the viall and played some*
> *things from one of their books, Lyra lessons, which they*
> *seemed to like well.*[26]

When he returned a couple of days later he did not call in again, but commented that 'The house stands very finely, and has a graceful view to the highway.'

Clapham in the Plague

The Great Plague did not hit Clapham as hard as previous outbreaks had done. It was certainly less badly affected than its neighbours, even taking account of its smaller size; only sixteen people were buried in Clapham at the height of the Plague from July to November 1665, at a time when over 60 died in Putney, 245 in Wandsworth and 113 in Battersea. Clapham's annual figure for 1665, at twenty-eight (less than 10 per cent of the population), was not much higher than the average annual death toll for that decade, and similar numbers were buried in both 1668 and 1669.

There are other indications that the Plague was not too serious at Clapham. In October 1665 the Court of the East India Company chose to meet in **Peter Vanderput's** 'mansion at Clapham in Surrey', although at ten hearths it was by no means one of the largest there. Vanderput was the first of a number of Huguenot Flemings in Clapham, and a neighbour of Pepys in London.[27] His Clapham residence was also used by the Court after the Fire of London the next year, and as a result his wife was presented with silks and fine calicoes to the value of £20, although at first he refused to permit this because of the grumbles of some Court members. Staying in Clapham may well have been of significant benefit to him, because he was probably the Dutch broker who wrote to friends in Amsterdam: 'My house among others was burnt; by God's grace my books and letters of credit are at my house at Clapham, but none know where I shall find the merchants to pay me the moneys due.'[28] He died in 1668 but his son, also Peter, stayed on for a few years before embarking on a distinguished career. Another Flemish immigrant, **John Baptiste Peters,** was tenant of the Manor House from 1667 until 1672. His chief claim to fame is that his daughter Frances married the composer Henry Purcell.[29]

Gauden and his children by his first wife also stayed in Clapham during the Plague, and were visited there by Pepys at its height, during a week in July 1665 when 1,700 died in London:

> We with great content took coach again, and hungry come to Clapham about one o'clock ... where a good dinner, the house having dined, and so to walk up and down in the gardens, mighty pleasant ... and I had a little opportunity to kiss and spend some time with the ladies above, [Gauden's] daughter, a buxom lass, and his sister Fissant, a serious lady, and a little daughter of hers, that begins to sing prettily.[30]

The 'buxom lass' was Gauden's daughter Sarah, who married the next year in Clapham, three weeks before her sixteenth birthday. The oddly named Fissant is Abigail Pheasant, the sister of Gauden's wife. The two women were daughters of the Presbyterian doctor John Clarke, President of the Royal College of Physicians. Two of their brothers were doctors, and their elder sister married their father's deputy, John Micklethwaite.

However bad or not the Plague in Clapham, the parish spent over £20 on building a pest house to isolate the infected, including those arriving from other parishes. The parish accounts for 1665 show that more than £45 was spent on dealing with the Plague, including food from the local inns, bedding and nursing for those in the pest house, as well as the cost of burying two of the helpers. This was comparable with what was usually raised to keep the parish going for a whole year. A further cost was a special rate assessment in October 1665 to raise £8/2/6 for the relief of the poor in nearby parishes 'visited by the pestilence'. Peter Vanderput gave an additional £13/8 for the poor. One of the nurses, Widow Gurney, whose husband had died of the Plague, survived but became ill the next year, and the parish paid eight shillings for a nurse to look after her. She recovered from this illness and ran her husband's inn for another twenty-five years.

We know something about decisions about whether or not to stay in Clapham from correspondence between Elizabeth Gauden and Simon Patrick.[31] Patrick, the future Bishop of Chichester and then Ely, had been chaplain to Walter St John, lord of the manor of Battersea and subsequently vicar of Battersea from 1658 to 1675, when he became close friends with both Elizabeth and Dennis. He became rector of St Paul's, Covent Garden, in 1662, leaving his younger brother John in charge at Battersea, and earned a reputation as an exemplary parish priest, not least because – unlike many – he stayed with his parishioners during the Plague, the period of his correspondence with Elizabeth.[32]

Elizabeth Gauden, having small children and being also pregnant, did not live in Clapham during the Plague but stayed with her sister-in-law, the widow of Bishop John Gauden, at Hutton Hall in Brentford, Essex, a safe eighteen miles out of town. Her child was born there in October 1665. She was well-educated, and her correspondence with Patrick often discussed the finer points of theology. Pepys described her as 'good', by which he usually meant religious.[33] Few of her letters remain, but Patrick's contain much discussion of the progress of the Plague together with advice on whether to return to Clapham – usually not to do so!

Towards the end of 1665 the Plague began to diminish, although there were still surges and stories of people returning only to die from the disease. It had moved south of the river, certainly as far as Lambeth, but by November there had been only one death in one week in Battersea, and Patrick could walk there from Covent Garden. Wandsworth, however, was still infected; twenty-four had died in the week ending 12 October and a further nine in the week ending 9 November, a fact that, Patrick said, had caused people 'to run away'. In contrast, there was no week during the Plague when more than three were buried in Clapham. Nevertheless, his advice remained not to go to Clapham:

*The physicians' rule is comprised in three words, when
they advised what to do about the plague; in plain
English they are 'Quickly, far off, slowly.' That is fly soon,
and far enough, and return late. To his counsel then I
refer you. When he returns to London you need not fear
to come to Clapham.*

Elizabeth finally returned to Clapham at the end of December
1665, although Patrick waited for a further drop in mortality before
visiting her. Following the Gaudens' return home, Pepys paid his next
visit there in January 1666, when John Evelyn dropped him off at
Gauden's house:

*He set me down at Mr. Gawden's, where nobody yet
come home, I having left him and his sons at Court, so I
took a book and into the gardens, and there walked and
read till darke with great pleasure, and then in and in
comes Osborne, and he and I to talk of ... great hopes
there is of a decrease this week also of the plague ... and
then I, in the best chamber like a prince, to bed.*[34]

Gauden was always very near the edge financially, and this was
exacerbated by the effects of the Plague. Soaring naval costs and
decreased tax receipts meant that both public and private sectors
were in difficulty. He was in debt to the tune of almost half a million
pounds, but the Goldsmith bankers were not able to help because the
Plague's effects on trade meant that their loans were not being repaid.
Nevertheless, Pepys was able to extract £125,000 from the Exchequer,
a sum that saved Gauden and for which he gave Pepys £500.

Gauden survived the Plague, and in 1667 he became Master of the
Clothworkers (also Pepys' livery company) and was elected Sheriff of
London, for which he must have been prepared to take the necessary
oaths. Pepys was pleased for him, not least because it brought an
immediate knighthood, but, he commented, 'as the city is now, there
is no great honour nor joy to be had in being a public officer.'[35]
Gauden had been highly regarded in the City, and the account of
aldermen in 1672 speaks of him as 'esteemed justly a man of great
justness and uprightness in his place of government'.

Elizabeth Gauden was not the only one to leave Clapham during
the Plague. Samuel Crisp, who had just moved to Clapham, described
1665 as 'the never to be forgotten year when the terrors of God

multiplied all the land over', and went with his wife and family to stay with his sister Mary Carleton in Addington, Surrey, for seven months. She was a pious lady, and their neighbours in Clapham, Dr Henry Wilkinson (of whom more in the next chapter) and his family, also joined them, as did other Puritan ministers such as Peter Sterry.[36] Crisp, who was somewhat obsessive, filled a hundred-page notebook with a memoir of his sister, who died at the age of forty-three having had seventeen children in twenty-five years of marriage. This memoir chiefly praised her piety and seemingly unceasing goodness and care for others, but also commented on the sermons that the two ministers had given in her house:

> The doctor laying the conscience open to the Law and
> Mr Sterry pouring in the oyle of joy, to heal it by the
> gosple; not but the doctor preached true gosple doctrine
> too. Her heart was wonderfully ravished at the sweet
> sound of the gosple which came from their lips, and
> sparkled out agayne at her eyes.[37]

One anecdote Crisp tells of his sister shows both how the risks of catching the Plague from others were perceived and his view of her piety:[38]

> One morning somewhat early a poore woman came and
> brought her daughter to her; and requested her advice
> and help for her daughter; whereupon she askt the poore
> woman how was it with her daughter; to which the
> poore woman readily replied, that she thought she had
> the plague, and that there was a great swelling under her
> arme, at which sudden and unlooked for answer she was
> not dismay'd; but bid the poore woman bring her daughter
> nearer that she might open her bosome, and see how it was
> with her; and though upon the sight of the sore, she found
> that it was not the plague, yet her courage was exceeding
> great; or rather I may say her faith was very great; for she
> never feared any danger, when engaged in a duty.

Conclusion

Clapham was an unusual London village in having a high proportion of large houses with merchant occupiers, most located off the main roads. These characteristics were established by 1650, and only a quarter of the merchant houses were built after the Restoration; all were constructed before the Plague and the Great Fire, which did not stimulate further growth. It was sufficiently free of the Plague for merchants to go on using it and for others to be prepared to come there for meetings, although some residents preferred to take refuge further from London.

Two thirds of the merchants in Clapham before the Restoration remained there afterwards, often for some considerable time. There was a relatively slow turnover, and any new arrivals already had strong political or business connections there. Meanwhile many of Clapham's former radical Puritans withdrew from political activity as they were imprisoned and/or deprived of their official posts. A number died, and others adjusted by returning to their businesses. This had the effect of maintaining the village's Puritan, now Nonconformist, character. Meanwhile Dennis Gauden continued Clapham's links with the Navy by becoming its chief victualling contractor, and Samuel Pepys became a frequent visitor to his house.

(Endnotes)

1. Ian Warren, *The London and Middlesex Hearth Tax*, vol. 1 (British Record Society, 2014), p. 121.

2. Dorian Gerhold, *Putney and Roehampton in 1665* (Wandsworth Historical Society, 2007), p. 20.

3. Peter Laslett, The World We Have Lost (Routledge, 2005), pp. 53–80.

4. F.M.L. Thompson, *Hampstead* (Routledge & Kegan Paul, 1974), p. 19.

5. Warren, *London and Middlesex Hearth Tax*, p. 128.

6. John Ogilby, map of the road to Portsmouth, in *Britannia* (1675).

7. Highgate was on the border of two parishes, St Pancras Kentish Town and Hornsey. It had twenty-six houses with more than ten hearths and seven with more than twenty, and between 161 and 179 properties in total, including many smaller dwellings. See T.F.T. Baker (ed.), *A History of the County of Middlesex*, vol. 6 (Oxford University Press, 1980), pp. 122–39, and *Survey of London*, vol. 50: *St Pancras* (Yale University Press, 2013), Appendix 2.

8. Dorian Gerhold, 'London's Suburban Villas and Mansions 1660–1830', *London Journal*, vol. 34 (2009), p. 233.

9. Michael Green, *Historic Clapham* (Tempus, 2008), p. 17.

10. Larry Kreitzer, *William Kiffen and his World*, Part 1 (Regents Park College, 2010), pp. 150, 159–60.

11. Samuel Pepys, diary, 18 April 1660.

12. The term Anglican will be used to describe those in favour of episcopal governance of the Church and the range of associated liturgical practices.

13. Percy Society, *Early English Poetry, Ballads and Popular Literature of the Middle Ages*, vol. 4 (1861), p. 237.

14. *A Compleat Collection of Farewell Sermons, Preached by Mr. Calamy, Dr. Manton etc ...* (1663).

15. Jeremy Walker, 'Calculating with Calamy', *Reformation 21* blog, 7 December 2012, www.reformation21.org/blog/2012/12/calculating-with-calamy.php.

16. William Birken, 'The Dissenting Tradition in English Medicine of the Seventeenth and Eighteenth Centuries', *Medical History*, vol. 39, no. 2 (April 1995), p. 198.

17. Gary S. De Krey, *London and the Restoration 1659–1683* (Cambridge University Press, 2005), p. 76.

18. William Kellaway, *The New England Company* (Longmans, 1975), p. 954.

19. Pepys, diary, 16 May 1667.

20. Ibid., 19 December 1660, 24 December 1662.

21. Ibid., 21 December 1663.

22. Ibid., 21 July 1664.

23. Ibid., 2 March 1668.

24. Ibid., 2 April 1666.

25. Green, *Historic Clapham*, pp. 171–214. For the painting, see p. 186.

26. Pepys, diary, 25 July 1663.

27. Ibid., 30 April 1668.

28. Quoted in W.G. Bell, *The Great Fire of London in 1666* (Bodley Head, 1923), p. 62.

29. Jonathan Keates, *Purcell* (Northeastern, 1996).

30. Pepys, diary, 27 July 1665.

31. For this and subsequent letters, see Simon Patrick, *Collected Works*, vol. 9 (1858), pp. 571–614.

32. A. Lloyd Moote and Dorothy Moote, *The Great Plague: The Story of London's Most Deadly Year* (Johns Hopkins University Press, 2004), passim.

33. Pepys, diary, 22 January 1668.

34. Ibid., 29 January 1666.

35. Ibid., 11 September 1667.

36. Vivian de Sola Pinto, *Peter Sterry, Platonist and Puritan, 1613–1672* (Cambridge University Press 2013), pp. 18–19.

37. Bodleian Library, Rawlinson D 106, ff. 33b, 34.

38. Ibid p 42-3

CHAPTER 6

A HAVEN FOR RADICALS

Clapham merchants

Former Puritans, whether merchants or ministers, continued to move into Clapham in the 1660s; they were all well connected to existing residents, and the Langhams provide a good example. **Thomas Langham** appeared in the early 1660s, also giving a home to his unmarried sister-in-law, daughter of the prominent Puritan Stephen Marshall. His sister Judith also lived with him after the imprisonment of her second husband, Colonel Edmund Harvey, a silk merchant who in the early 1640s had formed part of a radical group that also involved Abraham Babington and Joshua Woolnough. Langham's evidence that Harvey had not signed the king's death certificate saved his life after he was convicted of regicide. Meanwhile **George Langham**, who had been on the City militia committee with Moyer and others in 1659, and Harvey's younger brother **Charles Harvey**, both came to live in Clapham in 1666, and remain there until their deaths. Thomas Langham died in 1695, leaving his house to his nephew **Thomas Juxon** (great-nephew of the diarist Thomas Juxon) and the rest of his estate to his sister's daughter-in-law Jane Harvey, who then lived for five years in Clapham. Juxon was buried in the Langham family tomb.

Edmund White was a member of another prominent Puritan family who traded with North America. Like other Clapham residents, he had invested in the Massachusetts Bay Colony; his agent Humphrey Davy had moved to Boston in 1662 after marrying White's daughter. His son, also Edmund, became a member of the Society for the Propagation of the Gospel in New England in 1668, and it was through his account that the society transmitted funds to New England. Between them, father and son occupied from 1664 to 1690 the house in Clapham that had formerly been leased by William Sydenham. It was then lived in by the younger White's daughter, who had married **Thomas Hunt**, a merchant dealing with North America who invested £1,000 in creating a shipbuilding industry through Thomas Coram, the founder of the Foundlings Hospital.[1] Edmund's sister-in-law Mary Wilson married first the well-known preacher Rev. Tobias Crisp, one of whose sons was **Samuel Crisp**, who lived in Clapham from 1664 until his death in 1703. Samuel married Mary, the sister of Dennis Gauden's brother-in-law Nathaniel Pheasant, and will be covered in future chapters; he was later on the board of the Society for the Propagation of the Gospel in New England.

Another Nonconformist, **William Stonestreet**, rented a Clapham house from Charles Harvey from 1670. Stonestreet was an apothecary and had married one of the daughters of the Presbyterian George Thomason; another daughter, Grace, lived with them. **John Love** occupied a house owned by his father, **William Love**, who was a prominent Congregationalist MP described as 'faulty in the late troubles'. He had refused the sacrament in 1661 and so was excluded from being either an alderman or an MP, but even so he held many offices, including Commissioner for Trade, and later became a very active MP, serving on more than fifty committees. One of his apprentices, **Henry Harrington**, lived in the Manor House for three years around 1680, but moved out when his wife died. He shared it with **Richard Sherwin**, who married into the prominent Presbyterian merchant Thorold family but died shortly afterwards, in 1681. Sherwin was a cousin of Thomas Rodbard (Rodbard senior's nephew), with whom his sister Juliana moved in until her death in 1685. Harrington's trading activities extended to land deals in New Jersey with a consortium involving both John Love and future Clapham residents Arthur Shallett and Joseph Paice. The family connections were strengthened further when Harrington's son married John Love's daughter. Meanwhile, **Thomas Polhill**, who had been born in Clapham in 1636 and lived there in the early 1660s, returned to the Manor House from his family estate near Sevenoaks. Despite his family being from a Royalist part of Kent, and perhaps being influenced by his Clapham neighbours, he married the daughter of Cromwell's son-in-law Major General Henry Ireton.

More former residents returned to Clapham. When Sir Lawrence Bromfield died, Thomas Corbett returned to his father-in-law's house there, but disaster soon struck. He had been prevailed upon to lend his son Bromfield Corbett money to improve his estate and to purchase a good position for him in Jamaica, and had used his father-in-law's legacy of £1,000 to his daughter Sarah to assist in that purpose.[2] Bromfield's 'debauched behaviour' led to him forfeiting his job and therefore unable to repay his father, who found himself thrown into prison when the debts were called in. He spent at least eight years in debtors' prison, which cost him some £80 per annum.[3] Sarah lived on in Clapham and died a spinster in 1685, leaving her estate to the children of her sister and neighbour Anne Arthur.

George Foxcroft had also lived in Clapham before he left for India on being appointed governor of Fort St George, Madras. Edward Winter, his predecessor as governor and a committed Anglican Royalist, described him as 'of most rotten and unsound principles who had he loved the Church half so well as he did the lands thereof, could never have had so little allegiance for his king'.[4] Although insisting that he was loyal to the king, Foxcroft never denied the charge of religious nonconformity, and his approach led him to criticise the licentiousness of the Restoration Court. Winter, who had resented being replaced, took advantage of this to launch a coup, imprisoning Foxcroft for three years before he in turn was removed by the East India Company. While he was in India, Foxcroft's wife, Elizabeth, was companion to the philosopher Ann, Viscountess Conway. Foxcroft returned to Clapham in 1674 and his wife joined him and was buried there in 1679.

Richard Salwey also returned as a resident from 1683 to 1685 and was appointed an executor of Dorothy Arthur's will in 1677, as well as subscribing to a collection of almost £60 for repairs to the parish school in 1685, not long before his death. This was a sad one, reported by Dr Henry Sampson:

> *Major Salloway, a known and famous member of the*
> *Rump Parliament, a great preacher, a preacher in his own*
> *family, mightily versed in the Scriptures, yet when in his*
> *later days his son failed who had involved him in bonds*
> *and great debts, gave his melancholy thereupon. One*
> *morning he rose out of his bed very early went two or*
> *three closes off from his house to a pond onto which he*
> *threw himself and was drowned.*[5]

Salwey's suicide may account for the fact that his will, which was extremely short and written only three weeks before his death, took almost two-and-a-half years to be probated, and only after the intervention of the Earl of Clarendon on his family's behalf.[6] It contains the odd request that although he appoints his wife and eldest son executors, his son 'should forbear from taking the same upon him till my said wife shall thereunto require him or some failure should happen by her death or otherwise'.

A number of overseas merchants who came to Clapham were married to women who had been brought up there. **Anthony Stephens** returned to live with his mother-in-law Ann Hughes, while **William Sheldon** took a house to be near his daughters, both of whom had married Clapham merchants. He, too, was a Dissenter; he had been apprenticed to Edmund Harvey, the alleged regicide, and married the daughter of Joshua Foote, when she was living in Clapham with her Puritan father.

Two further merchants who moved to Clapham displayed the same characteristics. **John Doggett** had married John Beauchamp's daughter Alice, and moved into the house of his fellow Baltic trader and colleague Robert Whitlock. Doggett had been born in Hamburg, where his father ran a textile business with extensive trade with North America. A substantial merchant, he left property worth £11,500 when he died, but he was also owed a further £11,700.[7] His business was not confined to trading with the Baltic, and although the majority of his trade was in textiles, he also dealt in shipments of hemp, sugar, Smyrna galls (used for making ink) and barrels of swine bristles for brushes. He dealt extensively with the Levant, including Constantinople, Smyrna and Aleppo, and with New England, where he had dealings with one of his wife's cousins in Virginia and with Humphrey Davy of Boston, the brother-in-law of his Clapham neighbour Edmund White. This range of activity was reflected in the postage bill of more than £8 that his wife paid in the year after his death to maintain correspondence with all his contacts. He was an active Nonconformist, and referred in his will in 1680 to his being a member of 'the Church of Christ'. He had been an alderman from 1652 to 1662, but had to give it up for not being prepared to swear the oath, and was temporarily one again in 1670 until he paid a fine to avoid the role.

Henry Powell had married William Daniel's eldest daughter, Sarah, in 1649. He spent much of the 1660s in India as the East India Company's factor at Kasimbazar, one of the great trading centres of West Bengal. Robert Hooke used some of Powell's letters to his father-in-law describing an earthquake at Balasore after the appearance of a comet.[8] Sarah and their children may have lived with her father while Henry was abroad, but he returned in 1673 and was known thereafter as 'India Powell', to distinguish him from his brother Thomas. He leased the three-storey house that had previously been occupied by Hugh Forth, with a barn, a brew house, a garden and a field with almost fifty sheep.[9] He exported cloth to Barbados, but the inventory produced after his death shows a much wider trading pattern including cargo from Bengal, Aleppo, Smyrna and Constantinople. He spread his risk in a different way from John Doggett, underwriting whole ships and then paying insurance on them at the rate of 2.5 per cent for Constantinople and 1.5 per cent for Scandinavia; Doggett preferred to take only a small fraction of a ship, usually 1/64 or 1/32, but on occasion 1/16 or even 1/10. Powell was rich, too, being worth £9,900 at the time of his death, with outstanding net debts owed to him of £11,400. While his surviving son came to an unpleasant end, as we will see in Chapter 11, two of his daughters married long-standing Clapham residents. Mary married **William Lethieullier**, another Clapham Dissenter and Whig, and Sarah married **John Mitford**, a merchant from a Northumberland family, who moved to Clapham in the early 1670s.

Other Nonconformist merchants included **Christopher Redshaw**, a hop dealer. The inventory of his house at Clapham contains a number of tools for dealing with hops, such as hop hooks and a hop board, as well as the sign for his business in London, the Three

Brushes.[10] He was Common Councillor for the Bridge Ward in 1678–79 and 1681–83. **James Fowke** lived in Clapham for ten years and had a collection of books by Puritan authors. He left his house in Clapham for his wife, Elizabeth, to live in if she wished (and she did), but otherwise it was to be left to his 'loving friend' at a rent of £13 per annum. This friend was the somewhat improbably named **Guicciardini Wentworth**, private secretary to the Chancellor of the Duchy of Lancaster; he had lived in Clapham for a few years.

Ejected ministers in Clapham

The disasters of the Fire and the Plague tended to strengthen the hand of the Nonconformists. It was the ejected ministers, not their Anglican counterparts, who returned to London to deal with their flocks during the Plague. The Fire destroyed eighty-seven parish churches, but the ejected ministers were already used to using alternative buildings, and so missed them less. A later bishop of Salisbury wrote that 'in that time conventicles abounded in all the parts of the city. It was thought hard to hinder men from worshipping God any way as they could, when there were no churches, nor ministers to look after them.'[11]

From the late 1660s Nonconformist worship in the London urban area was extensive, well-known and rarely broken up. In 1667 Samuel Pepys was told that 'the Nonconformists are mighty high, and their meetings frequented and connived at; and they do expect to have their day now soon; … and it is certain that the Nonconformists do now preach openly in houses, in many places.'[12] Sometimes their interventions were more violent. Letters to the House of Commons reported 'the Fanatickes, in several places, coming in great bodies, and turning people out of the churches, and there preaching themselves, and pulling the surplice over the Parsons' heads.'[13]

The acquiescence of its rector, John Gurgany, coupled with long-standing Puritan residents made Clapham a relatively safe and attractive place for Nonconformists, despite being inside the five-mile limit from London.[14] It is likely that this rather than personal contacts was the driving force in bringing no fewer than fourteen ejected ministers to Clapham, although some of them were already well-known to Clapham residents.

Henry Wilkinson had known Lawrence Bromfield at the church of St Dunstan in the East when the former had been rector there. He had also been Lady Margaret Professor of Divinity at Oxford, and is supposed to have stamped on the medieval glass removed from Christ Church Cathedral. He preached regularly in Clapham, and a conventicle (unlicensed Nonconformist service) at which he was preaching was broken up at Camberwell in 1665. He was reportedly 'an excellent preacher (though his voice was shrill and whining), yet his sermons were commonly full of dire confusion'.[15] He died in 1675. Both his wives had been the daughters of earls, and Lady Anne Wilkinson, his second wife and the closest to an aristocrat who lived in Clapham, stayed there for only one year after his death. He was a friend of another ejected minister, **Robert Ferguson**, a serial plotter, who wrote to his wife, Hannah, in 1674 explaining that he had just met 'Dr. Wilkinson and my lady as I returned from thee on Friday. I was very much importuned that thou wouldst go to Clapham for a week, so, if thy neighbours and thou do not cotton, thou mayst promise thyself a welcome elsewhere.'[16]

Illustration 8. Thomas Lye, *c.* 1662
Fairclough Portrait Collection, University of Leicester

Thomas Lye was a Nonconformist minister from Somerset and a fellow of Emmanuel College, Cambridge. He was invited by parishioners to take charge of All Hallows, Lombard Street, where he would have known both Daniel and Wilkinson, and was ejected in 1662. He then came to Clapham, where his children were baptised and some buried. He ran a school there for some time and is said to have been popular and successful, particularly in catechising children.

The strong links among the ministers are illustrated well in the autobiography of the prominent Manchester Nonconformist Henry Newcome, who stayed in Clapham with Hugh Forth, a Presbyterian merchant and briefly MP for Wigan, his home town. Newcome records that in December 1668 Henry Wilkinson preached at Forth's house on a Sunday morning ('an excellent sermon on mortification') and Newcome himself preached in the afternoon. He returned the day before Epiphany 'to keep a fast the day thereafter, on behalf of Mr Bridges, who is in trouble. Mr Lye ... joined me.'[17]

Forth's second wife died in Clapham in early 1666, and he soon married Amy, the youngest unmarried sister of the strongly Presbyterian Gurdon family. Judith, one of her elder sisters, had married John Gould a couple of years before, and no doubt was on the watch for suitable husbands for her sister, who was, at twenty-three, relatively old to be getting married. Amy went on to marry the Nonconformist minister Dr Thomas Jacombe when Forth died in 1676, demonstrating the desire of the godly to find godly partners.

The Nonconformist preacher James Forbes was attached for some time to Gloucester Cathedral, and became pastor of a congregational church; he was ejected from the cathedral in 1660. The then Bishop of Gloucester described him as 'once a Presbyterian, afterwards an Independent, but always a sectary in Cromwell's time and ever since ... the source of all the schisms we have had in and about Gloucester.'[18] After two bouts of imprisonment, Forbes left for London in 1664 and was reputed to be living in Clapham and working as a shoemaker. A warrant for his arrest had been issued in Clapham in 1664 for distributing treasonable publications, but he had already moved on. Further arrests followed. Three more ejected ministers spent at least a little time in Clapham: John Pindar; Thomas Lisle, who had lived with General George Monck and tutored his son; and William Bridge. The last had been a fellow of Emmanuel College,

Cambridge, when John Arthur was an undergraduate, and was a well-known Independent. Ejected from his posts in 1661, he had moved by 1663 to Clapham, where he administered an Independent church. There are various stories that he started this church as early as 1640–50, and a sermon he preached there in 1646 still exists. The two portraits shown here give rather differing impressions of him, one stern and the other much more friendly.

Illustration 9. Philip Hobnes, *William Bridge*, late seventeenth century

Illustration 10. James Caldwall, *William Bridge*, late eighteenth century

Both images © National Portrait Gallery, London

The scope for Dissenting ministers increased as Gurgany grew older. In 1670, when he felt too infirm to conduct the whole of the church services, the parish agreed that the churchwardens should pay twenty shillings to each minister that preached on a Sabbath Day, and that every inhabitant should be free to bring a minister to preach. Gurgany himself promised to pay the churchwardens £20 a year to compensate them. This gave Clapham Dissenters ample opportunity to bring in a variety of godly ministers, and it will have encouraged such to come and live in Clapham. Perhaps as a result of this competition, by 1675 it was felt that the sermons were becoming rather long, and the churchwardens bought an hourglass for a shilling to assist with timekeeping.

Gurgany died in 1675, and his successor was **John Savill**, who stayed until his own death in 1706. Little is known of him, but he married the younger daughter of Anthony Stephens soon after his arrival and made the most of a rich parish to leave his wife and children the equivalent of about £5,000. Whatever Savill's own views, he must have acquiesced in continuing Dissenting activity in Clapham, and at least some of his lecturers, chosen and paid for by the parish, had clear Dissenting tendencies. One of them, **Rev. Stephen Charman**, was the son of an ejected minister but probably conformed in the end, when the St John family of Battersea appointed him to one of their livings.

The Nonconformist minister **Philip Lamb** was a lecturer in Clapham from about 1677. He had resigned from his parish in Dorset before being ejected in 1662, and moved to a nearby parish, where in 1672 he was granted a licence to be a 'Congregational teacher'. However, he was driven out and lived in Clapham until 1689, preaching to a congregation that met in Judith Gould's house after her husband had died in 1679. Another Nonconformist who preached there in 1682 was **Joseph Hussey**, who had been appointed domestic chaplain to Sarah Powell just before the death of her husband, Henry. Hussey lived with her for two more years, by which time she had become the third wife of Samuel Thompson. Hussey became a distinguished Nonconformist minister of an uncompromising nature, having written his ordination thesis arguing that the Pope was the Antichrist.

Both Lamb and Lye preached many funeral sermons in Clapham, and such occasions provided an important opportunity for teaching, with subsequent publication of the text. The point of such sermons was not to provide encomia for the dead or to describe their life, but rather to remind the living of the uncertainty of life, the immediacy of death and the need to prepare accordingly. Lamb explained in his sermon for Sarah Lye, 'Funeral sermons are not … cannot be for the help of dead Saints, they need no such little things; but they are for the comfort and solace of living Saints.'[19] Thomas Lye put it much more bluntly in another such sermon: 'When Ministers of the Gospel are called forth to improve funeral obsequies, their proper role is not so much to launch out into praise, and panegyric of the dead, as to excite and profit the living.'[20]

Illustration 11. John Faber Jr, *Joseph Hussey*, 1722
©The National Portrait Gallery, London

Religion and politics

The (temporarily) increasing openness was reflected in Dissenters being elected to City government positions. Forty-one of the Common Councilmen were Dissenters in 1669, almost double the figure of 1665, including two Clapham residents, William Daniel and Thomas Powell. In 1669 and 1670 Thomas Polhill, William Daniel and John Doggett were appointed aldermen for Farringdon Within, but all paid the fine as they could not swear the oath. A former resident, William Kiffin, was chosen as Sheriff in 1669, but also declined.

Dissenters also sought to influence King Charles the next year. He approached the city magistrates for a loan of £60,000, but the Corporation had been able to raise only a third of it. Stepping into the breach, Dissenters organized their own loan of £40,000 from 155 individuals, including two Clapham residents: John Gould and Andrew Crawley (a cousin of William Hewer).[21]

Such increased recognition of Dissenters was followed by Charles issuing on his own authority the Royal Declaration of Indulgence, which attempted to extend religious liberty to both Protestant Nonconformists and Roman Catholics by suspending the execution of the penal laws that punished recusants from the Church of England, and by providing for the licensing of Nonconformist ministers and buildings. This was immediately taken up in Clapham, Gould being one of the agents arranging such licences.[22] There were soon three licensed premises in Clapham, more than anywhere else in Surrey.

Henry Wilkinson took out a licence in 1672 for both his house and the Clapham schoolhouse to be used as a Presbyterian meeting house. Thomas Lye was also licensed that year, although only at the fourth attempt, as a Presbyterian teacher at his house at Clapham, where he would preach after attending service at the parish church.[23] He often preached at conventicles with Bridge and Wilkinson, and he was eventually charged for this offence and sent in 1683 to the Marshalsea prison, where he died the next year. A third licence for a Presbyterian preacher was granted in Clapham in 1672 to William Hughes, whom we came across earlier in connection with the foundation of the Clapham school.

The next year, however, Parliament compelled Charles to withdraw his Declaration of Indulgence, not least because it was viewed as unconstitutional. He was forced to implement, in its place, the first of the Test Acts (1673), which required anyone entering public service in England to deny the Catholic doctrine of transubstantiation and take Anglican Communion.

William Love was the only Dissenting MP from Clapham, and there were few such in City posts in the 1670s. The City's new governing elite was not well-connected to its commercial leadership, which remained in Presbyterian hands. It was harder for Dissenters to remain involved in the government of the City than in the various stock companies, and there were only three Anglican aldermen on their Courts. The continuing links between trading and Dissent worried an Anglican apologist, who wrote that 'the Fanatick Party' and 'the Trading part' of the nation were so much the same that 'the inriching of this sort of People' would only promote what he called 'Seditious Practices'.[24] This connection was reinforced by the Quaker William Penn some fifteen years later, when he wrote that Dissenters 'were a chief part of the trading people of the nation such as merchants, shopkeepers, clothiers, farmers etc.'[25]

Discrimination against Dissenters

The so-called Popish Plot of 1679 alleged a Jesuit conspiracy to assassinate Charles and support the succession of James by a French invasion. Although this turned out to have been largely fabricated by Titus Oates, different groups drew different conclusions from it. City Dissenters and their Parliamentary friends read the revelations as proof that the Court and the bishops were determined to bring in popery and arbitrary government, reinforced by the prospect of James succeeding as a Catholic king and the continued proroguing of Parliament by Charles. The Anglicans, meanwhile, saw the Popish Plot as demonstrating that Dissenters were trying to exploit the Catholic threat to undermine the settlement between Church and state. This led to the Exclusion Crisis of 1679–81, with attempts to prevent James from succeeding to the crown, and has been seen as the start of identifiable political parties; the Tory party included all those who had benefited from the coercive confessional state of the Restoration, while the Whigs consisted both of those who were excluded from that confessional state and those who wanted to replace it with a broader Protestant political order.[26]

The new Parliament, elected in 1679, was very different from the previous Royalist Cavalier Parliament, which had been elected in 1661, and had a definite anti-Court majority. The Commons passed legislation preventing James from succeeding Charles, but it was immediately rejected by the Lords, and this encouraged Charles to prologue Parliament, which worried those (largely Whigs) who were concerned about a movement to greater absolutism. There were repeated petitions in the City and, after a greatly contested election,

Whigs were elected Sheriffs in 1680 by the Common Council by a comfortable majority. Thomas Powell and Christopher Redshaw were two of the Common Councillors for Bridge Within. Charles continued to prorogue Parliament, so preventing his opponents from pursuing any legal way to exclude James, and he also demanded a new Charter for the City that would give him the power to appoint the Lord Mayor, Sheriffs and all other major office holders. He finally secured this in 1683 after the revelations of the Rye House plot to assassinate both Charles and James, and then moved on to remove and rewrite the charters of the livery companies.[27] Sir Peter Daniel facilitated this when he was Master of the Haberdashers that year.

The last years of Charles' reign have been described as the worst period of religious persecution in British history.[28] Thousands of Dissenters were fined or imprisoned (where some died), and some left the country for North America and elsewhere. Through the enforcement of the requirement for oaths of allegiance and the taking of Holy Communion, Dissenters were essentially eliminated from elected and nominated office, while denial of their role as liverymen also deprived them of the right to vote in City elections. The effects of this continued some long time; Anthony Stephens described himself in his will in 1686 as 'formerly a linen draper of Gracious St but now a private inhabitant of Clapham', and Thomas Tanner started his will as late as 1710, not with the usual rubric of his livery company and status as citizen of London, but with 'Gent, being long since disenfranchised and consequently no freeman of London'.

Dissenting schools

The schools in Clapham were well-known for their Dissenting character, and drew many Dissenting teachers. One of these was Elizabeth Birch, from 1675 the governess of Anthony Ashley Cooper, the future 3rd Earl of Shaftesbury. He was under the guardianship of his grandfather, who asked the philosopher and physician John Locke to supervise the boy's education. A woman tutor was unusual, but Locke chose Birch partly because of her ability to speak as well as read both Latin and Greek. Her father was Samuel Birch, a prominent Nonconformist schoolmaster and ejected minister, who ran a remarkable school near Burford, Oxfordshire, from which no fewer than fourteen of his pupils went on to occupy high government office. When he died in 1679 Elizabeth went to Clapham, and the future earl followed her.[29] He spent three years there with her from 1680 to 1683, learning to speak both Latin and Greek; Locke visited periodically to check his progress or to meet the school's head, **William Tanner**.

William Hughes and Thomas Lye continued to be active in Clapham, both teaching in schools and preaching there and elsewhere. The fact that they were both well-known, and obviously tolerated by the population of Clapham, is borne out by the story of Thomas Doolittle, another Nonconformist minister and teacher. His school had been moved on repeatedly as he was convicted for preaching to congregations in his own house. Ejected from Wimbledon and Islington, he came to Battersea in 1683 but the authorities there seized and sold his possessions. He then dispersed his pupils into a number of private houses in Clapham and continued his teaching there until 1687, when he moved to Clerkenwell.

Further evidence of the status of Clapham comes from the writings of Sir Roger L'Estrange, the outspoken Tory propagandist, known particularly for his widely read periodical *The Observator*, which was produced in the 1680s. L'Estrange campaigned against the Dissenting academies and schools, describing the academies that sought to provide the equivalent of a university education for future Nonconformist ministers as 'nurseries ... for the planting and cultivating of sedition and schism', and saying that 'the punishment of the present conspirators will never do the business, without cutting off seditious schools' and that the Church could not be safe 'so long as these seminaries are permitted'.[30]

Although in some previous editions of *The Observator* L'Estrange had concentrated his fire on Newington and Hackney as Dissenting centres, his ire now turned to Hughes and Clapham. He played a major part in the campaign to wrest St Thomas' Hospital away from the Whigs, and a number of editions of *The Observator* concentrated on the subject. L'Estrange made two separate charges. The first was to attack a sermon preached by Hughes almost thirty years earlier, in which he justified the execution of Charles I, and to use that as proof of Hughes' unsuitability.[31] The second was to use Hughes' apparent impersonation of another Hughes to cover up the fact that he had no licence to teach in a school. L'Estrange gave the story:

> *There was one Thomas Hughes, several years since, that*
> *had a licence to teach a School in Clapham in Surrey, in*
> *a school house that was erected by the parish. He stayed*
> *there a while, and then went on his way. And then Mr*
> *William Hughes took upon him to officiate there in the*
> *place of Thomas Hughes under colour of this licence;*
> *and to continue till Michaelmas term 1683. Appeared*
> *at visitations, as the schoolmaster at Clapham; and at*
> *the visitation exhibited the said Thomas Hughes licence;*
> *but in conclusion now was made appear that our*
> *William ap Thomas had no licence at all and he*
> *himself confessed as much.*[32]

This, L'Estrange said, was particularly hypocritical because 'Hughes had prosecuted William Tanner of Clapham for not coming to Church and receiving the sacrament according to the law and he likewise prosecuted Mr George St Cler for teaching in a private school in the said Tanner's house without a licence.'[33]

Hughes had indeed confessed to this charge in his response to an earlier L'Estrange onslaught, producing a pamphlet 'A Candid Plea to a Cruel Charge' in which he admitted that he had taken action against 'the Lord of Shaftesbury's school maintained and kept some years by Unlicenced and High Dissenters'.

Not everyone was Nonconformist

Although Clapham retained its Dissenting and subsequently Whig character, five of its residents can be identified as Anglican and, once the labels Whig and Tory emerged at the end of the 1670s, as Tory. Three of these were aldermen and all became Sheriff of the City of London. They were **Sir Richard How, Sir Peter Daniel** and **Sir Peter Vanderput** (son of the father of the same name). Daniel, despite the Dissenting beliefs of his father, William, was identified as a 'person of known loyalty and prudence'.[34] He was on a committee in the eastern part of the City that organized loyalist addresses in 1681, and was nominated as Sheriff by the Tory Lord Mayor in 1685, 'when no Whig appeared' to force an election.[35] All three men enforced the conventicle acts rigorously. None of them stayed long in Clapham, and Daniel, despite building a number of houses there – including his 'Great House' – never lived there as an adult, although his widow moved to one of his smaller houses. Both How and Vanderput were succeeded in their houses by other Anglicans/Tories: How by the returning William Sherlock; Vanderput by **William Hooker**, son of the Lord Mayor, Sir William Hooker. Sherlock soon moved back to London, being appointed to St Paul's Cathedral first as prebendary and then as dean, while Hooker stayed a little longer, until he came out clearly for the Tories to secure his own position as receiver general of the Duchy of Cornwall.

The varying loyalties of Clapham residents are illustrated well by the appointments made at St Thomas' Hospital. In 1677 William Hughes became its chaplain, being described as a person 'of fractious principles'.[36] He edged towards conformity, and was ordained in the Church of England in 1683, but was distinctly unenthusiastic. In July 1683 the king ordered the Bishop of Winchester to investigate complaints of 'the great disorderliness in the Church service as now performed in St Thomas Hospital', and a later report described Hughes' conduct of the services in graphic terms: 'the Form of Prayer made him puke, he sweat at the Litany … and he still hates everything in the Church except its preferments.'[37]

There was more to this than meets the eye. St Thomas' Hospital owned substantial property in Southwark, and its majority of Whig governors had a policy of letting the property to known Whig supporters to help in securing at least one Whig MP from the constituency. The investigation of 1683 was part of a move to change this state of affairs. Hughes was relieved of his position and left Clapham at the same time, and the Whig chairman was replaced by the reliable Tory Sir William Hooker, who joined the Tories Sir Peter Daniel and How as governor. Large numbers of Clapham residents who had been governors were also replaced, including William Daniel (who had in any case died in 1678), Thomas Polhill, Thomas Powell, Anthony Stephens and Edmund White junior; the Tories John Heather, William Hooker (Sir William's son) and William Sherlock were appointed after the change in control, and Edward Munns kept his place. Heather, Munns' son-in-law, later married one of Sir Peter Daniel's daughters, so they probably all had some Tory sympathies.

Conclusion

Although in the early 1670s it appeared as though there would be an increasing acceptance of religious diversity, this was not to continue. This chapter demonstrates Clapham residents' strong links with Nonconformity and the Whigs, shown by their known religious or political positions and, for example, their role as governors of St Thomas' Hospital and the Society for Propagating the Gospel in North America. This is given greater weight by the large number of ejected ministers who spent time in Clapham, by the frequency with which legacies were left not to the rector of Clapham, but to Dissenting clergy (whether in London or elsewhere), and by the presence of a number of schools with a strong Dissenting flavour. The requirements of the Test Acts reduced Dissenters' involvement in City and national politics in the later 1670s, with the result that the residents of Clapham at this time were less politically active than the earlier generation. Even so, they still produced eight common councilmen and eight aldermen, and were able to run successful businesses. Increasingly, they did so by commuting from Clapham or by using their partners' City premises.

One of the effects of the Exclusion Crisis was to develop social segregation, in that Whigs and Tories congregated in the same wards and frequented different taverns, coffee houses and clubs.[38] Clapham was an example of this. It continued to provide a home for a range of Dissenters as well as many ejected ministers, including those who had pursued other careers. They were integrated into the village community, presumably with the acquiescence of the rector, John Savill. Many of them played a full part in the vestry while still sustaining their own worship, providing funds to maintain ministers for meetings in their own houses. This was not entirely a private affair, and the village's character was well-known to the powers that be, being described by no less an authority as L'Estrange as 'Clapham which the Phanatiques (as Everybody knows) have turned into a kind of Whig-warren'.[39]

(Endnotes)

1. Gillian Wagner, *Thomas Coram Gent, 1668–1751* (Boydell and Brewer, 2004), p. 39.

2. Letters of Thomas Corbett to William Windham, Norfolk Record Office, WKC 7/8, 404 x 1.

3. Debtors in the eighteenth century who could afford the prison fees had access to a bar, shop and restaurant, and retained the crucial privilege of being allowed out during the day, which gave them a chance to earn money for their creditors.

4. Quoted in Stephen Pincus, *Protestantism and Patriotism* (Cambridge University Press, 2002), p. 327.

5. Dr Henry Sampson, day book, British Library, Add Ms 4460.

6. Earl of Clarendon, letter to Earl of Rochester, 14 March 1685/86.

7. Common Sergeant's Book 4, 134, 203b, London Metropolitan Archives.

8. Robert Hooke, *Philosophical Experiments and Observations* (1726).

9. Common Sergeant's Book 4, 197b.

10. Ibid., 233b, 234.

11. Gilbert Burnet, *Burnet's History of My Own Time*, ed. O. Airy, vol. 1 (Oxford University Press, 1897), pp. 400, 489.

12. Samuel Pepys, diary, 21 December 1667, 5 December 1668.

13. Ibid., 28 February 1668.

14. A.G. Matthews, *Calamy Revised* (Oxford University Press, 1934), p. 86.

15. Anthony Wood, *Athenae Oxonienses*, vol. 3 (1691), Col. 714.

16. Quoted by Eric Smith in *Clapham Antiquarian Society Newsletter*, 19 November 1970.

17. Henry Newcome, *Autobiography* (Chetham Society, 1852), pp. 177–78.

18. Quoted in Matthews, *Calamy Revised*, p. 205.

19. Philip Lamb, *Funeral Sermon for Mrs Sarah Lye* (1679).

20. Thomas Lye, *Funeral Sermon for Mr W. Hiett* (1681).

21. Gary De Krey, *London and the Restoration 1659–1683* (Cambridge University Press, 2005), p. 126.

22. Alexander Gordon (ed.), *Freedom after Ejection* (Manchester University Press, 1917), p. 273.

23. F. Reynolds Levett, *History of Clapham Congregational Church* (1912), p. 37.

24. Samuel Parker, quoted in De Krey, *London and the Restoration*, p. 129.

25. William Penn, *Considerations Moving to a Toleration and Liberty of Conscience* (1685), p. 4.

26. De Krey, *London and the Restoration*, p. 173.

27. Ibid., p. 325.

28. Tim Harris, *Revolution* (Penguin, 2006), pp. 28–29.

29. Robert Voitle, *The Third Earl of Shaftesbury* (Lousiana State University Press, 1984), p. 11.

30. Sir Roger L'Estrange in *The Observator*, no. 198 (1681); L'Estrange in *The Observator*, no. 270 (1682).

31. L'Estrange in *The Observator*, no. 128 (6 September 1684).

32. L'Estrange in *The Observator*, no. 163 (6 November 1684).

33. Ibid.

34. Earl of Sunderland, letter to Roger L'Estrange, 12 August 1684, Windsor, CPSD Chas II Entrybook 56, p. 125.

35. Mark Knights, *Politics and Opinion in Crisis 1678–81* (Cambridge University Press, 1994), p. 341.

36. Lindsay Granshaw and Roy Porter (eds), *The Hospital in History* (Routledge, 1989), p. 128.

37. Ibid.

38. De Krey, *London and the Restoration*, p. 313.

39. Sir Roger L'Estrange in *The Observator*, no. 163 (6 November 1684).

CHAPTER 7

CLAPHAM RESIDENTS
1688–1720

James and the Glorious Revolution

K ing Charles had grown more absolutist in the last few years
of his reign, and James, as a natural authoritarian, continued
the process when he became king in 1685. He did promote
toleration, chiefly as a means of making life easier for Catholics, but
his Declaration of Indulgence in 1687 gave complete toleration and
right of office for Catholics, together with the right of worship for
Presbyterian conventicles and a relaxation of penal law. Dissenters
were not allowed into universities or to serve as Army officers,
however. James used this to appoint Dissenters to City posts in
place of Tories who were less inclined to support toleration, and he
nominated two Clapham Dissenters as aldermen in 1687.

The first was **Thomas Rodbard**, who had moved into his cousin's
house in 1681. He was alderman from August 1687 until 8 October
1688. A cheesemonger like his cousin and uncle (both also Thomas
Rodbard), he supplied the Navy, so may well have known Samuel
Pepys, Dennis Gauden and William Hewer. The scale of his business
is shown by a Treasury instruction to the Excise Commissioners in
January 1691 requiring them not to press him for payment of £1,882
'till further order from my Lords[,] as the King is ... indebted to him
in a much greater sum for victuals by him furnished for the use of
the Navy'. The other was **Samuel Thompson**, nephew of the famous
Civil War merchant Maurice Thompson; Samuel was nominated

alderman by James II in 1687 and sheriff in 1688. The third Clapham resident appointed alderman, and later sheriff, was Sir Peter Daniel, who survived the purge of Tory aldermen in 1687 and was also appointed governor of the Irish society that administered the City's plantation in Ulster.

Pepys, who had worked closely on Navy matters with James when he was Duke of York, was well-placed when he became king. He was reappointed Secretary of Admiralty matters, often working with **William Hewer**, his former clerk but now a merchant and family friend. They both became MPs. Gauden, Pepys's former client, had finally met disaster, being arrested for debt in 1677, and there was nothing Pepys could do to avoid his bankruptcy. A by-product of this can be seen in Gauden's neighbour **Margaret Farmer**'s will of 1688. She left £10 each to the wife of Gauden's son Benjamin and to his other daughters-in-law, but required that this should not be paid until her estate had received the money due from one of Dennis Gauden's bonds for £80, which she held.

Illustration 12. Print of Godfrey Kneller, *William Hewer*, 1689

Hewer, perhaps at Pepys's instigation, had bought Gauden's house, Clapham Place, together with its contents, although he allowed Gauden to go on living in part of it with members of his family until his death. Hewer's mother, Anne, moved into the house at the end of 1684, after Elizabeth Gauden died, giving Pepys another chance to renew his acquaintance with it when he visited her there. Gauden died in July 1688, and Hewer then moved in himself. Pepys was to follow.

Although James was becoming increasingly unpopular, he continued to perform the functions expected of the king, including the ceremony of touching.[1] The Clapham parish register includes at the end of one volume a list of 'Children touched by his Majestie for the evil'. There were only five names on it, including two small children, all on different occasions in 1687 and 1688, the last only three days before William of Orange landed at Torbay.

After the Glorious Revolution

A number of present or former Clapham residents were affected personally by the Glorious Revolution. Sir Peter Daniel might have expected to become Lord Mayor, since he was by then the senior alderman, but the Whigs blocked his election three times after bitter contests. In 1691 they circulated strongly anti-Tory material that accused him of being a 'pragmatical spy upon the Court of Aldermen and the City in the last Reigns', attacked his role in the changes at St Thomas' Hospital, accused him of using his power as Sheriff to pack the jury for two controversial trials, and claimed that he had been a supporter of the standing army under command of Popish officers.[2] It ended by saying that 'being a sneaking Prostitute to King James, he promised him to comply in taking off the Tests and Penal laws.' Faced with this, Daniel ordered the (controversial) arrest of two common councilmen who had distributed the literature.

Hewer and Pepys were affected by the Glorious Revolution because of their close association with King James, and both resigned their posts a week after the proclamation of the new monarch. Pepys was one of those (relatively few) who refused to swear the oath to the new king on the grounds that they were still bound by their existing oath to James. Hewer did the same. They were both arrested in May 1689 and accused of 'dangerous practices against his Majesty's government', but were released from the Gatehouse Prison after six weeks. It was the end of Pepys' involvement with government, while Hewer continued as a successful businessman and became a director of the East India Company.

On the other hand, the Revolution increased the opportunities for Nonconformists, and **Thomas Rowe**, who had come to Clapham for safety, was able to move his school near St Paul's. The saga of William Hughes and St Thomas' Hospital continued after the Revolution. He had been replaced as chaplain, but complained to the governors that he had been erroneously dismissed under the last regime and should be reinstated. Finally, after more pamphlets on both sides and only after Hughes' death in 1689, his daughter was paid £10/12s for his salary, a further £10 in consideration of 'his long sickness[,] age and poverty', and allowed a further quarter's salary. The governors were refreshed and a series of Clapham residents were appointed.

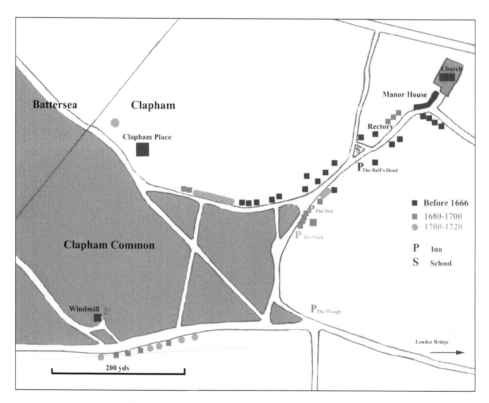

Map 7. Merchant houses in Clapham, 1720

Clapham grew rapidly after the Glorious Revolution, and again at the end of the seventeenth century. It numbered almost two hundred houses in the rate assessment by 1720, double that of the early 1680s, and a total of seventy houses for merchants and their equivalent. This more than doubled the thirty of the early 1680s, and still provided roughly a third of the total in the village. These houses were filled by Nonconformist merchants who had dealings with the existing residents, but with a wider spread of occupations, including lawyers, bankers and some superior artists and craftsmen. Map 7 gives the location of about 80 per cent of the merchant houses, including those added during 1680–1700 and 1700–20; it shows building creeping along both north and south sides of the common, a process that would be completed only towards the end of the century.

It has not been possible to locate exactly the twelve or so houses that were along the road to London Bridge, which, together with the east end of the common, was increasingly taken up with shops of various kinds. By 1720 there were five inns, including the one on the old windmill site, most of which advertised in the London papers.

Clapham merchants

A number of the merchants had close ties with the slave trade, and four of those moved to Clapham in the mid-1680s. **Urban Hall,** son-in-law of Anne Redshaw (who had remained in Clapham after the death of her second husband, Christopher), had been a factor in Stockholm for some years before he returned to England; he moved to Clapham in 1686.[3] In common with other large Baltic traders, he was involved in the re-export to Africa of Swedish iron and copper, which were used to pay for the slaves transported to the West Indies and North America. Slaves from the Gold Coast cost £3–£5 each at the end of the seventeenth century, and the Royal Africa Company needed access to the goods used to pay for them.[4] Many of its shareholders were the merchants who supplied these goods, and belonging to the Court of Assistants naturally gave them an outlet for their imports from the Baltic States. Despite the time-consuming nature of the posts – the Court met twice a week, with subcommittee meetings on top – Hall was on the Court for seventeen years, including holding the top two operational posts of deputy and sub-governor for six years.[5] **John Bull** was also on the Court, and **John Cooke**, who took over the house of his father-in-law, Abraham Babington, was a long-time assistant in the Court of the Company. **Anthony Tournay** had close links to the Royal Africa Company and exported almost £4,000 worth of iron to Africa during the first decade of the eighteenth century.[6] He had shipped 34 tons of iron trade bars on the *Henrietta Marie*, which sank off Florida in 1699.[7] The ship was a regular on the triangular slaving route between England, the Guinea Coast and the Americas, and the wreck also contained over eighty shackles or bilboes, supplied by Tournay, which were used to shackle the adult men in pairs.

Other Clapham slave traders operated largely independently of the Royal Africa Company, including the ironmonger **Sir Robert Dunkley** and his two brothers; John Mitford; **Sir Thomas Cuddon**; and **Robert Bristow**. **Dormer Sheppard** was involved in the Baltic trade and also active in North America, visiting Maryland in 1677. He moved to Clapham in 1683 and by 1694 had built a house in Mile End; it is still used as private house. He owned slaves and, when a black boy ran away from his London house in 1707, he advertised in *The Post Man* for his return. The first time the boy was recaptured after seventeen days trying to return to Guinea, but he ran away again, and the editions of 13–16 December contained a fuller advertisement for his return:

> *Run away from Dormer Sheppard Esq ... a black Boy named Lewis, about 16 years old, with a Hat on, in a darkish fine Cloth Coat lin'd with Red, without a Waistcoat, Leather Breeches and Blue Stockings: he speaks English very well. He has already been advertis'd of in this Paper of the 27th and 29th of November, and the Gazetter of the 4th instant; and on the 5th was brought home from Her Majesties Ship the Roebuck at Sheerness, aboarde of which he had continued several days, attempting to enter himself, having change'd his name to Scipio. He is now supposed to be Aboard some Man of War. Whoever secures him and gives notice of, or sends him to the said Dormer Sheppard shall have their charges paid and a Guinea Reward. Masters of Ships, and all other persons are forbid to harbour him at their peril.*

Baltic connections brought other merchants to Clapham, including those from the Flemish and Huguenot communities. Both John Doggett's daughters married merchants from the Dutch Church in London, Austin Friars. Elizabeth had married Justus Otgher, who started his career doing business from Doggett's house. His family had originated in Ghent, and his brother **Abraham Otgher** was a witness to Doggett's will and himself came to live in Clapham. Doggett's other daughter married another merchant of Flemish extraction, **David DeBarry**, who was deacon at the Dutch church in 1690 when Otgher was an elder. DeBarry was an interloping merchant in the Baltic trade and had lived in Hamburg, where Doggett had been born. Other Clapham residents who were elders of the Dutch Church were **Peter van der Meersch**, who lived in Clapham for sixteen years, and **Jean de la Chambre**. One of the latter's cousins, **Nicholas Oursel**, moved into DeBarry's house in 1696, before giving it to one of his partners, **Stephen Mason**; the two of them later lobbied the Council of Trade and Plantation to allow them to import pitch and tar from America.

John (Jean) Dumaistre, another established Huguenot silk merchant, was naturalised in 1684 and occupied a house in Clapham from 1692 to 1732. In 1697 he was impeached with others by the House of Commons for trading with the French, in particular in various kinds of silk.[8] Dumaistre pleaded guilty and was fined £1,000, although he pleaded in mitigation that 'he had a Wife and Six Children and was … always a Well-wisher to this Government.' This contretemps does not seem to have damaged his standing, and the next year his daughter Anne married the Goldsmith Edward Lambert and, when he died, his partner **Nathaniel Woolfreys**, both of whom were from Huguenot families. Dumaistre himself was churchwarden in Clapham in both 1702 and 1703, which would hardly have been open to someone in disgrace, and Woolfreys later lived in Dumaistre's house. Other Huguenots were the slave trader Anthony Tourney and the haberdasher **John Cheere**, who served in many of the parish offices, staying in Clapham until his death in 1756. His two sons, Henry and John, became well-known sculptors and used their merchant connections to create thriving businesses. While both moved away from Clapham, they chose to be buried there with some of their children.

As we have seen, William Lethieullier, a member of another prominent Huguenot family, had married Henry Powell's daughter Mary, and by 1694 had come to live in 'The Great House' built by her uncle Sir Peter Daniel.

Illustration 13. Sir Peter Daniel's 'Great House',
Clapham, date unknown

The Lethieullier family were rich merchants trading with Turkey and descended from Protestants of Flemish extraction who came to England from Frankfurt in the early seventeenth century. William was the sixth of seven surviving children. Two of his brothers were prominent in the City and both knighted; although he lived on a more modest scale, he too was a successful Turkey merchant, and died worth almost £60,000. All were Nonconformists and Whigs.

The family remained in Clapham until Mary's death in 1741, and acted as a focus for many of the substantial number of Lethieullier relations who visited or lived there. As well as four children who died young, William and Mary had two sons and five daughters, many of whom lived in or near Clapham. The Lethieulliers are a good example of a rich merchant family marrying within its own kind, rather than its daughters – with their good dowries – marrying into the aristocracy. William's eldest daughter, Mary, was the second wife of **Edmund Tooke**, the secretary to the Salters' Company. Although the couple had their own estate in Hertfordshire, they spent much time in Clapham, and Tooke appears as a lodger with the lawyer Edward Fryer in 1700. Their eldest son, Lethieullier Tooke, subsequently had a house in Clapham.

William's second daughter, Sarah, married Thomas Loveday, and their son John, best known for his accounts of his Grand Tour in the mid-seventeenth century, kept a diary in which he recorded regular visits to his grandmother and other family members.[9] William's third daughter married **Richard Hopkins**, a rich Turkey merchant, who also had a house in Clapham for three years from 1718. The fourth daughter, who never married, lived in Clapham until her death in 1754; the fifth daughter married the son of the rector of Clapham. These were not the only Lethieulliers to live in Clapham. William's niece Jane Lethieullier married **Thomas Burrow** and moved to Clapham in 1687, taking the house formerly occupied by William Hooker, whose sister was married to William's brother Sir John Lethieullier.

The Lethieullier and Otgher families provided the hub of a significant Huguenot and Fleming community in Clapham. They were very different from the Huguenot community in Wandsworth, which consisted principally of craftsmen and was well-known for hat-making and associated trades, such as dyeing.[10] The Clapham families were more affluent and better connected, and family connections continued to bring other prominent Huguenots to the village, including those associated with the French church in London. Jane Ducane had married William Lethieullier's brother Christopher, and first **James Ducane** and then his brother **Peter** lived in Clapham for almost fifteen years. Both **John** and **Daniel Dorville** turn up as lodgers in the early eighteenth century; they were business partners of DeBarry, who was close enough to the French Protestants to be entrusted in 1692 with distributing £800 to the Vaudois on behalf of Queen Mary. Daniel Dorville would also have known William Lethieullier because they were both Common Councilmen of Dowgate Ward at the same time. The **Longuet** family also lived in Clapham from the early eighteenth century. It is difficult to believe other than that they consciously made Clapham their joint country getaway. The presence of so many rich people of Huguenot extraction also explains the enormous donation of £126 collected in Clapham for the Vaudois Protestants in March 1698.[11]

Not all connections were solely among Huguenots. Robert Bristow's son followed him to Clapham, together with his brother-in-law Wight Wooley, who had moved into the house of **Henry Cornish**, whose father was executed for alleged complicity in the Rye House Plot of 1683. **Thomas Carleton** had many business contacts with North America, and his sister had married into the Otgher family. He lived in the house formerly occupied by Francis Bridges and then Gabriel and Ann Carpenter and which was still owned by their son Joseph, a slave trader. Carleton's daughter married a highly regarded clockmaker, **James Markwick**, whose daughter married his partner **Robert Markham**; both couples lived in Clapham. Markwick had been brought up in Clapham by his father, also **James Markwick**, and another distinguished clockmaker. Markwick senior had started coming to Clapham to look after John Doggett's clocks, but had then bought himself a house and lived there for seventeen years.

Michael Mitford was related to John Mitford, but from another branch of the Northumberland family. He was not a freeman of London, having been apprenticed as a mercer in Newcastle. He began as a coal trader, working with Arthur Shallett, but as a member of the Eastland Company was also active in the Baltic and other trades. He lived in Danzig for some time and returned to London in 1696, already a wealthy man. We know something about his activities because one of his letterbooks has been preserved, giving his correspondence with a wide variety of agents and other merchants around Europe. He and many others in the Baltic trade used an Amsterdam notary, Heinrich Outgers, as a clearing house for their bills; Outgers was related to the Clapham Otghers, and one of Mitford's apprentices was Abraham Otgher's nephew David. Mitford's letters include ones to (or about) other Clapham residents such as Urban Hall, Arthur Shallett and John Dumaistre, confirming his business links with them.

Hall used his previous Swedish contacts to write to the mayor of Bergen recommending Mitford:

> My good friend Mr Michael Mitford of London merchant
> designing to send his ship the Mitford Castel ... to load
> tarr and some stockfish hath desired my recommendation
> unto you in which we pray serve him according to your
> wonted integrity ... He is a man of honour and ability
> that you need not doubt but the bids drawn ... on him
> the said Michael Mitford payable in London will be
> punctually and duely complied with.[12]

Mitford had also done business with his neighbour Jean Dumaistre,[13] but his letters subsequently report Dumaistre's bankruptcy:

> I doubt not but you will have heard of Mr Collins and
> du Maistre and Mr Hoyle who all broke in a few days
> time one of another. These gentlemen and others who
> did over risk and trade were always obliged to sell at any
> rate for to raise ready moneys and thereby did not only
> use themselves a mischief but did much harm to all the
> Eastland and Russia walks but the business I hope all is
> past and gentleman begin to see into the folly of it.[14]

Mitford reports that Dumaistre made 'a prodigious loss' on hemp, which also caused Mitford to lose money, and he complains that 'a great run was made on several honest merchants.'[15] He goes on:

> John Du Maistre is indebted to them above £9000 ... I
> am very confident he will never be able to pay ... I bless
> God I got clear of all these bankrupts, not concerned
> with any of them ... John Du Maistre his business looks
> very ill, the creditors do not expect above 1/3 from him.[16]

Dumaistre may well have had trouble paying his debts, but to judge from his will, almost thirty years later, he was able to deal with that, since he was still comfortably off.

These strong links through the Baltic, Levant and slave trade, as well as through their families, made Clapham an obvious place for merchants such as Mitford, Hall, Henry Powell and John Doggett to take a house when they returned from abroad. Many of them spoke foreign languages, and Mitford's letterbook contains letters in both French and German. It is not surprising, therefore, that in 1688 a foreign merchant, John Bode from Bremen, died in Clapham, visiting a customer or partner, hurriedly writing a will on his deathbed appointing two London merchants as his executors. Another merchant was **William Brooke,** who had lived much of his working life in Lisbon but returned to Clapham three years before his death. His memorial (now gone) in the church described him as 'merchant', and 'a tender husband, an indulgent father, a sincere friend and a good Christian'. His son, also William, was apprenticed to another Clapham resident, **Roger Lillington,** a merchant with strong family and trading connections to Barbados, where his cousin George owned a number of plantations and was another slave trader.

A number of brewers came to Clapham. Samuel Rush's father had started a vinegar distillery in Castle Street, Southwark, and it remained in family ownership until 1791. **Benjamin Hooper** owned a brew house in the parish of St Giles in the Fields, and moved to Clapham in 1705. His daughter married **Benjamin Mee,** who later became a director of the Bank of England, and they too lived in Clapham. **Nathaniel Collins** was a distiller, but a better-known one was **Josiah Nicholson.** The latter was prodigiously wealthy and able to give his daughter Mary a marriage settlement of £40,000 to marry a younger son of the Verneys who became the 1st Earl. Another daughter, Christian, had married Nicholson's partner, Felix Calvert, of another brewing family; their son, also Felix, later came to live in Clapham.

Clapham lawyers

We find more lawyers living in Clapham later in the seventeenth century than in the earlier decades. **Edward Fryer** witnessed sixteen wills of Clapham residents, conducted the inventory for one of the testators, and was probably the attorney who helped them to write the wills in the first place. He lived in the Manor House for three years between the tenures of Thomas Polhill and Samuel Crisp, and his daughter married Crisp's eldest son. Fryer witnessed Polhill's will, a circumstance that may explain a summons in 1685, with a security of the large amount of £300, to appear as a witness at the trial for treason of Polhill's brother-in-law Major General Henry Ireton. Towards the end of the period covered in this chapter, the amount of religious rubric in Clapham wills declined and was increasingly entirely absent. Of the sixteen wills written and witnessed by Fryer between 1683 and 1715 only two – those of the Nonconformist minister Henry Sampson and the young baronet Sir Henry Atkins – have a substantial religious rubric at the start; the rest have little or none. This suggests that Fryer was prepared to include such text when asked to do so, but that either his standard practice was not to or most did not ask for it. His reward for preparing the will of Dame Rebecca Atkins in 1711 was a legacy of 'so much black cloth at twenty shillings a yard that will make him a mourning suit and coat'. At that price it would have been the best possible cloth.[17]

Henry Markinfield of Furnival's Inn, also a Clapham lawyer, had married Hannah, the daughter of Anthony Stephens, and moved into his house; he too witnessed a number of wills. Another was **John Barnard**, who died in 1711, having acted for Thomas Carleton and no doubt others in Clapham. His widow, Isabella, stayed in the house for another twenty-five years. **Charles Perkins**, who had a house on the south side of Clapham Common, was clerk to the King's Bench Court and managed to use his post to refuse the position of Overseer for the Poor Law.

Many people had a Clapham connection that cannot be picked up from the formal rate books and other documents because they only rented their properties for a short time. One such is the Lord Chancellor **Lord John Somers**, and correspondence in 1697 refers to him:

> *The Lord Chancellor Somers hath been lately very ill at his country house at Clapham in so much as yesterday being the first day of Term the writs which should have been sealed in Westminster Hall were carried to Clapham to be sealed[,] but I am told he is a way of recovery.*[18]

Somers is known to have owned the manor of Reigate, and had previously tried Mortlake for a retreat, but Clapham may have been a useful stop on the way, allowing him the benefits of the country as well as ready access to Westminster.

Clapham bankers

One of the first bankers in Clapham was **Andrew Stone**, son of the jailer at Winchester gaol, who used the perquisites of that post to finance his son's apprenticeship to Richard Smith, a goldsmith at the sign of the Grasshopper on Lombard Street in the City. Stone married his master's niece and became senior partner on Smith's death in 1699, taking a house in Clapham the next year_until his death in 1711. His fellow clerk in the Bank was **Thomas Martin**, who became a partner in 1703 and to whom Stone left his share of the bank on his death in return for the payment of £9,000 to his wife and sister, his own sons all being under the age of ten at the time. Two of Martin's brothers joined him as partners, and the bank eventually became known as Martin's Bank. Thomas also came to live in Clapham, in 1717, and stayed there for almost fifty years. While he was buried with other members of the family in Cheshunt in Hertfordshire, the inscription on his memorial there records that 'the last 49 years of his life he spent at Clapham in Surrey in great hospitality, without pomp, doing much good and being much beloved, warm in friendships, liberal in his benefactions, in his benevolence unbounded.'

The year 1703 brought another scion of a major banking family to Clapham: **Elizabeth Hankey**, widow of the goldsmith Samuel Hankey. He had started what was effectively a bank at the sign of the Ring in Fenchurch Street, taking on his nephew **Henry Hankey** as apprentice in 1683. Samuel died in 1685, when his nephew was only nineteen, and Elizabeth remained active in the business, which became known as Widow Hankey and Co. By 1704 Henry had taken charge and renamed the firm Henry Hankey and Co., and his aunt moved to Clapham, where she remained for the rest of her life. This was the start of a long association of the family with Clapham; Henry himself, by then knighted and an alderman, later had a house in Clapham, as did his son **Sir Thomas Hankey**, who married the daughter of Clapham resident and Lord Mayor John Barnard.

Another Clapham banker was **Abraham Atkins**. Although the family was Baptist, he played a prominent part in parish matters, holding most of the parish offices, including churchwarden, during his twenty-four years there. The Huguenot Nathaniel Woolfreys became a partner in the firm of goldsmiths at the Golden Fleece in Lombard Street in 1696, having been dismissed by the Bank of England from his position as a teller because he refused to withdraw his request to have his salary doubled.[19] He will surely have made more money at the goldsmiths than his £50 salary at the bank.

There were many Barnards who lived in Clapham. The most famous was **Sir John Barnard**, who became a highly respected Lord

Mayor in 1737. His parents were Quakers, and he went to the Quaker School in Wandsworth before moving to the counting house of his wine-merchant father at the age of fifteen. He was baptised into the Church of England in his early twenties and soon took over the business, moving into marine insurance, which became his major preoccupation. He moved into John Jackson's house in 1723, and his two daughters married Sir Thomas Hankey and the Hon. Henry Temple, grandfather of the prime minister, Viscount Palmerston.

Anglican clergy

Nicholas Brady was the successor to John Savill as rector of Clapham. The son of a Protestant Irish Army officer, he became a strong supporter of King William and moved to England. He was commissioned as chaplain to Colonel Sir Richard Atkins' foot regiment, and soon afterwards became chaplain to William and Mary. He was a minor poet and wrote the 'Ode to St Cecilia's Day' that was set to music by Henry Purcell. His metrical translation of the Psalms, in collaboration with another Protestant Irish clergyman, Nahum Tate, steadily replaced the previous version and ran to more than 300 editions. It especially pleased Whigs because of its occasional political allusions, such as its translation of psalm 107 verse 40, which read:

> The prince, who slights what God commands
> Expos'd to scorn must quit his throne.

This 'New Version of the Psalms of David' was dedicated to William himself, who made an Order in Council shortly after its publication allowing it to be used 'in all such churches ... as shall think fit to receive the same'.

Brady was then appointed perpetual curate of Richmond chapelry, having been invited 'by the gentlemen of that place, in consequence of a high esteem they had conceived for him during a retreat which he had made thither, while he was translating the psalms'.[20] He had preached Richard Atkins' funeral sermon in 1696, stimulating his mother, the widow Dame Rebecca, to appoint Brady to Clapham when Savill died in 1706. He immediately sought and obtained permission for his metrical version of the Psalms to be used in Clapham church. He continued to hold his Richmond curacy and lived there, where he kept a school that was promoted by Richard Steele in The Spectator. His son, also **Nicholas Brady**, was ordained too, and his first church post was as a lecturer at Clapham (albeit voted in by a majority of a single vote in fifty-three); he retained the post when he was appointed rector of the next village, Tooting.

Political positions

Clapham residents were overwhelmingly Whig, reflecting both their Nonconformity and, as in the case of Henry Cornish, their family tradition. They supported, and were members of, Whig organizations. They continued to provide trustees of the Society for the Propagation of the Gospel in North America; twenty-four were among the first subscribers to the Bank of England; and seventeen sometime Clapham residents were governors of St Thomas' Hospital in 1719. Michael Mitford was on the Court of the Whig New East India Company.

Clapham residents also continued to play their part in livery companies. They provided three Prime Wardens of the Fishmongers and three Masters of the Clothworkers (four if we include Samuel Pepys, who was Master in 1677/78). However, there was less representation in the governance of the City, with only seven Common Councilmen and four aldermen, three of whom were nominated by James II and held the position for only a year; the other was the long-standing Sir Peter Daniel. No Clapham resident was an alderman between 1700 and 1724. Even so, and taking only the Nonconformist post-holders, these amounted to a fifth of all Presbyterian and Independent office-holders between 1685 and 1715, a remarkable proportion for such a small village.[21] One such was Sir Thomas Cuddon, a Presbyterian involved in a terrific struggle for election to the post of City Chamberlain in 1696. He stood in the Whig interest, and a mob of armed youths 'exclaimed promiscuously against Mr Cuddon, and the Whigs, etc., calling them damned dogs, with other such villainous language'.[22]

There were few MPs from Clapham in this period: four around the turn of the century and none between 1702 and 1724, when Sir Richard Hopkins and Sir John Barnard became MPs for the City of London. This reflected the requirement introduced in 1711 that

MPs should have an annual income of at least £300 from land, or £600 for a county seat. The earlier members do not seem to have had a great enthusiasm for the job, and few remained for very long, although Arthur Shallett's desire to be an MP was largely driven by attempts to stave off bankruptcy with parliamentary privilege. Joseph Paice helped to provide the majority of one for the Act providing for the Protestant succession after Queen Anne, but he began to be sick of 'court and country' squabbles and did not seek further election, writing in his diary:

> As I never sought it at first, so I can appeal to my God
> that I never had any vain glory in it, and have in all my
> votes acted according to the best of my judgement and
> conscience, without the least partiality or favour to any
> party or cause.[23]

Pepys and Clapham

One of the few non-Whig residents of Clapham was Samuel Pepys, who had come as a result of his friendship with Dennis Gauden and William Hewer. Clapham Place had been seriously affected by Gauden's bankruptcy, with much of its contents sold, and once he took possession Hewer promptly improved it, disposed of the farms used by Gauden to supply his victualling contracts, and retained only sixty acres, which were largely devoted to gardens and pleasure grounds.[24] Pepys retreated to Hewer's house for several weeks in the summer of 1697, a much longer period in 1700, and then permanently in the summer of 1701; all his books were moved there the next year, a sign that he would not return to London.

While Pepys was very much an urban animal, there were significant benefits to remaining in Clapham. It had good air and its height above sea level of one hundred feet, coupled with its distance from the City, provided considerable improvement for those used to the stench of London, as well as much less noise. John Evelyn commented: 'I do most heartily congratulate the improvement of your health, since your change of air,' and later 'while I mourn your absence here, you are at Clapham, enjoying better health, a purer air, nobler retreats.'[25] The Earl of Clarendon wrote along similar lines:

I hope your being thus long in Clapham (for I think you
were never so long in the country before, since you knew
the world) will make you relish the pleasure of a garden,
which will be no burthen to your other perfections.[26]

Pepys himself, having remarked on the improvement in his health,
'perfected by the air of this place', went on to write: 'if I must be
left to philosophise by myself, nobody, I fancy, will blame me for
choosing to do it in a serene air, without noise, rather than where
there is nothing of the first, and nothing else but the last.'[27]

Hewer had made the house much more pleasant to live in,
decorating it with fashionable ornaments and furniture, and
improved the gardens. Evelyn wrote: 'I went to visit Mr Pepys at
Clapham where he has a very noble and wonderful well furnish'd
house, especially with Indian and Chinese curiosities. The offices and
gardens well accommodated for pleasure and retirement.'[28]

Some of this approval may have come from the fact that Evelyn
himself had had a hand in the improvements. William Nicolson, about
to be consecrated as Bishop of Carlisle and visiting Pepys in 1702,
made clear that Evelyn had 'kindly met him there [and] owned himself
the causer of a deal of Luxury in these matters'. Nicolson's diary
contains a description of the house and particularly Pepys' library:

In the house mighty plenty of China-ware and other Indian
Goods, vessels of a sort of paste; hardened into a Substance
like polished Marble. Pictures in full pains of wainscot; which
(by having one moveable, painted on both sides) admits of
three several Representations of the whole Room. Models
of the Royal Sovereign and other Men of War, made by the
most famous Master-Builders; very curious and exact, in glass
Cases. Mr Pepys's Library in 9 cases, finely gilded and sash-
glass'd; so deep as to carry two Rows ... of Books on each
footing. A pair of Globes hung up, by pullies. The Books so
well ordered that his Footman (after looking the Catalogue)
could lay his finger on any of them blindfold. Miscellanies of
paintings, cuts, pamphlets, etc in large and lesser Volumes.[29]

Nicolson also admired the 'Garden, Walks, and Bowling Greens,
Ponds'. In the light of his own hand in the comfort it gave Pepys,
Evelyn's reference to 'your Paradisian Clapham' in a letter to Pepys
comes as no surprise.[30]

Pepys played a full part in the community. In 1701 he contributed two guineas to a subscription to pay for the parish lecturer; he reported the death of Sir Peter Daniel in a letter to his nephew John Jackson; and in his will he gave £5 to the poor of Clapham and a series of mourning rings to Clapham residents (the rector, John Savill, the two lecturers who had been in post during his time there, and his neighbours Urban Hall, Thomas Juxon and Benjamin Gauden, the eldest son of Dennis. Pepys left his estate to Jackson, the son of his sister Paulina.

Illustration 14. John Jackson, date unknown

Hewer lived on in the house until his death in 1715, together with Jackson, who was described by the writer John Aubrey as 'a Gentleman of most singular Humanity and Goodness'.[31] Jackson had made an offer of marriage to one of Evelyn's granddaughters, but he was not a good enough match for the family. Seven years later, at the age of thirty-nine, he married Anne Edgely (a niece of Hewer and daughter of the vicar of Wandsworth), but the couple in the house for a few years. Aubrey recorded: 'In this house are still carefully preserved by Mr Jackson an excellent collection of Curiosities, much augmented by Mr Jackson himself ... which consist of various subjects relating to English History, Maritime Affairs etc.'[32] However, Jackson preferred a more modern house, and he built one in the grounds, The Cedars, a three-storied red-brick structure with a platform on the roof, guarded by an ornamental wrought-iron railing and giving extensive views of the City and river and southwards towards the Surrey hills.

Illustration 15. The Cedars, 1850s, photograph
by Henry Deane
Courtesy Wandsworth Heritage Services

Clapham place remained empty when Jackson died in 1722, and was finally knocked down in 1762. Many of Hewer's relations, even distant ones, were buried in his family vault at Clapham.

Conclusion

Clapham grew by over 50 per cent after the Glorious Revolution, but with the same high proportion of merchants and other professionals. Family and business links remained the most important factor influencing those who moved there, whether it was slave trading, links to North America or marriage to children of existing residents. There was a substantial Huguenot and Fleming community, and newcomers already knew many of their future neighbours either socially or through business. The vast majority were Whigs, and although political activity was still constrained, many supported a wide range of Whig organizations. Clapham maintained its Nonconformist character in which both Anglican rectors appear to have acquiesced with Nicholas Brady, who was in any case living in Richmond. But while the merchants included in this chapter were certainly Nonconformist, a substantial number of Clapham residents were extremely active in Nonconformist circles, and they are covered in the next chapter.

(Endnotes)

1. It was widely believed that the king's touch would cure the skin disease scrofula, which was in fact a swelling of the lymph nodes caused by tuberculosis. Kings would hold grand ceremonies at which they would touch hundreds of people, each of whom usually received a small gold coin called a touchpiece. Charles II touched more than 90,000 during his reign.

2. Advice to the Liverymen of London in their choice of Lord Mayor in 1692, British Library, L.R.404.n.5.(53).

3. Sven Erik Astrom, *From Cloth to Iron: The Anglo-Baltic Trade in the Late Seventeenth Century* (Helsingfors, 1963), p. 140 and passim.

4. K.G. Davies, *The Royal Africa Company* (Longmans, 1957), p. 237.

5. Ibid., Appendix A.

6. Ibid., Appendix B.

7. Corey Malcolm, 'The Iron Bilboes of the *Henrietta Marie*', *The Navigator: Newsletter of the Mel Fisher Maritime Heritage Society*, vol. 13, no. 10 (October 1998).

8. *Journal of the House of Lords*, 8, 30 June 1697.

9. Sarah Markham, *John Loveday of Caversham, 1711–1789: The Life and Tours of an Eighteenth-century Onlooker* (M. Russell, 1984).

10. R.A. Shaw, R.D. Gwynn and P. Thomas, *Huguenots in Wandsworth* (Wandsworth Borough Council, 1985).

11. John Batten, *Clapham with its Common and Environs* (1841), p. 92.

12. Urban Hall, letter to Mr Lydder Fasting, 31 August 1706, Michael Mitford, Letterbook, London Metropolitan Archives.

13. Mitford, letter to Robert Baily, 24 February 1704, ibid.

14. Mitford, letter to Richard Green, 13 April 1704, ibid.

15. Mitford, letter to William Shipard, 12 September 1704, ibid.

16. Mitford, letters to Mallabar and Lowther, 6 March and 13 April 1705; letter to Messrs Bland and English, 17 April 1705, ibid.

17. Peter Earle, *The Making of the English Middle Class* (Methuen, 1989), p. 286.

18. Richard Lapthorne, letter to Richard Coffin, 4 June 1697.

19. Anne L. Murphy, 'Learning the Business of Banking: The Management of the Bank of England's First Tellers', *Business History*, vol. 52, no. 1 (2010), p. 150.

20. A. Kippis, *Biographica Britannica*, vol. 1 (1778), p. 564.

21. Gary De Krey, *A Fractured Society* (Oxford University Press, 1985), p. 87.

22. Quoted by P. Gauci in History of Parliament online, www.historyofparliamentonline.org.

23. Quoted in Anne Manning, *Family Pictures* (Arthur Hall, Virtue and Co., 1861), p. 13.

24. John Aubrey, *The Natural History and Antiquities of Surrey* (1692).

25. John Evelyn, diary, 10 May 1700; 10 December 1701.

26. John Smith (ed.), *Memoirs of Samuel Pepys*, vol. 5 (1828), p. 337.

27. Samuel Pepys, letter to Dr Gale, 13 June 1700.

28. Evelyn, diary, 23 September 1700.

29. William Nicolson, diary, 17 June 1702.

30. John Evelyn, letter to Samuel Pepys, 29 January 1703.

31. Aubrey, *Natural History and Antiquities of Surrey*, Appendix, p. 1.

32. Ibid.

CHAPTER 8

A WHIG WARREN

D issenters had been wary of James II's attempts to reduce religious discrimination because they distrusted his motives. This changed after 1688, but not completely. A Toleration Act gave Dissenters immunity from prosecution for holding their own religious services, if they licensed their meeting houses and kept their doors open when they met to answer charges that they were plotting against the Crown. They also had to subscribe to the declaration in the Test Acts against transubstantiation, take the oath of fidelity and allegiance and swear against the right of the pope to depose sovereigns. None of these conditions normally caused any difficulty for Nonconformists, and Quakers were allowed to subscribe to these declarations to get round their refusal to swear any oaths. It was still compulsory to participate in religious observance on a Sunday, but going to Church could be avoided by attending a Dissenting meeting. While Independents and Congregationalists were essentially gathered churches catering to the like-minded, Presbyterians still wished to be part of a national Church. However, attempts failed to create a single national Church that included Dissenters as well as traditional Anglicans. This made inevitable the creation of Nonconformist churches in England, with or without a national structure.

Clapham continued to attract committed Nonconformists. **Arthur Shallett** was a younger son of a minor Hampshire family who became a successful merchant, moving in 1696 into what had been Anthony Tournay's house.[1] He did business with David DeBarry and was a leading figure in the Newcastle coal trade, where one of his connections was his Clapham neighbour Michael Mitford. Mitford told one of his correspondents of a shipment of tar and that 'Mr Arthur Shallett is concerned with me in it. Several of the colliers would be glad to serve him in carrying it.'[2] He also passed on the 'kind love' of Mr Shallett and family to the commander of one of his ships.[3]

Shallett was a member of an Independent congregation and also played a full part in many Whig activities. He held £2,000 stock in the New East India Company, being one of the merchants who petitioned for a charter in 1698. He was a governor of St Thomas' Hospital and served as an assistant in the London corporation for the poor (workhouse); he was attracted to the movement for the reformation of manners and in 1693 joined a group of gentlemen who pledged to promote the execution of the laws against profaneness and debauchery. He was one of three patrons of a Nonconformist charity school set up in opposition to an offer of free education for the poor by the Jesuit Andrew Poulton.

Shallett described his business in 1688 as

> *possessed of a considerable estate, and yearly sold in this port of London fifty thousand chalder of coals and traded much in exporting the manufactures and produce of this kingdom, together with great quantities of fish from the west of England and Newfoundland, to Spain, Portugal and other foreign dominions; and for return thereof did yearly import considerable quantities of wine, brandy, etc.*

The Spanish brandy was the output of a large distillery he had constructed in partnership with Sir Gilbert Heathcote, and another of his partners in trade with Spain was John Mitford. Shallett's brother Joseph was the English Consul in Barcelona and a frequent visitor to Clapham, where his local knowledge of Spain was doubtless put to good use. After the Revolution Arthur Shallett was known as 'a great dealer in shipping' and hired out his vessels to the government, supplying ships for the Irish war of 1689–91, the campaign in Flanders in 1693 and the evacuation of the Army from the Continent after the peace of 1697. Business deteriorated later in the 1690s, however, and a number of his ships were captured by the French. He ended up deep in debt to Customs, although he argued that this should be offset by what he was owed for the use of his ships by the armed forces. He had been protected from prosecution by being an MP, but when he was defeated in the election of 1701, Customs had him delivered to the Marshalsea prison, to be released only on the surety of 'five credible merchants'. The Treasury finally allowed him to do a deal in March 1703, noting that 'he has lost £20,000 by losses in the war, and is reduced so low that he and his wife and children want bread.' His will suggests that he had little to leave above £50 in small legacies, and his wife's will nine years later makes a number of references to those who have helped her with 'the great charge and pains of managing her troublesome affairs'. Their son, also Arthur, became a Nonconformist minister but left the ministry in 1718.

Samuel Crisp lived in Clapham until his death in 1703. He was described as 'a man who cared more for high-Calvinist doctrine than for peace among the churches',[4] and he republished the sermons of his father, Tobias, works that had been viewed as heretical by some sections of Nonconformism. He included in the same volume a tract of his own, setting out his version of the doctrine of justification. The sermons reopened past controversies, essentially about which came first, repentance or faith, and their publication prompted the eminent and elderly theologian Richard Baxter to write:

> But I see the corrupting design is of late grown so high,
> that what seemed these thirty four years suppressed,
> now threatneth as a torrent to overthrow the Gospel and
> Christian faith and to deny it the true office of Christ as
> Mediator and his Grace and righteousness by seeming
> ignorantly to extol them. And Satan designeth to make us
> a common scorn to papists and malignants by palpable
> grossness of such men's undeniable errors.[5]

The sermon at Crisp's funeral, preached by the Nonconformist Edward Grace, used the same text as had been used for John Gould, 'Mark the Perfect Man', but there was not as great a sense of warmth. While Grace mentioned that Crisp was one of the longest-standing members of the Nonconformist church in Clapham, he admitted that 'in some things he was a man of a warm temper', and another comment emphasised Crisp's straight talking:

*Yet such is the prevailing Atheism and Impiety of the
Age, that many think not themselves genteel enough in
conversation, unless they make bold with the name of God.
This he was wont to reprove in all Company where he was
present; and such was his resolution and courage in the cause
of God, that he would not spare those of the highest rank.*[6]

It was Crisp who had complained 'especially' in 1697 about the
activities of the Adams family, who by then lived in the little house
next to the church. He said, the vestry minutes reported, that 'it
was very inconvenient for the parish, and not only offensive on the
Lord's Day, but that they do break down the hedges and fences of
the Churchyard for firing'. As a result the house was taken down and
moved elsewhere on the common.

Crisp was not just a devout man, but also well-read. Grace said
in the funeral sermon that

*He took singular delight in the Holy Scriptures; he read
them diligently, and for his own entertainment wrote
them over in the original languages (in which he had
no mean skill) that they might have the more powerful
impression on his mind.*

He took great care in his will to dispose of his library. He left his
Bibles with their copious annotations to two of his sons; and to his
son Stephen,

*to furnish him somewhat in the blessed work of the
Ministry, I give all of my Manuscripts of Hebrew and
Greek in my three times writing out the Bible in Hebrew
and Greek in English letters and rendering the whole into
proper English correcting the same each time as I could
with the help of authors and hoping it may on perusal be
printed as an essay to a more punctual rendering of the
Bible into English than any former by public authority
for a general benefit to the Land and some particular to
my family in compensation of sixteen years pains 4 hours
a day tho this was by itself through God's assistance hath
been a blessed and great reward.*

Crisp went on to leave Stephen his 'Book of the list of 7000 and
odd sermons from 1646 to 1701', about 300 books of sermons, and
finally his much-annotated copy of a Bible printed in 1576.

Joseph Paice was born in Exeter to Dissenting parents, but, following his father's early death, was adopted by his uncle, who later sent him to a counting house in St Malo to learn French. He was apprenticed to a Turkey merchant but was still struggling financially, and when he married, the combined capital of his wife and himself was only £50. He left for Jamaica when things became difficult for Dissenters after Monmouth's rebellion, but found the climate uncongenial and returned to England, where he became a successful merchant and ship owner. He lived in Clapham from 1694 to 1698, and returned to the Manor House a few years later, after Crisp's death. He accepted an offer to stand as MP for Lyme in 1701, and prepared himself for the parliamentary session by praying privately with two Presbyterian ministers. In general he supported the Whigs, writing:

> *I have with great diligence attended my duty the whole session and found in a little while the Members principally divided into two parties; the Court and Country – an unhappy distinction. Upon an impartial observation, in my weak judgement the Court party were those who did most heartily espouse the true interest of His Majesty and the nation; and, therefore, from my own judgement and not to espouse a party, I voted usually with them. It seemed to me that the Country party (Sir Edward Seymour etc) were offended that they themselves had not the preferment and had particular resentments against some whom his Majesty had preferred and ... therefore obstructed the King's affairs in the House greatly.*[7]

Paice acted for Dissenting friends in 1706 when he supported a petition asking that Dissenters should not be excluded from membership of the General Assembly of South Carolina, an Assembly for which 'all sorts of people, even servants, Negroes, Aliens, Jews and Common sailors were admitted to vote in Elections.'[8] Stephen Mason, another Clapham merchant, also signed the petition.

John Gould's widow, **Judith**, lived on in Clapham until her death in 1704. She was a great supporter of the Independent church, whose members met for many years in her house until they built their own. Her will has an extended religious piece to start with, and was written about a month before her death, 'being desirous to have nothing to do but die when that time cometh'. Her two younger sisters, **Anne**

Joliffe and **Amy Jacombe,** had married older men, and they came to live with her when they were widowed; **Richard Jennings** lived with them as her chaplain from 1690. He was another ejected minister who had spent a short time in North America. He was popular with widows, and a number left him legacies.

Judith's will asked the executors to work out whether it was best to sell the remaining eleven years of the lease of her house or extend it for letting. In fact, her sisters continued to live there. When Anne died in 1715, her son **Thomas Joliffe** took over the house. He died in 1722, but his aunt Amy lived there until 1726. The Nonconformist minister Moses Lowman was one of the witnesses of his will, and Joliffe was very firm about limiting the expense of his funeral. He was a friend of Henry Hankey, whom he chose to be his executor, giving him £1,000 for his trouble.

The church supported by the Goulds was very active and had its own ministers. **Edward Grace** succeeded Philip Lamb in 1689 as the minister for the congregational chapel (a position he held until his death in 1714) and married Henry Tatham's young widow, Ann, in 1691. Not much is known about Grace, but he identified himself in his will as 'gentleman'. He had inherited half the estate of his uncle, a Draper, and his brother, a London merchant. Grace was well-known at the time, and a minatory letter addressed to 'the rest of the Eminent Teachers of the Congregation of Anabaptists' included him as an addressee.

Moses Lowman followed **Edmund Batson** to become the assistant minister in 1710, and succeeded Grace as chief minister there until his death in 1752. He was known for his scholarship but, although an active and public-spirited pastor not only serving his own congregation but also assisting other chapels in a poor financial position, he had a poor reputation as a preacher, as the *Protestant Dissenter's Magazine* recorded in 1794:

> *His discourses were obscure, the respect and esteem of his congregation must be due not on evidence for the acceptableness of his sermons [but] to the excellence and weight of his character, and the candour of his hearers who, possessed of high sentiments of the latter[,] passed over the unpleasing defects of the former.*[9]

Lowman seems to have been a very eighteenth-century cleric, sometimes being seen as Presbyterian and sometimes as Independent, and was a founder member of the London Congregational Board in 1727. His style matched the sentiments of the time, as the same magazine explained: 'His piety was rational, not superstitious; the effect of principle not enthusiasm; grave not morose; and serious without being disfigured by sourness.'[10]

Another Clapham Minister was **John Mottershed,** who trained under Thomas Doolittle and was described as 'the son of an opulent father ... [with] a great estate now entering preaching'.[11] That father was **Thomas Mottershed,** a younger son of a well-known Chester family; he came to London in the 1650s and traded with Virginia, where his elder brother Samuel had emigrated. Thomas owned a number of properties in Clapham, including the first coffee shop there, which later became an inn.

Two Nonconformist ministers-turned-doctors came to Clapham. **John Hutchinson** had been ejected from his fellowship at Trinity College, Cambridge, but subsequently became a fellow of the Royal College of Physicians. He practised in Hertfordshire for thirty years, but in 1701–2 he lived in part of the Manor House in Clapham with Samuel Crisp.[12] Another very distinguished doctor was **Henry Sampson.**[13] He was a fellow of Pembroke College, Cambridge, and was presented to a Suffolk living even though not ordained. He was ejected in 1660, but continued to preach and developed his own congregation; he also trained to be a doctor, which he did very successfully, particularly treating fellow Nonconformist ministers. He published a series of papers on morbid anatomy, but his chief interest was in producing a history of Puritanism Nonconformity, in which he presented Nonconformists as 'a Considerable, an injured and misjudged people'.[14] His many contacts with Clapham Nonconformists naturally led him there at the end of the seventeenth century, and he died there a rich man, worth over £8,000. His will thanks God for 'the recovery of me from the grand Apostary' and asks for his body to be buried in the Nonconformist graveyard in Bunhill Fields, where he had already purchased a place and where his second wife was buried. He recognised, however, that 'if God wills that I should die in some place remote from London', he should be buried at the discretion of his executor. He left a life interest in his property to his wife, with one of his old Bibles, instructing that 'she should read therein all the days of her life, leaving it to some one of my kindred with the like charge.'

Many of Clapham's Nonconformists played a major part in national approaches to supporting the development of new ministers. It had been difficult to provide new blood systematically when Dissenters were prevented from teaching at universities or taking degrees, and there was a real need for more and younger ministers. This became increasingly important, since although many ejected ministers continued to preach and support the laity – often, as in Clapham, holding positions as chaplains in individual houses or as schoolteachers – they were described as 'though wonderfully preserved to this time, are aged'.[15] Without a national structure there was often little practical difference between Congregational churches on the one hand and isolated Presbyterian churches on the other. Once moves to achieve a single national Church failed, it became natural for the two to work together, and they formed what was known as the Common Fund to relieve the poverty of Nonconformist ministers and to assist in the education of new ones. Arthur Shallett was the treasurer and manager of the Common Fund, which was used to fund the education of Nonconformist ministers, and later the Congregational Fund.

By 1693 the Fund had split into two factions representing the different streams, stimulated in part by arguments over the writings of Tobias Crisp, Samuel's father.[16] Clapham laity played an important role in the structures of the Nonconformist church, representing both branches. Henry Sampson was the largest individual donor, at £50, while Edward Grace gave £25 and Thomas Powell also contributed. Grace succeeded Shallett as manager of the Congregational Fund in 1696, while Thomas Cuddon and Thomas Rodbard (the nephew) were on the board of the Presbyterian fund.[17] One Clapham minister supported by the Fund was **John Troughton**, son of a father of the same name; the former entered into a number of controversies in support of his father from Clapham, where he was described as 'teach[ing] school and preach[ing] occasionally'.[18] These close connections must have been one of the elements in bringing many of these people to Clapham.

Clapham school

The large number of Nonconformists in Clapham generated some tension about the appointment of the schoolmaster. The school had been running successfully since 1648 under a body of trustees. The first trustees were essentially those who ran the vestry and had no difficulty in appointing Nonconformists such as William Hughes and Thomas Lye as masters. It was, at least in part, a boarding school for boys, and one Francis Hunlocke, whose mother had lived in Clapham for ten years and had known the school since 1662, explained:

> The school had a very good reputation and was well filled with scholars ... Mr Lye has usually during that time some boarding and Town scholars, about fifty belonging to said school, whereof thirty were boarders in the said Mr Lye's house at Clapham.[19]

The trustees, who were by this time the successors of the original body, naturally saw the appointment as their responsibility, and chose one Robert Forbes. It is not clear what his religious views were, but a body of prominent residents wanted a Dissenter, in particular a Mr John Hunt from Epsom. Hunt had worked with Benoni Rowe, the Congregational minister at Epsom and brother of the Thomas Rowe who had moved his Dissenting school to Clapham for a short while just before the Glorious Revolution. This dispute eventually led to a court case.

At first it was too late for the parishioners to do anything, as Forbes was successfully in place. Many witnesses at the subsequent case held that he was 'sober, kindly and learned', came regularly from school between 8 and 9 o'clock whatever the weather, and had even been known to arrive soaking wet rather than be absent. This seems to be confirmed by the fact that Dr Samuel Edgely, the vicar of Wandsworth and himself a trustee of the school, sent his son Hewer to school there as a preparation for Eton.

Then Richard Fulker, the former blacksmith and then pub owner, brought in 'a public coffee house' a charge of cruelty, alleging that Forbes had beaten one boy about the head so hard that he died, and had twisted the arm of another, and that because of this and his negligence people were taking their children from the school. No proof was brought to support these charges, and Fulker later withdrew them, but they gave Forbes' opponents their chance. A written proposal to replace him with a Mr Samuel Billingsley, an under-teacher at Christ's Hospital, was circulated, and a vestry meeting arranged for noon on Ash Wednesday, when the supporters of Forbes would be at church. Billingsley's Dissenting qualities are not clear, although his father and grandfather were of known Dissenting views. He was eventually sufficiently orthodox to have gained preferment as Archdeacon of Surrey.

The new appointment was agreed by those present who maintained that it was the parishioners who had the right of appointment. William Hewer, Dennis Gauden, Forbes and the rector, John Savill, arrived too late to overturn the decision. Forbes then refused to give up the key, so the churchwardens changed the lock. Billingsley lasted two weeks, until the Trustees arranged for a blacksmith to break open the lock and Forbes was reinstalled.

The vestry minutes in March 1700 record that Hewer proposed that the case be referred to arbitration, since the four Counsel appointed had failed to resolve it. Hewer had been churchwarden recently (ironically with Richard Fulker as the other one) and was about to take over again, on 21 March, but the meeting tried to find one of the existing churchwardens to come for the vote. Alderman Rodbard was away, but it was discovered that the other churchwarden, the lawyer Edward Fryer, was 'in the Bull Alehouse'. The rector sent the parish clerk to fetch him but he refused to come, and the meeting endorsed Hewer's proposal unanimously. In the end, the case went to Chancery, which ruled in favour of the trustees. Fryer was friendly with Thomas Polhill and Henry Ireton, and it may be that he had Dissenting sympathies and so opposed Forbes' appointment. Forbes, meanwhile, went on to be Hewer's own chaplain.

It is perhaps noticeable that this is one of the few records of a major dispute within the parish. Only a few months later, the vestry minutes for Saturday morning, 28 December, read: 'At 11 of the clock the Vestry meeting ... nothing was done: the morning very Rayny and Blustring.'

Charitable legacies

Charitable legacies can also give an indication of the commitment of Clapham residents to Nonconformism, and the most obvious example is a legacy to Dissenting clergymen. This is very common, and local Nonconformist ministers such as Edward Grace, Philip Lamb and Thomas Lye were included on many occasions. Both John Gould and Henry Tatham gave £20 to allow distribution to such poor ministers, or ministers' widows, as their executors should choose. Gould also left £5 a year each to a number of Nonconformist ministers, including Lamb and Lye, as part of an agreement he had made with his wife, Judith, 'and her friends' on marriage. Mary Daniel and Dorothy Arthur are the only people to have left a monetary legacy to the rector John Savill. Samuel Pepys did leave mourning rings to Savill and the two Anglican lecturers present during his stay in Clapham, but no legacy; he gave nothing to the Dissenting ministers.

Many wills included a legacy for the poor of Clapham, ranging from £5 to £20, and required it to be disbursed at the discretion of either the executors or a minister and churchwardens. Lye ordered the selling of his books, with the first £30 of the proceeds going towards the funeral costs and the remainder to be given to the poor.

There was also much emphasis on the 'deserving' poor. Judith Gould left

> the sum of ten pounds of lawful money of England to be laid out by my executors in linen and in woollen cloth for shifts and garments for the poor in [Clapham] and it is my will that in the distribution [t]hereof a special regard will be had for widows and aged persons and such as are in greatest want and who in the time of their strength were industrious for a livelihood and have not brought themselves into poverty by idleness or vicious course.

In the same way, Michael Mitford left £50 to generate an income to pay for

> Two grey cloth coats against the first Sunday in December yearly forever for two such poor old men as the Minister and churchwardens aforesaid shall judge to be the greatest object of charity in that parish who shall

attend divine service in Church frequently which said
coats are to be marked with the letters M M and set in
green cloth and affixed to each such coat.

A few left capital sums, either to their livery company or to Christ's Hospital, to pay for annual donations to the poor in their parish. Thomas Langham left £10 for the poor in Clapham, but additionally £400 to his own livery company, the Mercers, on condition that they spend four shillings a week for ever on providing twelve fourpenny loaves for distribution to the poor after Sunday morning service, with the odd twelve shillings going to the churchwardens for overseeing the distribution. He also ordered his executors to pay for a wainscot shelf to be put in some convenient part of the church to hold the bread. He also left £100 to Christ's Hospital.

Sometimes involving livery companies in this way was a means to influence the way the money was spent. Henry Colborne left a large sum for a school in Kirkham, Lancashire, to be administered by the Drapers Company. This was a deliberate attempt to secure the appointment of Puritan ministers and schoolmasters against the wishes of the parish worthies, who fought the terms of the legacy in court unsuccessfully for many decades.[20] Colborne also left £1,000 to create a school in Ashwell, Hertfordshire, to be administered by the Merchant Taylors, and £50 for the school in Clapham.

However, although such wills do contain donations to charity, these are generally small, and most amount to less than 1 per cent of the estate. This might seem surprising given the religious persuasions of these testators, but it is very much the same as found for a larger selection of merchants, suggesting that Nonconformists were no more – or less – generous than others.[21] Nevertheless, this may be unfair, since, as was often the case, they continued to give directly to the poor in a spontaneous response to an individual appearing before them.[22] More than twenty Clapham residents were also governors of St Thomas' Hospital in 1719, a post that usually entailed a donation of £50, and there were contributions to the Poor Law assessments, and regular collections through the churches to assist various disadvantaged groups.

Those who wanted funds could apply to the monarch for authorisation of an appeal for donations. Once permission had been given the appeal would be read out in churches within a particular county or area. These were called 'briefs', and were frequent enough for the Prayer Book of 1662 to give instructions that they were to be read out after the Creed and before the sermon, together with citations and excommunications. In 1663 Clapham had twelve such briefs, averaging eight shillings each and covering the rebuilding of churches in Pontefract, Bridgnorth, Lithuania and Strasbourg, relief for a sailor and his family, and money for the redemption of Christian captives or slaves in Turkey. The most exotic was for the support of a prominent Turkish Muslim convert, Rigep Dandulo.

Substantial sums were raised in this way, and congregations often felt hard done by, not least because the administration costs were high and the system was open to abuse, whether by forged approvals or through the money going astray. After witnessing collections of this kind for fourteen consecutive weeks in his church, Pepys wrote in his diary: 'To church, where we observe the trade in briefs is come now up so constant a course every Sunday, that we resolve to give no more to them.'[23] Nevertheless they continued throughout the seventeenth century and longer. It may be, therefore, that the better-off felt that they had done enough for the poor in their lifetime. Henry Sampson's will scandalised his Nonconformist contemporaries because

> He should not leave one penny to pious and charitable
> uses. All that can be said is, his wife made, or forced him
> to make a new will ... and if she can be made a lady by
> it, she will think it as much for his honour.'[24]

By far the most generous Clapham resident was Joseph Paice, who had a particular reason for leaving a very large sum of £1,200, set out in his will:

> During the war in King William and Queen Anne's reign
> I were greatly concerned in shipping and in husbanding
> of ships, many of which were taken by the French, some
> afterwards ransomed and others retaken before they were
> carried to the Enemies' port, some were stranded and
> some stored on shore whereby I had vast trouble to adjust
> the ransom of some and the salvage of others and really
> saved to the proprietors many thousand pounds which
> by their own confession have been absolutely lost. Now

by reason hereof many seamen, passengers and others
on board some of those ships were carried into France
and died there. Others took unto other devices and after
my utmost endeavours I could never hear of them or the
next heirs who might justly claim a right to the wages or
effects of such seamen or passengers to whom I might
safely pay the same though it will appear by the accounts
in my ledgers that after many years diligent search I found
out [several of] their widows children or legal heirs and
paid them, yet by the best calculate that I can make, and
a strict review of my ledgers, I judge that at least one
thousand pounds is yet in my hands belonging to such
seamen and passengers and in all likelihood will never be
claimed. I therefore thought myself bound in conscience
to state an account as I have done in my ledger ff folio 99
entitled the account of God's Poor in which I have made
myself debtor twelve hundred pounds and do hereby
order my executors to pay the said sum of twelve hundred
pounds according to a memorandum paper which they
will find with this my will, being to widows and children
of seamen deceased and old decayed seamen and to
dissenting Ministers in poor circumstances and to their
widows and children and to the widows and children
of pious Church of England Ministers deceased and to
some other particular persons there named and whatever
those payments when made shall fall short of the said
twelve hundred pounds it is my will that my executors do
distribute and pay the same to such objects as they shall
judge most deserving.

Conclusion

This chapter has demonstrated that many committed and active Nonconformists had houses in Clapham, often for an extended period. There were extensive family and business connections between them, and the ease with which Nonconformists were able to take services or provide schools also attracted a range of Nonconformist ministers. The next chapters draw together a range of other information about them to give a broader picture of them and of how they compare to other London merchants.

(Endnotes)

1. D.W. Hayton, in History of Parliament online, see www. historyofparliamentonline.org (and subsequent quotations).

2. Michael Mitford, letter to William Proctor, 13 January 1704, Michael Mitford letterbook, London Metropolitan Archives.

3. Mitford, letter to Thomas Linskill, 20 October 1704, ibid.

4. Peter Toon, *Puritans and Calvanism: The Crispian Controversy* (Reiner Publications, 1973).

5. Richard Baxter, *The Scripture-Gospel Defended and Christ, Grace and Free Justification Vindicated against the Libertines who use the Names of Christ; Free Grace ... to Subvert the Gospel and Christianity and Humanity ... In Two Books* (1690), postscript.

6. *A Funeral Sermon Occasion'd by the Death of Samuel Crisp, Esq; Who Died the 20th. of June, 1703. by Edward Grace*, British Library, 1417.a.4.

7. Quoted in Anne Manning, *Family Pictures* (Arthur Hall, Virtue and Co., 1861), p. 14.

8. Address by Parliament to Queen Anne, 13 March 1706.

9. *Protestant Dissenter's Magazine*, 1794, pp. 465–69.

10. Ibid.

11. Alexander Gordon, *Freedom after Ejection* (Manchester University Press, 1917), p. 2.

12. Edward Cleal, *The Story of Congregationalism in Surrey* (J. Clarke, 1909) p. 278.

13. David Wyles, 'Henry Sampson', in *Oxford Dictionary of National Biography*.

14. Henry Sampson, letter to R. Thoresby, 9 May 1699, Yorkshire Archaeological Society, MS 7.

15. Quoted in David Wykes, '"The Minister's Calling": The Preparation and Qualification of Candidates for the Presbyterian Ministry in England, 1660–89', *Dutch Review of Church History*, vol. 83 (2002), p. 272.

16. Walter Jeremy says in his *History of the Presbyterian Fund* (p. viii) that in the eighteenth century wind guards fixed on chimney pots were called Presbyterians in 'derisive allusion to the want of fixedness in the theological opinions of the Denomination of that name, who were charged with turning with every wind of doctrine'. He goes on to deny the charge, saying rather that the 'motion was progressive in a tolerably straight line ... from Calvinism through Arminianism, Arianism, Humanitarianism, to Unitarianism'.

17. Gordon, *Freedom after Ejection*, p. 2.

18. A.G. Matthews, *Calamy Revised* (Oxford University Press, 1934), p. 494.

19. Quoted by Eric Smith in *Clapham Antiquarian Society Newsletter*, 16 January 1971.

20. Joseph Ward, *Culture, Faith and Philanthropy* (Palgrave Macmillan, 2013).

21. Peter Earle, *The Making of the English Middle Class* (Methuen, 1991), p. 316.

22. Steve Hindle, *On the Parish? The Micro-politics of Poor Relief in Rural England c. 1550–1750* (Clarendon, 2004), p. 120.

23. Samuel Pepys, diary, 30 June 1661.

24. J. Hunter (ed.), *Letters of Eminent Men*, vol. 1 (1832), p. 400.

CHAPTER 9

PARISH AND COMMUNITY

Houses and population

M uch of the book so far has concentrated on who lived in Clapham and the various connections that brought them there. This chapter looks at how the village community functioned over the period 1660–1720, what part the merchants played in it, and how they related to one another. Figure 1 shows how the number of houses in Clapham increased over this period.

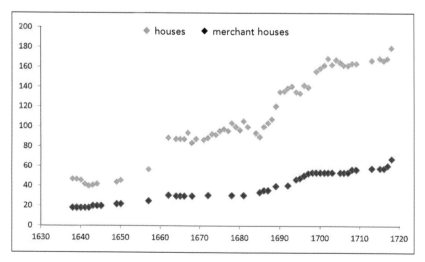

Figure 1. Number of houses in Clapham 1640–1720
Source: Clapham Parish rate assessments

The scatter demonstrates the limitations of this data, particularly in relation to the smaller houses, although the trends are clear. Merchants' houses increased from 25 to 32 during the period 1657 to 1662, and then stayed roughly constant until the late 1680s. There were two rapid rises in the number of houses: from 1650 to 1662, most of which were small houses either just built or being rated for the first time, and from 1688 to 1702. This second expansion, after the Glorious Revolution, produced a substantial increase in merchants' houses from 36 to 56 and then to about 70 as a row of twelve terraced houses was completed by 1720. Smaller houses were also built, but the proportion of merchants' houses never strayed far from 30 per cent.

Illustration 16. 39–43 Old Town, Clapham

Although a few smaller seventeenth-century houses remain, albeit now converted to shops, no larger ones survive.[1] They were viewed as inconvenient long ago; in 1811 a local builder described the old rectory as

> a very ancient building erected at different times, the
> newest part having been built a century ago … the
> rooms are small and inconvenient, the roof, walls and
> foundations in several parts very defective and ruinous,
> and it will require a considerable sum of money to be

*still laid out upon it in order to render it thoroughly
commodious and a respectable residence for the rector of
so opulent a parish as Clapham.*[2]

Not all the larger houses were detached and within their own
grounds, and two sets of terraced houses still exist from the start of
the eighteenth century, both put up by local builders as a speculative
venture. The first dates from 1706 and is shown in Illustration 16.

The two end houses were first occupied by William Brooke senior
(the merchant from Lisbon) and a widow, Mary Astell. The other
terrace, shown in Illustration 17, consisted originally of twelve houses
built between 1713 and 1720, of which two have been demolished.

Illustration 17. Church Buildings, 12–21 Northside,
Clapham Common

It is the equivalent of the contemporaneous terraces Church Row
in Hampstead and Montpelier Row in Twickenham.[3] Most of the
houses have three bays, but there were at least three larger ones with
five bays or even more. Their occupation was not confined to the
relatively less well-off, and many rich merchants, such as Abraham
Atkins, John Bullock and Benjamin Mee, and lawyers, such as
Benjamin Portlock, lived there.

While more houses meant an increased population, there is little information about household size. A common estimate of the average household size outside London at this time is 4.3 people, but this would be low for a village with such a high proportion of merchant houses.[4] For such villages, estimates range from seven people to fourteen or more, since the richer households contained a number of servants and often other members of the extended family, such as widows or unmarried women.[5] Taking an average of nine people for the merchant houses and four for others gives Clapham a population in 1664 of about 500; an average of seven for merchants and 3.5 for the others would give a population of 420, and it is probable that the population lay within this range. In any case, it was 50 per cent larger than the estimate of 300 for 1630, and this explains the parishioners' decision to increase the size of the church even as early as 1650. On any of the above assumptions, the merchants' houses supplied approximately half of Clapham's population. Applying the same calculations to the village in 1720 gives a significantly larger population range of 875–1,070, but this can be no more than indicative.

The other indication of population comes from the record of baptisms and burials in the parish register, which is fairly complete from 1553 although with some gaps in the 1670s and around the end of the seventeenth century.[6]

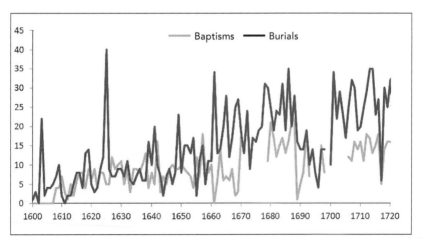

Figure 2. Clapham baptisms and burials
Source: Parish register, Holy Trinity, Clapham[7]

Figure 2 shows a rising trend in both baptisms and burials, with more buried than baptised in two out of every three years from 1600 to 1660; after 1660 there is only one year for which there are complete records when there are more baptisms than burials. The burial peaks corresponding to the outbreaks of plague in 1603 and 1625 are very obvious; twenty-two people died in the former outbreak and even more died during the latter, when forty were buried. The peak corresponding to the plague in 1665 is considerably smaller, and fewer were buried then than in 1661. It is tempting to link the other peaks in deaths to winters that are known to be severe, but the only substantial winter peaks were in 1641/42, one of the coldest ever recorded, and 1683/84, when the Thames froze for two months with up to eleven inches of ice.

The rising number of burials put pressure on the vestry to find more space, and in 1678 it decided to make better use of the Frost burial chapel, claiming that the building

> *hath been repayred and amended constantly at the parrish charge, contrary to agreement, and upon consideration that the Parrish Church of Clapham is so full of greene corps not fit to be stirred and also that the vault is of large dimensions and but little use made by the family of Frosts and may very well serve for the use of others.*

The parish decided that while the Frost family would continue to be able to use the chapel free of charge – and two members were buried there in 1685 – it should be thrown open to burials for anyone. Parishioners were to be charged twenty shillings and strangers forty shillings, although there was an argument later because the rector had been keeping the fees for himself rather than passing them on to the parish.

The parishioners were horrified a few years later to learn of plans to use the church by the dowager lady of the manor, Lady Rebecca Atkins, whose husband had died in 1689. Although the Atkins' main residence was in Newport Pagnell in Buckinghamshire, they were usually buried in a vault in the Clapham graveyard. Eschewing this, she, the 'most mournful relict', wished to give her late husband a large monument inside the church, with two large effigies of herself and Sir Richard to be placed at the foot of the memorial to their three deceased children, which her husband had already commissioned from the sculptor William Stanton. They were to be surrounded by iron railings, almost completely filling the Clerke chapel and leaving only one pew there. The parish, which had already had to use the Frost chapel, did not want to lose the space in the church, and began litigation. Dame Rebecca won the case, however, and the effigies of herself and her husband, also by Stanton, were in place by 1691.

18. Maquette for Atkins memorial
© Victoria and Albert Museum, London

Rebecca lived for almost twenty years after her effigy was placed in the church, and was keen to maintain the memorial properly, leaving a legacy of an annual income of thirty shillings to the churchwardens on condition that they spent fifteen shillings a year for cleaning and looking after her tombs and figures. Ironically, the Clerke chapel was pulled down some thirty years after the new church of Holy Trinity had been built in the 1770s. By then the last remaining member of the Atkins family had died, and their more distant relations had little or no interest in the grave. The parochial authorities opened the Atkins vault in the churchyard and put the statues and much of the other stonework inside it. They were rediscovered in 1886 and are now in St Paul's Church. The maquette of Rebecca's figure is shown in Figure 18.

The parish register continues to contain entries for merchant families in the winter, confirming that Clapham was not just a summer home. Some did genuinely retire there, for example William Sheldon and Francis Bridges, and increasing numbers were commuting from Clapham rather than maintaining a City residence. The inventory for Henry Powell shows no London address, and John Gould's entry in a register of merchants gives his address as either the Turkey Walk in the Royal Exchange (the part of the Exchange used by merchants trading with Turkey) or Clapham. The same register also shows another four Clapham merchants whose City address was that of a neighbour and business partner, while others, such as John Doggett, continued to maintain a house in the City. The women and children may have spent more of their time in Clapham, but there was regular travel to and from the City.

The river was of no use for travel to Clapham, which at four miles from London Bridge was forty minutes or more by horse. Walking was of course much more prevalent then than now, and Simon Patrick, the future Bishop of Ely, regularly walked from the City and West End to and from his Battersea parish. Many Londoners walked to Dulwich and Streatham at weekends. However, horse was the usual means of travel. The larger houses had stables and the richer merchants maintained their own coaches. Joseph Paice kept a 'a pacing mare with all suitable accoutrements' for his wife until she became more weighty and less active, when he provided 'a chariot and horses, which cost £150'.[8] He kept a horse for himself and rode it every day to and from the City, confirming that daily commuting was well established by the early eighteenth century. James Fowke left one of his grandsons 'my horse, all my saddles, two bridles and the colt I give to my wife'. John and Judith Gould, Henry Powell, John

Doggett, John Mitford, William King, Thomas Langham, Thomas and Juliana Rodbard and Rebecca Atkins all had coaches, and no doubt others did too. Samuel Pepys came out to Clapham in John Evelyn's coach. Joseph Comfort ran a livery stable to meet demand.

There were also stagecoaches. Some of these went through Clapham on the way to Portsmouth or Newhaven, but others were specific to Clapham, and Thomas Delaune's guide of 1681 gives the first known example.[9] It ran daily from Clapham to the Spread Eagle in Gracechurch Street and was operated by John Day, described as 'coachman' in the Clapham rate book. By 1690 another Clapham resident had started a second daily run to the Cross Keys in Gracechurch Street. Although crossing the river at London Bridge was almost bound to take one to Gracechurch Street, it is instructive that the coach for Clapham went to the heart of the merchant district, while the stagecoaches from Hampstead went to Holborn or Gray's Inn Road, the haunt of lawyers. These stages became more established, and in 1710 two rival groups advertised in the *Post Man* within a week of each other. Both ran coaches leaving Clapham at about seven in the morning and four in the afternoon, returning at eleven in the morning and seven in the evening, catering for those who wanted to spend either a whole or part day in the City or Clapham.

Community

The relatively slow turnover of residents continued. John Gould, Dennis Gauden, William Daniel, Anthony Stephens and Abraham Babington all stayed in the village for thirty years until their deaths. Some pre-Restoration residents, such as Richard Salwey and George Foxcroft, returned for the last few years of their lives. For all years except shortly after the rapid expansion starting in 1688, half of the residents had been there for more than ten years and a quarter for twenty years. This continuity, coupled with the fact that incomers already had substantial connections to the village, helped to maintain its character of merchant Nonconformists.

Wills show that they were well-off, with property in many locations including the City, whether house, shop or investment property. Some of them also owned land outside London, often in the county from which their family originally came. Marie Oresby had property in Gloucester, William Molins in Cambridge, William Tanner in Oxfordshire and Thomas Rodbard (the nephew) in Suffolk and Somerset, while the richer ones, such as Dennis Gauden and Francis Bridges, were both lords of the manor in Essex. Gould and Thomas Frere both owned shares in plantations in Barbados, as well as slaves.

There is a distinct flavour of an affluent community at ease with itself and supporting its members. Many widows remained in Clapham after their husband's deaths. **Ann Carpenter**, Gabriel's widow, survived him by almost twenty years, while **Martha Furlonger**, **Rebecca Meacham** and **Ann Hughes** also stayed on a long time, sometimes with other family members. Dorothy Arthur, the widow of the former rector of Clapham, returned to live there in 1671, but Mary Daniel returned to London after her husband's death. In many cases the married daughters and their husbands moved into the houses when the widow(er) died. Richard Steele moved into Mrs Daniel's house, John Cooke into Elizabeth Babington's, Henry Markinfield into Anthony Stephens', and John Arthur junior into his mother's. This could result in the same family staying in a house for a very long time; when the last of Gould's sisters-in-law died, the family had been in the same house for seventy-five years.

Residents also shared their neighbours' lives. They were witnesses or overseers of one another's wills, were appointed executors, guardians or trustees, and were referred to as 'loving friend'. Lawrence Bromfield's will was witnessed by his neighbours Hugh Forth and Charles and Thomas Langham, William Sydenham's by John Arthur, and Thomas Langham's by Henry Sampson. Thomas Lye chose the minister Philip Lamb and Anthony Stephens as overseers. Lamb's widow chose the merchants Stephen Mason and William Sheldon as executors. Abraham Otgher was John Doggett's witness ten years before he moved to Clapham. Children married one another, and a very high proportion of the merchant residents were related in one way or another.

Clapham wills do not bear out the contention that it was rare for women to witness wills.[10] Approximately one third of men's wills and two thirds of women's wills were witnessed by one or more women. Often these were female servants, but it was common also to use friends or neighbours. It is very rare indeed for a will to have only women as witnesses, and only one man's will does, that of Roger

Lillington, where one of the witnesses was his partner's wife. So large a difference between the samples suggests either that Nonconformists were more prepared to accept female witnesses or that, at least for those wills drawn up in Clapham, it was just that bit harder to find witnesses in a small village.

One of the favourites in the community was John Gould, who was often at the forefront of the promotion of Nonconformist interests. He was at the nexus between three major Puritan families – the Thorolds, the Joliffes and the Moyers – and three of his sisters-in-law became wives and then widows of prominent Nonconformist minsters, ending their lives living together in Clapham. Even though funeral sermons did not normally eulogise the deceased, Philip Lamb dedicated the published version of his sermon at Gould's funeral to 'the truly Pious and Religious Gentlewoman, Mrs Judith Gould', with the words: 'I did not know how to pay my respects to the memory of so eminent a saint, and worthy a person, as our late (too early) deceased friend.'[11] He chose as his text 'Mark the Perfect Man, and behold the Upright, for the end of that Man is Peace' (Psalms 37:37). Unusually, he did include an encomium:

> *I need not tell you of his eminency in religion, his love to Christ, his zeal for the Gospel and for the house of God; his free and generous mind to the faithful Ministers and members of Jesus Christ, which you know better than I; I shall only say this of him, He liv'd a pious life, he died full of gracious breathings after God, and is entered into his glorious, never ending enjoyments.*

The vestry paid its tribute by recording in their minutes in 1680 Gould's thirty years in the parish and his legacy for the poor, albeit not unusual at £20, adding the explanation that 'when we are removed or laid in the dust the inhabitants that shall succeed us may know that such a parrishioner wee have had soe long a time in the parish of Clapham.'

The merchants played a full part in running the parish, taking the roles of churchwarden and overseer of the poor, although in 1675 one was allowed to appoint a deputy as churchwarden because 'his business required attention in London'. Over the period 1660–1720 there are only five years when there were no merchants as churchwardens, and only eight when none were overseer of the poor. Even so, many of them took the opportunity to pay a fine to avoid the post: Edward Munns paid a fine of £5 to be excused in 1667, and John Doggett and Edmund White senior paid a fine of £8 in 1671, when finally two locals, John England and Thomas Davis, were elected. No fewer than five potential candidates, including Samuel Crisp, paid a fine of £3 at the same time to be exempted from the post of overseer of the poor, even though these fines gave an exemption of only two years. These problems continued, and in 1673 John England was actually paid £5 to take on the job; later the farmer Joseph Hazard was excused from the office of constable on the basis that he had been upper churchwarden in 1677. Perhaps because of this, a practice grew up of the elected churchwarden appointing and paying a deputy to avoid doing the work himself, and Thomas Wilson paid the innkeeper William Smallpiece to act for him, as he did later for James Fowke, whose 'bodily infirmity' prevented him from continuing. Deputies were banned in 1687, however, and Thomas Carleton had to pay the fine of £8 to be excused from being churchwarden, while Thomas Rodbard (the nephew) paid £10 to be excused for two years.

In 1675 John Doggett managed to get the fine for Peter Costin excused on the grounds that the latter was not living in the parish that year, because he was churchwarden of his London parish. This is an illustration of how people came and went from Clapham. The parish then chose Frere, but that did not work since Samuel Crisp and William Daniel returned to the vestry and 'alleged that in regard of his bodily indisposition, he was not able to discharge the said post'. A fine was duly paid and Hazard chosen as a replacement, which was just as well because Frere died shortly afterwards.

Merchants also contributed regularly to fundraising activities. As well as paying some £30 annually for the parish lecturer at the church, they raised £60 to repair the school, over £50 for 'Beautifying the Church' (in 1685), and almost £40 for buying church silver to replace that sold under the Commonwealth. A number of wives contributed directly, as well as their husbands. William Hewer, Sir Richard Atkins and Lady Gauden all gave generously, and this might suggest a move away from strict Puritanism, although there was clearly still a Communion table rather than an altar in the church itself.

Other occupants of Clapham

Less information is available about those occupants of Clapham who were not merchants, but longevity in Clapham is even more marked for the yeomen, artisans and others who were in any case less likely to be mobile. Many appear frequently as churchwardens or other parish officials, but we have no direct evidence about their religion. Rate books and wills show that one John King was a shoemaker and another a chandler, Richard Fulker a blacksmith and John Clarke a poulterer. Jonas Roberts and Richard Norman were bricklayers, Francis Preston and David Arthur 'Gardiners', and John Bowne and his son carpenters, as was Thomas Morris. Only two were members of a livery company and thus freemen of the City of London: Richard Norman; and Samuel Green, a Glazier, but manifestly a working one, given his bills for reglazing the church. Inventories show debts from Clapham residents outstanding to many of these artisans. John England was a mealman or grain dealer, and there were also yeoman farmers such as Hazard and John Chalkhill; Thomas Noakes is explicitly referred to as managing Dennis Gauden's farms, which were used for victualling the Navy.

Many of the residents who were not merchants provided infrastructure for the village. Both William Gurney and Henry Sharpe ran inns, and, after Sharpe's death, Smallpiece took over the White Hart Inn, as well as filling many parish offices. He issued the first known Clapham token, which shows a white hart on one side and the initials of Smallpiece and his wife, Ann, on the other.[12] He died in 1691 and his widow moved to smaller premises nearby, where she too kept an alehouse. Smallpiece's inn was then leased by William Wigsell, who renamed it the Bull's Head, by which sign it is still known until recently (it is currently the Calf). The inventory of Wigsell's widow contains little to show that it was an inn, although one room is described as 'kitchen and bar room' and its contents include a set of nine pins and a copper coffee pot. The parlour next to the yard also contained 240 beer bottles, 26.5 barrels of beer and six barrels of stout.

In 1693 the parish took steps to prevent Thomas Floyd, who ran the Sun inn, from holding a bull-baiting, getting a warrant from a Justice of the Peace to punish him if he held 'such riotous disorderly and unlawful assembly'. The Sun continued its enterprise, and advertised a few years later:

*At the Sun in Clapham is to be had Alehouse Ale mixed
with several other ingredients, particularly that herb
which Sir William Raleigh made use of in his excellent and
famous cordial which kept the late King alive for several
days. It is rightly prepared, according to an approved
receipt of an eminent physician: it purges gently, cures
the scurvy, sweetens the blood, prevents the dropsy, and
several other distempers, too long to enumerate here. The
master of the house assures us that he sells it for the public
good and not for any private gain at Three pence a quart.*[13]

Drinking on Sunday, at least where it might be observed, was
also frowned upon, and in 1697 the farmer John Pether was fined
three shillings and fourpence for drinking and tippling in the house
of Richard Newman, who was fined even more at ten shillings.
There are other indications that the parish was turning its mind to
entertainment: the *Post Man* advertised to 'Gentlemen and others'
that the Clapham Bowling Green opened in March 1710; and the
Daily Courant announced that there would be a race for maidens
from the Plough at Clapham, with the first two prizes a Holland
smock and a pair of silk stockings.[14]

Clapham also had its own coffee houses. The rate book for 1693
contains an entry for 'John Wood his coffee house', and William
Wigsell also had one before becoming the lessee of the Bull's Head.
In 1701 Richard John, druggist, took widow Roberts' son as an
apprentice 'to be imployed in grinding and other business as he shall
think fit in his coffee and chacolett trade'. In 1718 the auditors of
the highway accounts met at Harwood's coffee house.

There were other shops in Clapham. Mrs Jane Philips offered
'Streatham Waters', which were drawn from Streatham Wells and
were supposed 'to be the best sort of purging waters',[15] and the
following advertisement appeared for a local apothecary:

*The famous Virgin and Antidote PILLS, formerly made
by Mr Anthony Smith, Surgeon, deceased, are now truly
prepared by his grandson Mr Thomas Davis, Surgeon
notwithstanding it hath been already published, they are
prepared by other Persons; the Receipt for making these
PILLS having been in the hands of the said Mr Thomas
Davis some years past; who does likewise know all the
alterations the said Mr Smith ever made therein; but*

concealed the same out of respect to his said grandfather.
They are to be had at Mr Davis house in Clapham and
also at Fishmongers' Hall, where the said Mr Smith
formerly dwelt and where Mr Davis will be on Tuesdays
and Thursdays any week.[16]

Thomas Davis appears in the Clapham rate books for 1699 and 1700, living in the house that had been occupied by the merchant Stephen Mason, but there is no record of Mrs Philips. **Francis Richardson** was also an apothecary, as was his father of the same name; the latter's inventory after his death in 1679 shows a number of debts outstanding from Clapham inhabitants, the largest just over £3 owed by Judith Gould.[17] A later apothecary was John Barton, who turns up on a number of occasions as a witness to a will together with Edward Grace, the incumbent Nonconformist minister, and John Gwillim, the resident barber surgeon; the three of them may well have been a regular deathbed trio.

A number of other businesses catered for the needs of the merchants and others, not least to support transport. As we have seen, Joseph Comfort ran livery stables; there were also two stagecoaches and a blacksmith. There is a significant increase in the number of carpenters, bricklayers, gardeners and other crafts linked to house-building. Although not as rich as the merchants, they were by no means poor. London was experiencing a massive building boom after the Great Fire, and it was the carpenters and the bricklayers who supervised the whole process and who often managed the financing and took the risk themselves, including for houses in Clapham. Although their main business was in the City and closer suburbs, they too had close connections with one another.

One example is **Richard Norman**, the middle of three generations of Richard Normans, all bricklayers. Although he described himself in his will as a bricklayer, his wife a few years later described him in her will solely as 'Cordwainer and citizen of London'. He left his wife his house in Clapham and his various children six houses in the Minories, near the Tower of London. One was leased to the Clapham clockmaker James Markwick senior. Norman had taken on the guardianship of the orphaned son of his cousin and son-in-law Francis Richardson junior. Other Clapham cousins included the merchant **John Walker**, whose wife, **Frances**, remained until her death in 1680 and left her house and household goods to her cousin and companion **Ursula Goddard**, whose daughter had married yet another Clapham merchant, **John Hately**. The next Richard Norman married the daughter of **Francis Preston**, a gardener and owner of four brick houses in Clapham.

We know very little about the servants who lived in Clapham, although they must have made up a fair share of the population. Many received legacies. Elizabeth Mottershed left her maidservant '£10, and decent mourning, a chest of drawers four pairs of coarse sheets other linen with the furniture for a chamber', while Elizabeth Pheasant left hers 'all my wearing apparel, one chest of drawers, my dressing box, red trunk and a box iron'. Henry Powell, whose sons were still children, left 'his man Thomas Blake all my woollen wearing apparel'. Some, such as Gabriel Carpenter, were concerned to ensure that their widows had continuity of service; he left his three servants ten shillings each, but only if they stayed with their mistress for a year after his decease. Others, being the last of a married couple to die, were concerned to give their servants time to find another post, and Judith Gould wrote: 'It is my will that in case I die a householder in Clapham the family be kept together for the space of one month after my death that servants have time to dispose themselves.' She left up to £20 from her estate to pay for this. John Dumaistre was thoughtful enough to leave 'the weeder woman' and her son five shillings, and £2 to both the gardener and the carter, 'to help his numerous family'.

Some people were extremely generous. Lydia Moyer left £120 to her servant, and Ann Yates managed to pick up £50 from Michael Mitford, with whom she had lived as housekeeper for ten years, and then continued to work for his wife for another fourteen years, when Margaret Mitford left her

> *£50, £10 for mourning, a quarter of a year's wages and one month board after my death, all wearing apparel for head and body, silk woollen and linen clothes in London with my chest of drawers and bedstead bedclothes and all household goods in my lodging in Eltham and one silver spoon marked M M and six other silver spoons, all to be paid as soon as possible.*

But the record must surely go to Dame Rebecca Atkins: for her coachman 'who shall then be living with me I do give to him my coach mares and coach and chariot with the harness to them belonging'.

Pressure on the parish

There are also snippets of information about the very poor, usually in connection with their support under the Poor Law or the continuing desire to keep out those who might prove to be a charge on the parish. One example appears in the accounts for 1665 as an 'extraordinary expense', showing that it cost three shillings and sixpence to remove a family to the adjacent parish of Streatham. In 1665 the churchwardens and constable were ordered 'to take special care for prosecuting the law against all idle people who harbour in and around the parish', and this was backed up by appointing the clerk of the parish

> to be a warden for looking after vagrants and poor
> children that may be a charge to the parish and to be
> helpful to the churchwardens and constable for the
> hindring of and timely removing such poor as are driven
> by law from other parishes and shall take small houses or
> rooms in this parish for this service and he shall be paid
> four pounds a year quarterly starting at Midsomer 1666.

From time to time babies were abandoned in the parish, and the custom was to baptise them with the surname of Clapham. In about 1666 Michael Clapham 'was found at the door of one Smallpeece … and was laid in a Fish Baskett being a weakly infant'. As they grew up they would be placed as servants or given an apprenticeship, and Eliza Clapham was placed with Elizabeth, Lady Gauden, in 1679/80 for eight years. It was reported in the vestry minutes in 1680 that Lady Gauden was 'pleased to accept 30 shillings to buy her clothes this year and 30 shillings next year; then to discharge the parish from expense'.

The parish authorities were determined that they would not become a soft touch, and recipients of alms were expected to work unless it was physically impossible. Mary Tickner, described as 'sick, lame, deaf, and dim sighted and almost past labour', was still granted only twelvepence a week. Edward Preston's wife had died in childbirth, leaving 'seven children to be maintained by his labour'; the youngest was put out to nurse and Preston received three shillings a week to continue at 'the pleasure of the parish'. The vestry ordered that he 'should not be allowed parish relief until he submitted himself and his two eldest boys to the disposal of the parish, as they think fit; or satisfy the parish why they should not be disposed of.' One of his sons, Robert, was later bound apprentice to John King for nine years, and because he was so young, King was given £3 for clothing, which sum would be passed to the apprentice at the expiration of his time.

Many different methods were adopted of ensuring that strangers did not become a burden on the parish. The simplest was for the constable to hire a cart and remove them bodily, following them if necessary to ensure that they did not return. The vestry accounts for 1687 show that the constable, Robert Goodwin, incurred costs

> *for passing a vagabond to Westerham 6d*
>
> *for passing away a woman and 2 children and straw for them lodging in town all night 1/7*
>
> *for passing a poor man that had been 6 years in slavery in Turkey 1/-*

There were also careful checks that Clapham inhabitants did not wittingly or otherwise allow to stay in the village people who might become liabilities, and substantial bonds were often required as security. In 1691 a widow with several children came to live in the parish and Samuel Green, a Glazier, and William Green, Polterer of London, were both required to give a bond for £50 'to save the parish harmless' against any cost that might fall upon it as a result of her presence. Barbary Anstell, who had previously been allowed to live in the little house adjoining the church, and who eked out her living by doing weeding in the various gardens in the village, was granted instead a weekly twelvepence on top of the sum of two shillings that was already paid to her.

In 1693 the problem reached such a pitch that every landlord or inhabitant letting houses under £4 per annum had to give security to the parish that the tenant would not become chargeable to the rates. Armed with a warrant, Mr Justice Evans attended at the Bull's Head in 1695 and interrogated a number of people who had tenants. Thomas Langham had hired a coachman who had held himself out to be a single man and then brought a wife and three children. The coachman had to leave. Arthur Radborne agreed not to take a Mrs Cave as his servant because the parish disapproved, presumably because she had family whom she might bring with her; Robert Gibbs and John Gardon agreed to send their tenant away, while a Mr Moore agreed to ensure that his farm workers would be no charge to the parish while he held the lease on his property. A few years later, in 1698, the parish decided that all those receiving the poor rate should 'have a Roman P on the right sleeve of their outer garments to act as a badge that they received support from the parish.'

The public watch

The movement between Clapham and the City, and greater wealth in the village, increased the need to keep out vagrants seeking benefits, as well as to deter robbers. The vestry decided to build a new Watch house in 1693 (costing £13/9/6), to strengthen the Watch, and to extend it after the existing Evening Watch from 5 until 8, to go through the night from mid-December to mid-February. Some 125 householders in the parish contributed to the cost, ten shillings each being given by Dame Rebecca Atkins, William Hewer and Sir Samuel Thompson, the last of whose house had been robbed five years earlier.

The Watch met in the new building that had been constructed for the purpose, and the watchers were under orders to keep anyone arrested there, rather than in one of the Clapham alehouses as had presumably been the practice earlier. They were provided with coal to keep them warm. There were nine watchers in total, including the constable or headborough, and they were expected to walk along three separate 'Rankes' or routes, from 10 or 11 at night until 5 in the morning:

First	from Mr Crisp's house to Mr Hall's
Second	from Mr Hall's to Preston's
Third	from Richard Fulker's to Coles and Trimmers.

This description shows very nicely the social distinctions: Samuel Crisp and Urban all were rich merchantgs,Hall were rich merchants; Richard Fulker was the blacksmith; while Edward Preston was in receipt of financial support from the vestry and Cole and Trimmer were farmers.

The constable was supposed to be present at 10 pm every day to check that the Watch had turned up and to walk with them, but gentry holders of these offices often paid someone to do it on their behalf, and one of the debts outstanding at Henry Powell's death was eleven shillings for 'the watch and petty charges'. At least three of the men selected for the Watch were on the list of people in receipt of parish relief, so it is not clear how able they would have been. Each watchman was paid twelvepence a night, but the Watch shared twenty shillings if they produced a successful prosecution. Other rewards included one occasion, in 1703, when almost nine shillings was spent on drink 'for the watch for looking after the two thieves'.

The Watch was also needed to reduce the risk of robbery. In 1688 the *London Gazette* reported that a number of items had been lost from Samuel Thompson's house, including, as well as linen and other goods,

> *nine gilt spoons, three porringers with two trencher chafing dishes, two large plain salvers, a mug, a cup with two handles, a pair of monument candlesticks, two small trencher salts, two plates, a set of callees, and an orange strainer, all of silver and all except the cup with two handles having a coat of arms.*[18]

Seven years later the vestry ordered, 'That the Parish Clerk shall not leave the Surplice, Cushion, and Communion cloth in the Church, but carry them to the Parson's house.' A new surplice consumed about eighteen yards of Holland cloth and cost £4/16/-. The *Daily Courant* reported a few years later that 'two green bays window curtains and a surplice' had been 'lost out of Clapham Church'; a reward of £2 was offered – no questions asked.[19]

Not all villains were from outside the parish. The sad will of Jonas Roberts, a local bricklayer, explains:

> *Whereas I have been lately robbed of the sum of about one hundred and fifty pounds I have had great season to suspect my serving maid Sarah Winterbottom who lived with me at the time the said sum of money was taken out of my house.*

He left his remaining money to his landlord, Thomas Powell junior, who had allowed him to defer his rent after the theft.

On another occasion, following a number of break-ins in Clapham and Camberwell, where the robbers had left behind 'a knife, a brace of pistols loaded, and also a coat, hat and periwig', the king's pardon was promised to any person concerned whose information led to the arrest and conviction of the others.[20] There were also regular reports of horses being stolen, sometimes from Clapham Common, but also from Mrs Joliffe's orchard and Madam Brooke's grounds, and mostly belonging to the livery stables of Joseph Comfort.

These problems continued, and in 1718 an advertisement announced a reward of £3 for the successful prosecution of a thief and £10 for a housebreaker or highwayman (on top of the £40 given by law for highwaymen). The rewards were to be paid by 'Mr Wight Woolly of Clapham'.[21] Such rewards were not without risk, as was reported only nine days later:

> We hear from Clapham that a Journeyman Shoemaker
> who took on Athorp, a Highwayman, being himself
> entitled to the Reward of £40, and being in great want
> of money, sold the presentation to the said reward
> for sixteen guineas to his master, an old cautious
> Presbyterian of that town; but the said Athorp becoming
> an evidence for the King and convicting three of his
> associates the reward was entirely cut off which we
> hear has so mortified the religious stock jobber that he
> threatened either to turn Tory or to hang himself.[22]

Travel could be risky; the *Post Boy* reported on 2 July 1698 that 'the roads around Town continue to be very unsafe', and thirty-eight people had been robbed that Saturday between Lambeth and Clapham. Four people were robbed coming from Clapham by three footpads who 'stript them stark naked and left them bound in the Lane'.[23] On another occasion the Clapham stagecoach itself was robbed between 5 and 6 in the morning.[24] The wealthy hid their money in their shoes; one newspaper reported that when Mr Houlton from Clapham and his lady were robbed when driving in their chariot, the footpads removed their shoes and were so disappointed with the results that they removed the coachman's shoes and took all he had, namely three shillings and sixpence. Sometimes those robbed would offer a reward, no questions asked, for the return of their property, as when three highwaymen took 'from a Gentleman a silver watch the makers name Clements shows the day of the month and silver chain and seal all with coat of arms'.[25] One correspondent reported:

> *As I returned home the last night I met with two highway men between Clapham Common and Fox Hall.[26] They took away what money I had about me, which was under three pounds and my cloak but were so civil as to leave me my watch and my sword.[27]*

There are also advertisements reporting objects that have fallen off the coach, which may have been designed to secure the return of stolen goods. Sometimes these items were jewellery; on another occasion it was 'a black trunk about a yard long with drawers at the bottom with wearing apparel of a young gentlewoman almost 14 years of age, 3 gowns and petticoats, pair of stays, 5 shifts and divers other items', for which a reward of five guineas, no questions asked, was offered.[28]

Conclusion

The number of Clapham merchants did not increase markedly until towards the end of the seventeenth century, and this was coupled with a propensity to spend more time there. The village gradually acquired shops and local services, including inns, a coffee shop and a livery stable, as well as regular stagecoaches to the City. However, while the village could provide for much of its day-to-day activity, there is no doubt that the merchants still focused on the City as the source of their livelihood. They played their part in the administration of the parish and were keen to protect themselves from the demands of the poor looking for support, from robbers and from the more riotous forms of entertainment. Merchant houses contained the majority of the village's population, and wills demonstrate a degree of consideration to the servants both in legacies and in providing for continuation of their jobs.

(Endnotes)

1. Alyson Wilson (ed.), *The Buildings of Clapham* (The Clapham Society, 2000), pp. 55–56.
2. E.F. Smith, *Clapham* (Borough of Lambeth, 1976), p. 20.
3. Bridget Cherry and Nicholas Pevsner, *London 2: South* (Penguin, 1983), p. 385.

4. Dorian Gerhold, *Putney and Roehampton in 1665* (Wandsworth Historical Society, 2007), p. 17.

5. Peter Earle, *The Making of the English Middle Class* (Methuen, 1991), p. 212.

6. Clapham Nonconformists were married in the Anglican parish church, and many chose to be buried in the churchyard in Clapham and to have their children's baptisms recorded by the parish.

7. The data is for calendar years beginning in January.

8. Anne Manning, *Family Pictures* (Arthur Hall Virtue and Co., 1861), p. 12.

9. Thomas Delaune, *The Present State of London: or, Memorials Comprehending a Full and Succinct Account of the Ancient and Modern State Thereof* (George Larkin, 1681).

10. Richard Grassby, *Kinship and Capitalism* (Cambridge University Press, 2001), p. 131.

11. Philip Lamb, *A Funeral Sermon Delivered upon the Sad Occasion of the Much Lamented Death of John Gould, Late of Clapham, esq., Who Put on Immortality, Aug. 22, 1679*, British Library 1417.c.22 (and subsequent quotations).

12. Seventeenth-century tradesmen's tokens were the first genuine trade tokens to appear in this country, as a result of Parliament's failure to provide sufficient small denomination coinage; the commonest denomination was the farthing, followed by the halfpenny and some pennies.

13. *Post Boy*, 2 May 1702.

14. *Post Man*, 6 March 1710; *Daily Courant*, 14 July 1712.

15. *Daily Courant*, 15 May 1708.

16. *Post Boy*, 26 August 1699.

17. London Metropolitan Archives, CLA/002/02/01/1877.

18. *London Gazette*, 30 January 1688.

19. *Daily Courant*, 18 August 1714.

20. *London Gazette*, 10 June 1718.

21. *Daily Courant*, 19 February 1718.

22. Ibid., 28 February 1718.

23. *Post Boy*, 17 August 1700.

24. *Daily Courant*, 21 September 1717.

25. Ibid., 7 March 1712.

26. Fox Hall was another name for New Spring Gardens, the most celebrated pleasure garden in London; in the eighteenth century it became known by its present name, Vauxhall.

27. Lionel Herne, letter to Thomas Howard, 30 October 1697, Norfolk Record Office, How 825 349.

28. *Daily Courant*, 14 June 1712.

CHAPTER 10

POSSESSIONS AND EXPENDITURE

A number of Clapham residents in this period were covered by the Court of Orphans, and three in particular have inventories that cover their house in Clapham: John Doggett, who died in 1680; Christopher Redshaw, who died intestate in 1681 (both of whom also had a house in London); and Henry Powell, who died in 1682. Doggett and Powell were substantial merchants, while Redshaw was a hop dealer without major involvement in international trade, although his inventory does show that he owned a ship. The value of the contents of each room is given in the inventory, and the most valuable of the furnishings are the textiles. A number of other orphans' inventories, or those prepared in connection with probate cases, exist only in part and give limited information about the testator's financial affairs but not about the detail of the houses.

The houses give a good picture of the way they lived. Powell's was on three storeys with a Great Dining Room, a Great Parlour and even a Great Counting House. It was the most highly rated house in the parish after Sir Dennis Gauden's and the Manor House, and had twenty hearths in 1674. It had previously been occupied by Hugh Forth. As was usual in merchants' houses in the seventeenth century, the major pieces of furniture were the beds, which were a symbol of the wealth and status of the owners. The beds with their hangings provided a private space, often essential given that the chambers were used for a variety of functions, including as a thoroughfare to other rooms. In many cases the beds were used during the day as a place to receive guests. Most of the rooms except the dining room, parlour and counting house contained beds of some kind, and no room was described as a 'bedroom'.

The beds were substantial four-posters, usually made of oak, with accoutrements including rods to hang the curtains; the hangings were often made of serge, but in one case were of Indian silk. There were counterpanes, valances and silk quilts, also of Indian origin, which would have been readily available to any well-off merchant. The importance of the bed in the seventeenth century is shown by the fact that it is often the only piece of furniture to be made the subject of a specific legacy. Henry White left his sister 'one feather bed and bolster one pair of sheets and two blankets', and Henry Sharpe, an innkeeper, left both his children 'a featherbed and six pewter plates a piece and a pair of sheets'. Francis Preston, a Gardiner with four brick houses in Clapham, left each of his four children 'a feather bed, a feather bolster curtains and vallance, a rug blankets and sheets with all furniture belonging thereto'. But the rich also made a point of leaving their beds, and Henry Tatham left his daughter Elizabeth 'a bedstead with red and white curtains and valance one featherbed bolster and pillow and all chairs stools and other furniture in my said daughter's now lodging chambers' – as well as a large chunk of Knightsbridge. Margaret Farmer left her 'best bed' to one person and her 'other bed' to another.

Fires were an important aid to comfort, and each room had a full set of equipment for dealing with them, including fire dogs or andirons, shovels, tongs and forks, together with firebacks in the more important rooms. 'Curtains' referred to the hangings around the four-poster beds; any drapes at windows were referred to specifically as 'window curtains' and were less elaborate than those round the bed. In fact, they became common only towards the end of the seventeenth century. There were also tapestry hangings in a number of the rooms, and serge hangings with leather gilt ornamentation. These were critical to keeping the house warm in winter, particularly important as Europe was in the middle of the 'Little Ice Age'.

Powell's 'Great Dining Room' contained twenty chairs and six Spanish tables (very simple, small folding tables). There was little other furniture in the house: the occasional chest of drawers (a piece of furniture that had come into fashion only by the 1650s); two desks and a scrutore, the forerunner of an escritoire, in the Great Counting House; and a clock and case in the Great Entry. Some of the rooms had what were called 'close stools with pans', or what we know as commodes. There were rugs, including ones made of leather, which probably correspond more to our blankets and would have been placed on the beds, and turkey carpets, which would normally have been placed on a table or cupboard rather than on the floor.

Powell's wealth is also illustrated by the amount of plate and jewellery he had: 421½ ounces of silver plate valued at £105/7/6 and £200 of jewellery, comprising a string of forty-five pearls, a locket with seventeen diamonds, a diamond ring with seven stones and a cornelian ring. The most expensively furnished room in his house was the 'Chamber over the Great Parlour', for which the inventory was valued at £57/1/0, more than twice that of the next most expensive room, the Dining Room. The contents of the parlour were:

> One bedstead matt cords and rods, serge curtains, valance
> and tester and headcloth and counterpane, one rug,
> three serge window curtains, a room of hangings Indian
> flower and silk for furniture of a bed, chair, 4 pieces of
> tapestry hangings, one cabinet and frame, one side table
> and carpet, one looking glass, two pairs of andirons with
> brasses one silk Indian quilt and one calico quilt.

The kitchen had the full range of jacks, chains, pothangers, spits and spit racks, as well as a range of cooking pans, but only two knives are mentioned. There is almost no china, but the kitchen contained pewter plates and other dishes weighing a total of 211 pounds. This is very comparable to Doggett, who had 203 pounds of pewter in Clapham and 312 pounds in London. Kitchens tended to have a pair of bellows for speeding up the cooking, as well as other fire furniture, and these are found in only one room elsewhere. Powell's cellar was well-stocked with glass bottles and beer casks, but there is no record of any wine. The house also had a brew house, barn and banqueting house in its grounds, as well as a field with thirty-four ewes and seven lambs. The barn had room for three horses and a quantity of oats for them to eat.

Doggett's house is slightly less grand but still one of the more highly rated in Clapham, and was assessed at eleven hearths in 1664 and 1674. It had its own Great Parlour, and the rooms have names such as Red and Green Chambers, Wrought (meaning embroidered) Chamber and a 'Best' Chamber. The contents of the last were:

> *6 pieces of tapestry and wrought suite of curtains and valance and counterpanes, 2 cupboard cloths cases for chairs white calicoe curtains and valance, a bedstead matt cord rods, one feather bed a bolster 4 pillows, one rug 3 blankets, one table one pair of stands one chest of drawers, 14 chairs and stools with cases, one looking glass, brass shovel and tongs, one picture, one window rod. Valued at £19-4-6.*

The rooms were furnished in much the same way as Powell's, with limited furniture apart from beds, but plenty of hangings and some pictures. The inventory also gives details of Doggett's house in London. There is not a great deal of difference between the contents of the two houses, except that his plate (799 ounces of it) is all in London, where the rooms are furnished more expensively. Doggett had a watch, a seal, four diamond rings and some plain gold rings, but the jewellery was worth less than a tenth of Powell's.

The most expensive room in Doggett's London house is 'The Widow's Chamber', a significant part of the inventory because its contents were automatically left to the widow:

> *One bedstead with sackcloth bottom and rods a cloth furniture embroidered lined with sarsnet 12 cases for chairs one couch four white case curtains one chest of drawers one feather bed a bolster 3 pillows one rug 2 blankets 2 pieces of tapestry one iron back a chimney piece one looking glass one close stool and pan. Valued at £35-10-0.*

There was little decoration other than fabrics; Powell had 'some pictures' in his Little Parlour, but they were valued at almost nothing, and Doggett four pictures in one of the passages of his London house – but the value of the contents of this passage, including a clock case and a few other items, was only just over £1. Powell also had four 'images' in the garden, valued at £5; these were presumably statues of some description, but, given his Nonconformity, not likely to be of saints or angels.

While giving low values for probate may well have been the norm then as now, the apparently low valuations attached to wooden furniture do seem to correspond to the prices at the time. A turkey-work-back chair cost about 11/6 new, of which the turkey-work upholstery cost 4/8; caned chairs cost about ten shillings in the 1680s.[1] They were much lighter as well as cheaper than turkey-work chairs, and had the advantage of not being edible by moths. Cane chairs did not start appearing in the inventories of the middle classes until the 1680s, which suggest that both Powell and Doggett were in the forefront of fashion.[2] They both owned oval tables, which were only just filtering down to the middle classes in the 1670s, when they must have been bought. Some idea of their cost can be gained from the fact that 'a very large strong oval table with a double set of twisted pillars' was purchased for a royal palace in 1680 for £3/10/-; no doubt those owned by Clapham merchants were both smaller and less grand, and therefore much cheaper. What is more of a puzzle is the valuation of the clocks, at most only about £1 apiece, since these were still desirable and expensive objects. Finally, a number of inventories and wills mention cabinets, pieces of furniture that became an emblem of wealth and status.[3] These were chests set on an integral table with assorted drawers behind one or two doors. It was they that gave rise to the term 'cabinetmaker' to describe the more highly skilled joiners. Judith Gould left 'my great cabinet' to one son and her cabinet to another.

The inventories also include references to a range of fabrics not usually available now, such as pintado, an Indian block-printed cotton cloth; damask; bayse (baize); shalloone, a lightweight wool material used for linings; and serge curtains. By our standards there were large amounts of linen, but that reflects the number of beds. Doggett has eight beds in his Clapham house, while Powell had ten. Powell had twenty pairs of sheets (of two grades – fine and coarse), four dozen towels, sixteen pillow cases, nine dozen napkins and four damask tablecloths. Doggett had even more, with forty-one pairs of sheets in Clapham and twenty-eight in London. Candlesticks are rarely mentioned, although Doggett left an outstanding bill for over £4 with the tallow chandler.

The inventory for Redshaw, who left no will, covers both Clapham and London houses. They were less elaborately furnished than those of the other two, and the most expensive room was in fact in his Clapham house, with embroidered valance and curtains as well as damask inside curtains around the bed. His plate, 228 ounces that was worth just over £58, was less than that of the others, and he had only 112 pounds of pewter in each house. It may have been that he spent more time in Clapham, since there was almost twice as much linen there and more brass in the kitchen.

We can also get a good idea of the merchants' lifestyle by looking at the list of their debts. Doggett had a coach and horses at his London house and rented a coach house in Clapham, paying his coachman £3/10/- a year in wages. On his death Powell's coachman had wages of £2 outstanding. Both men paid gardeners at the rate of five shillings a week, and Doggett had someone to do the weeding as well. Doggett left outstanding bills for glaziers in both London and Clapham, showing that some at least of his windows were glazed. Bills were also paid to the plumber, and to James Markwick, the 'clockman' who looked after their watches and clocks. A year's outstanding wages for the chambermaid was £1.

These inventories can be compared with that for Dennis Gauden at his death in 1688.[4] His house was very much larger, being assessed for thirty-nine hearths in the hearth tax of 1664, compared with only eleven for Robert Whitlock's house (into which Doggett moved), and almost twice the size of Powell's. Yet the value of Gauden's contents by the time of his death was less than those of Powell and gives very little suggestion of affluence, although there was a folding screen constructed from the Chinese Coromandel lacquer that had been fashionable for a short period earlier in the century.[5] The bankruptcy in 1677 had hit him hard, and he had given up his coach. William Hewer is unlikely to have made any effort to improve the house before he lived there himself, although the inventory shows that his mother, Anne, had moved into the best room, perhaps after Gauden's wife, Elizabeth, had died in 1684.

It is not easy to put these valuations in context. Not only are the sums extremely hard to translate into modern equivalents, but also there must be a question of the extent to which the valuations were low, deliberately or otherwise. Tables 9 and 10 give average valuations for household goods, excepting plate, and valuations of the contents of various rooms based on Orphans' inventories.

Wealth (£)	Value of Household Goods	
	1660–90	1690–1730
Less than 500	59	70
500–999	69	80
1,000–1,999	102	98
2,000–4,999	120	108
5,000+	250	206

Table 9. Average value of household goods for probate,
1660–1730

Source: Peter Earle, *The Making of the English Middle Class* (1989), p. 291.

Both Powell and Doggett (if we take both houses) have household goods of about £300, excluding plate, and fit easily into the top group, and they were indeed worth over £10,000. John Blake was also worth over £10,000, but the value of his household goods was concentrated in his London house (at £142); his house in Clapham was very small, possibly even just part of his father-in-law's house, and the goods worth only just over £10. This suggests that it was very much a place to spend the weekend, although after his death his widow, Penelope, took over the whole house when her father, Thomas Chamberlain, died. Unlike Doggett, Redshaw kept almost twice as much of his household goods at Clapham as at London, and the total was worth just over £140. The inventory shows that he was worth about £1,350, much less than the others. Table 10 confirms that Powell, Doggett and Blake were among the more affluent merchants, while Redshaw was not.

Room	Average valuation (£)
Best bedroom	23.3
2nd bedroom	10.6
3rd bedroom	6.9
Dining room	12.2
Kitchen	13.1

Table 10. Average probate valuation of contents of rooms,
1660–1730

Others for whom we have an inventory are less well provided. Thomas Carleton did not live in great luxury, probably because he had passed on much of his worldly goods already and had let his London house. The most expensive room in his house in Clapham was the chief bedroom, whose contents were valued at about £12/10/, including hangings lined with silk. The Great Parlour had contents valued at only £8, but it did contain three family pictures and thirteen pictures 'with glass'. Even so, the overall value excluding plate was about £100.

Henry Knight's most expensive room was the parlour chamber, valued at £9/16/3, which contained a bedstead with all the accoutrements. It had three pictures, and the hangings were of the more modern calico, rather than serge. He had leased his London house, and we can presume that he had retired. We have both a will and an inventory for Mary Foster. There is no record of her in the rate book, but her house had two fore and two back garrets, a fore and back chamber, a dining room and a parlour as well as a kitchen and a wash house. The dining room and parlour are well decorated and contain a number of tables and a walnut chest of drawers. She had three family pictures, india pictures and prints and a series of china toys, as well as cups and saucers; the total household value was £87.

An inventory exists for the household of the rector, John Gurgany, made after his death in 1675. The contents were valued at just over £55, but there is very little to suggest any degree of luxury, even though the Hearth Tax for 1674 assessed the rectory for twelve hearths. The Hall has a clock and a map, but neither was of any significant value. He had very little silver, which was valued at £4 including a tankard and five spoons as well as a candlestick. As usual, most of the value of the household goods comes from the textiles, including a suite of green hangings with gilt leather and nine green chairs to match in the Great Parlour.

As we move into the eighteenth century, household contents become more varied and sophisticated: Sarah Kent left an olivewood chest of drawers; Peternel Weston a 'walnut tree chest of drawers', which was valued in her inventory at £2 and included a table looking glass and stand; and Elizabeth Crawley left an Indian japan cabinet. Jane Pritchard, second wife of Hez Pritchard, the lecturer at Clapham, left 'the organ in the parlour' to one of her daughters. This is also apparent in the comfort of the furniture, with cane chairs rather than turkey-work, and more couches – Blake even had an 'easy chair'.

The type of hanging material mentioned becomes lighter, with less emphasis on serge and more on lined but lighter material. There are more looking glasses (mirrors), which begin to come in frames, even gilt, and would have helped to make the rooms lighter, and there is also more purely decorative material such as pictures and china ornaments. These are not valued at much in inventories, but we come across them in wills, which suggests that they were valued by their owners. There are increasing references in both inventories and wills to apparatus for making and drinking tea, including tea tables, a tea kettle, cups and saucers, and, in the case of Jane Pritchard, a silver teapot. There are almost no references to coffee, however, although John Comfort, the Clapham farrier, does have a coffee mill in his inventory in 1715.

There are also more references to china, used both for tea and for decoration. Blake's inventory shows 'a forell', or box, of china over the chimney. Both Sarah Shallett and Sarah Kent left their daughters 'my china and all belonging to the tea table', while John Dumaistre divided his china between his granddaughters, with 'the china and figures on the chimney in the parlour' going to one, and that on the chimney in the dining room to another. The rest of the china, 'with the table on which it stands which is the great table', went to a third. Martha Jenney left two glass cabinets, which may well have been for displaying china. Mary Foster's inventory listed twenty-one cups and saucers, a tea kettle, and china and toys over the chimney in three rooms. She also had two sets of six knives and forks, one with white handles and one with buckshorn, the first Clapham inventory to include such table utensils.

None of the inventories that refer to paintings ascribes any significant value to them, a fact that reflects the prices of the time. Few pictures at auction in the 1680s sold for more than £4–10;[6] Gerard Soest, who painted the portrait of Richard Salwey (see Illustration 2), usually charged no more than £3, while etchings and prints would have been cheaper still.[7] There are no specific references to them in any of the seventeenth-century wills, although a number of the inventories contain pictures. These were owned not just by the rich, such as Powell and Doggett; Knight had three, and Blake seven in the front parlour. This changed in the eighteenth century. The most extensive reference is in Dumaistre's will, which refers both to his own collection in Clapham and to a number of pictures by his uncle 'Mr James Rousseau'.[8] Jane Pritchard made a number of specific bequests: her daughter Jane was left eight family pictures; Rebecca received 'her own picture'; Anne got eight pictures, three of which belonged to her cousin and were *The Gentleman's Dressing Table* by Gobo Caracci, a picture of King Charles II and a Dutch picture, as well as a picture of her brother; while Isabel got a picture of her father. Mary Foster's inventory, as we have seen, showed some india pictures as well as a family picture and small prints, but with very little value attached to them. Susanna Lillington left her grandson the picture of her cousin George Lillington, the prominent Barbadian plantation owner. Samuel Crisp left his eldest son two fine pictures, 'the fine picture of the Madonna which I frequently lent him, and the great picture of persons washing in the Blood of our Lord Jesus and then fighting against the world the flesh and the Devil'.

Religious books were of great importance to Nonconformists and often feature in wills, with great care taken over their disposal. As early as 1657, Gabriel Carpenter's will made special provision for his substantial library, leaving the books to his two sons but, because they were still young, asking his wife to 'take the fittest time to let them enjoy them and when there is a division of them she should choose out 40 of the big English books and I give them to her daughter Susanna. 'To such of my children as shall be professed in Divinity,' Sir Henry Atkins bequeathed 'all my Divinity books, and to such of my children as shall be professed in Physick I bequeath all my Physick books.' Many of them were also keen to leave children Bibles with their extensive annotations.

Henry Sampson owned a remarkable collection of English and Hebrew Bibles, including a copy of William Tyndale's translation and the Bishops's Bible printed in Geneva. He also had a collection of Books of Common Prayer, including two from Edward's reign, 'one commonly called the first in folio that in 4° which is the second in that reign but this is translated into French and is therefore the greater rarity'. James Fowke demonstrated his Nonconformist views by distributing his books by leading Nonconformist ministers among his three grandchildren with the caveat, 'but if my wife desire any for her own reading to have them while she lives'.

Thomas Lye ordered the selling of his books 'within a convenient time of my decease', and expected them to make good sum because, as we have seen, he required £30 of the proceeds to go towards the funeral costs and the remainder to be given to the poor at the discretion of his executors. They were sold at Bridges Coffee House five months after his death. Edward Grace's widow took the earliest opportunity to sell off his books; the sale was advertised in the *Daily Courant* only a few months after his will was probated:

> *Library of Rev Mr Edward Grace, Minister at Clapham*
> *and learned schoolmaster, consisting of a collection*
> *of valuable books on Divinity, History, Physick,*
> *Mathematics, Poetry, Classical Authors and their*
> *translations, Grammars, Dictionaries, Hebrew Greek,*
> *Latin, French and English (prices put on front page).*[9]

Women's wills

Most of the studies of the middling classes have considered merchants and the material relating directly to them. By concentrating on people associated with a geographical area such as Clapham, it is natural to look at the wills left by the women, in most cases widows. It might be expected that these would be of less interest, since the main shape of inheritance had been determined by the husband in his will and often widows had only a life interest in much of the property. In fact, many widows did have property because of the operation of marriage settlements, and some had considerable sums to leave. Twenty per cent of all wills in the early modern period were written by women.[10]

One woman who left a will, with the agreement of her husband, Dormer Sheppard, was Sarah, who died in 1694 after eleven years of marriage. She gave £40 of her original marriage settlement back to her father, a further £60 to her sisters and other family; the rest, with her jewels, was to be divided among her children. Anne Edgely, the cousin of William Hewer, exercised the right given her under Hewer's will to allocate £1,000 'the better to secure unto myself the duty and obedience of my children and grandchildren', to leave it to her daughter Anne, the wife of John Jackson. Her husband witnessed the will as evidence of his consent.

There are two other reasons why women's wills can be of interest as well as those of men. Very often a man would leave all his goods to his wife or to one of his sons, or substantial legacies would already have been passed to children for their marriages or to set the sons up in business. The widow was virtually bound to pass on to the next generation, and that often gives a greater insight into the family structure. In addition, women were generally more concerned to pass on particularly prized possessions to selected friends or relations, and so we can learn much more about what those possessions were. One example of this was John Gerard's *Herball*, running to 1,700 pages and profusely illustrated with high-quality drawings of plants, with woodcuts largely taken from an earlier Dutch herbal. Judith Gould left one of her sons her copy, while Abigail Macey, who had lived with her brother Stephen Crisp after the death of her husband, left her herbal to her niece Ann Crisp as part payment for what she owed her.

Women also left specific pieces of silver and jewellery. Frances Walker specifically refers to 'a piece of plate called a spout pot',[11] while Susan Marshall left her 'great cawdle cup'[12] to her nephew together with her silver bowl and silver salt, and her small cawdle cup to her niece together with a small silver wine cup, a gold chain and rings and a silver inkhorn. Mary Daniel left a silver basin and ewer as well as her 'best table diamond' to her son Peter, while a small diamond ring went to her daughter Winifred and a small table diamond to her daughter Sarah.[13] One of the few men who mentioned particular items of silver was John Hately. Recognising that he had left only real property to his wife, Frances, and all his goods to his son, he made a codicil leaving a variety of personal silver to Frances, including 'a silver comb, two silver powder pots, and two small silver bowls and a silver pin cushion and my looking glass with a silver frame'.

Women were also much more likely than men to mention their clothes in legacies, and were more ready to give a legacy for mourning clothes as well as rings. Many, even the relatively well-off, left their clothes to a relation, friend or servant, and many mothers left clothes 'linen and woollen' to one daughter or another, or 'to be lovingly divided between them'. By the eighteenth century some of the women were making a point of leaving their more decorative clothes. Margaret Mitford left her great-niece her sable muff and tippet;[14] Margaret Shrows gave her great-niece a 'silk gown and petticoat'; Peternel Weston left her sister Hannah Lambert the residue of her estate, which included a silk waistcoat flowered in gold, a silk gown and petticoat with ten gold laces, an old quilted silk petticoat and one with a silver fringe, a waistcoat with a gold fringe and a silk mourning gown. These were not mentioned specifically in her will, but appeared in the probate inventory valued at about £5. Jane Pritchard left one of her daughters 'a striped poplin gown and petticoat with a black satin lining, a pair of stays and a camblet riding hood, a striped calamanco night gown ... one silk crape gown and petticoat for mourning'. Elizabeth Fowke left her niece 'my best black silk suit and my quilted petticoat and lined scarf and ... my best stayes six of my best shifts and half a dozen of my best aprons (except the flowered ones)'.

If we go down the social order, the bequests of clothes become more specific. Elizabeth Curtis gave her best woollen apparel to her sister, her black hat and sasnett (a soft silk) hood to Mrs Chalkhill and one of her best white aprons to Sarah Webb. Some men also made explicit reference to their clothes: Henry White, a tailor, left his sister a blue gown and his brother-in-law 'my best hat and coat the suit I wore therewith and my best pair of stockings'. John Chalkhill, yeoman, left his brother Thomas 'my worst[ed] suit and some of my shifts'.

The cost of dying

While most testators claimed to be 'of good heath in body', others admitted to being 'old and weak in body', 'somewhat indisposed in body' or 'weak through infirmity of age', but in all cases they were sure to be 'of sound and perfect mind and memory', usually with an acknowledgement of thanks to God for that. Ann Salwey, aged sixty-seven, began her will 'considering my great age and the infirmities that accompany it'. Inventories show that falling severely ill was costly, at least for those who could pay professionals for help. Doggett's bill after his death came to over £55 for the doctor/surgeon and £12/10/- for the apothecary, while Powell owed £25 to the apothecary.

Funerals could be extravagant affairs, occasionally costing as much as £700 – a massive sum for those days – and most wills contained instructions for the testator's burial. The expense of a funeral was related to the number of people attending, and whether or not there was a big procession, possibly from their livery company hall to their chosen church. They might choose to be buried next to the grave of their spouse, parent or children, or in the family vault, which, as for the Hewer family, could be used for a very extended family. Unusually, Humphrey Davy had written his will some twelve years before he died, but he added a codicil on his deathbed asking his father-in-law to agree to his being buried in the Buckingham family vault.

Margaret, the widow of Michael Mitford, chose to be buried from Clothworkers Hall in 1722, her body being put in the vault in St Mary-at-Hill, where her sister was buried. She specified 'that only my nearest relations and some few friends' would attend the funeral. Richard Palmer's tomb recorded that he had served King Charles II, King James, King William and Queen Mary, and Queen Anne as Yeoman of the Guard. He clearly attached much importance to this because his will directed that he be buried as a Yeoman of the Guard and that all his fellow yeomen be invited to the funeral; he clearly expected them to come part of the way by river, since he instructed that their 'wateridge' should be paid. He duly set aside £50 for his funeral costs. Occasionally gravestones were requested, and Michael Mitford specified a 'brick grave turned over with an Arch with a marble stone upon it in such parish church or church yard where I shall happen to die and that no other body be laid in the same grave but my own'. This turned out to be in Clapham, and the stone had his arms on it.

Puritans had campaigned against extravagant funerals, and some make clear that they wanted only a few people to attend, explicitly asking for privacy. Martin Lister's will directed that his body should 'without pomp and in a private manner be carried in a hearse attended by only one mourning coach to Clapham in Surrey and there be buried in the grave of his first wife'. Philip Lamb wanted to be buried 'without the least show of pomp'; Thomas Juxon asked to be buried 'decently and privately'; Edward Fryer wanted his burial to be 'decent but free from excess in both numbers and charges' and imposed a cost limit of £30. William Lethieullier asked for 'as much privacy as decency will admit', while Urban Hall asked to be 'privately buried at Clapham according to such private instructions as I have left or shall leave for that purpose'.

William Brooke senior wanted his funeral to be 'without escutcheons or any other pomp', and Henry Powell wrote:

> *And my mind and will is that after my decease my bodie*
> *bee decently interred in some publique burying place*
> *of friends according to the discretion of my executors*
> *hereinafter named but without any worldly pomp or*
> *ostentation and without any mourning clothes rings*
> *ornament or attire to be given used or worne by my wife*
> *children or other relations or kindred whether at my*
> *funeral or at any time after my decease.*

Even though he later added a codicil overriding this and giving discretion solely to his brother-in-law William Meade, rather than jointly with his widow, the fact that his funeral cost only £8/9/8 suggests that his original stipulations were adhered to, except that his name does appear in the parish register of burials in Clapham, suggesting that he was not buried elsewhere. The reference to a 'publique burying place of friends' may suggest that Powell was a Quaker, and it may be relevant that despite his obvious piety there is no legacy in his will for any minister, at Clapham or elsewhere. In addition, the £10 that he left to the poor of Clapham was to be distributed by his executors, not a minister.[15]

The majority left all funeral arrangements to the discretion of their executors, although Marie Oresby asked that she be 'decently buried as I did my husband but not more'. The issue then turned on the extent of the money that should be spent on mourning, which could cover rings and mourning clothes. This could be extensive: Samuel Pepys' will provided for over £100 to be spent on 129 rings carefully graded at twenty, fifteen or ten shillings each. Clothes could be a considerable expense, and women were more likely to leave money to buy mourning clothes. Mary Wright left her aunt Ann Hughes and cousin Hannah Stephens (all three lived with her cousin Anthony Stephens) £50 each to buy their mourning clothes, which, to judge from other wills, might cost up to £5. Dorothy Arthur left £3 to her daughter Susanna Rodbard to buy a gown but forty shillings for a ring to her daughter-in-law Anne Arthur.

We can get some idea of what a more lavish funeral might involve by looking at the testators who went out of their way to avoid it. Thomas Joliffe declared:

> *I will have no pall or escutcheon, nor will I have my corps carried into the church and I will that but one coach shall accompany the hearse thither and I positively order my executor that there be neither rings hatbands gloves nor anything given away at my funeral and that he doth not pay to the parson of the parish any more than the remaining parish dues.*

However, there is one record of what must have been the most lavish Clapham funeral, that of the matriarch Dame Rebecca Atkins in 1711. Her will gave a careful prescription:

> *And as to my Body I desire it may be buried in my Vault at Clapham which I have recently erected in the Church Yard there and that it may be carried thither in a hearse drawn by six horses and that there may be at my funeral twelve mourning coaches each drawn by six horses and as many poor women as I shall be years of age at the time of my death and that every one of the said women shall have a black bayes gown and petticoat with other necessaries that shall be of the value of forty shillings and my desire is that all other persons that shall be invited to my funeral by my executor amounting to the number of three hundred shall have every one of them a gold ring to the value of ten shillings and those persons that shall hold up the pall shall have scarves and gloves.*

Since she died a week after her seventy-seventh birthday, the funeral costs ran to more than £300, even before the coaches and hospitality.

Table 11 gives the distribution of funeral costs compared with the wealth at death, estimated from inventories of those freemen of the City whose wills were covered by the Court of Orphans.

Funeral cost	Wealth at death				
	Under 1,000 (%)	1,000– 1,999 (%)	2,000– 4,999 (%)	5,000– 9,999 (%)	Over 10,000 (%)
Under 50	66	26	14	4	5
50–99	27	53	51	17	0
100–199	7	15	31	55	18
200 and over	0	6	4	24	77
Average cost	43.3	64.3	98.2	152.6	299.3
No. of cases	71	34	51	29	22

Table 11. Funeral costs (£) and estimated wealth at death (£)
Source: Peter Earle, *The Making of the English Middle Class* (1989), p. 312.

Henry Powell's funeral costs were clearly extremely low by any standards, and this is also true for those of Thomas Carleton, for whom we have evidence from a probate inventory containing the debts and other bills that were paid by his son-in-law and executor, James Markwick junior. Although the inventory suggests that Carleton was worth slightly under £200, this was probably because his various houses were left to his son-in-law and were excluded.

	£	s	d
Azariah Reynolds/Gilbert Page: under-takers		16	10
Claret and Canary		19	8
Gold rings	12	12	9
George Powell, parish clerk for fees	1	1	6
Pall-bearers		6	0
Total	15	16	9

Table 12. Thomas Carleton's funeral costs, 1709

On top of this Carleton left a legacy of £10 for mourning to his cousin Mary Cholmley, who lived with him. No rings are mentioned explicitly in his will, however, so it may be that these were taken for granted, at least for close family.

Michael Mitford paid for the funeral of Anthony, the brother of his apprentice John Lowther. They were the two youngest sons of Anthony Lowther, who had married Margaret Penn in Clapham in 1667. John was living in Danzig and, his father having died earlier, had obviously raised some questions about the style of funeral, because Mitford wrote to him in strong terms, having discussed it with Lowther's uncle the Quaker William Penn, and 'I think satisfied him':

> *Mr Nisbet only paid 25 for the funeral but it cost me*
> *over 5 times 25 [pounds] the charges of your brother's*
> *funeral and I must have you to know that I did not spare*
> *for anything that is in fashion at funerals but had all to*
> *the height of the mode and so as he made a good exit he*
> *is well provided for and needs no more portion.*[16]

A funeral costing £125 would have been entirely in line with any but that of the very rich.

This allows us to put into context the various specific limits on funeral costs included in about a tenth of all wills, and to conclude that in most cases they were genuine attempts to keep the costs down. This must be true of Ann Carpenter, who set a limit of £20 (her husband, Gabriel, had set a limit of £30 twenty years before). Roger Hughes set a limit of £30, and both Elizabeth Babington and James Fowke one of £40. Martha Jenney, a widow who had come to live in Clapham with an annual income of £200 from her late husband, set a limit of £50, more than the £40 her Draper husband had set for his a few years earlier. Samuel Moyer's mother, Lydia, undoubtedly had a family of considerable wealth, so her limit of £100 probably was a genuine attempt to reduce costs. There were two relatively high limits, the first being £200, by Juliana Sherwin (cousin of Thomas Rodbard and sister of the Richard Sherwin who had lived briefly before his death in the Manor House), and £300 by Samuel Moyer. Even for Moyer, who was very wealthy indeed and would have had many obligations to meet – his is the only will that explicitly leaves mourning for the coachman of each of his two brothers and his brother-in-law – it seems likely that he intended to impose a limit rather than to spend excessively. The sense of a limit being imposed is reinforced by all these cases involving a testator of strong Nonconformist views. A limit of £300 was also set by William Hewer for his funeral.

There are also limits placed by the less well-off. Two widows, Alice Johnson and Elizabeth Wiggsell (the latter the widow of the landlord of the Bull inn), decreed a limit of £20 and another, Mary Day, one of £25. Although they were not the widows of merchants, they were not poor and had property. Mary Day, the widow of John Day, who had provided the daily stagecoach service to the City, specified that she be interred as close as possible to her husband, and that the £25 should also cover the charge of 'a handsome gravestone to be laid over the place of our interment with a proper inscription thereon'. It was a second marriage for both of them, but had lasted almost twenty-seven years.

Conclusion

Descriptions of the houses and their contents confirm that Clapham merchants were indeed well-off. The two principal houses, the Manor House and Clapham Place, were large by any standards; for comparison, there were only thirty-four comparably sized houses in all the environs of London in 1674.[17] The inventories show the wealth of many of the merchants, with rooms furnished and decorated with current material and fashions. Art or china became common only towards the end of the seventeenth century, but many of these houses contained extensive collections of books, particularly religious ones. But, despite their wealth, the merchants were not extravagant, particularly when it came to their clothes, and they prided themselves on an outward appearance of modest refinement.[18] In all the inventories and wills there is only one reference to men's clothes other than those of wool or cotton, and that is to a satin doublet belonging to Lawrence Brinley in 1662. The portrait of William Daniel demonstrates their sobriety. Their funerals also avoided show, with the marked exception of Dame Rebecca Atkins, who was neither a merchant's wife nor a Nonconformist.

(Endnotes)

1. Adam Bowett, *English Furniture* (Antique Collectors Club, 1988), pp. 76, 84.
2. Ibid.
3. Ibid., p. 38.
4. National Archives, PROB 5/3027.

5. Michael Green in *Clapham Newsletter*, no. 3 (2013).

6. Gordon and Philippa Glanville in Mireille Gallinou (ed.), *City Merchants and the Arts 1670–1720* (Oblong, 2004), p. 12.

7. Ellis Waterhouse, *Painting in Britain 1530–1790* (Yale University Press, 1994), p. 101.

8. Jacques Rousseau was the most celebrated and sought after *trompe l'oeil* perspective artist of the time, and had painted the Salon de Venus in Versailles and rooms in the Duke of Montagu's house in Bloomsbury.

9. *Daily Courant*, 24 September 1715.

10. Lloyd Davis, 'Women's Wills in Early Modern England', in Nancy Wright et al., *English Women and Property* (University of Toronto Press, 2004), p. 204.

11. A spouted vessel used for consuming posset, a beverage of hot milk curdled with wine or ale, usually spiced or sweetened, and thickened with oatmeal or bread. The drinker sucked the liquid through the spout and ate the residue with a spoon.

12. A small, two-handled silver cup, usually with a cover, originally made in England during the second half of the seventeenth century and possibly used for caudle (warm ale or wine mixed with bread or gruel, eggs, sugar and spices), which was administered to women after childbirth, and to convalescents.

13. A 'table cut' for a diamond was introduced in the mid-fifteenth century when the point or top of the diamond would be sawn off, leaving a flat top. This did not reveal what a diamond is prized for today: its strong dispersion or 'fire'. At the time, the diamond was valued chiefly for its adamantine lustre and superlative hardness; a table-cut diamond would appear black to the eye, as they do in contemporary paintings. For this reason, coloured gemstones such as ruby and sapphire were far more popular in the jewellery of the era.

14. A woman's fur cape, often the whole fur of an animal such as a sable fox.

15. This William Meade is not the Quaker of the same name. Although also a Merchant Taylor, he gained his freedom by servitude with Joshua Woolnough, not by patrimony as the Quaker Meade did. This Meade was another son-in-law of William Daniel.

16. Michael Mitford letter to John Lowther 21 December 1703. Michael Mitford letterbook, London Metropolitan Archives.

17. Dorian Gerhold, 'London's Suburban Villas and Mansions 1660–1830', *London Journal*, vol. 34 (2009), p. 236.

18. Perry Gauci, *Emporium of the World* (Hambledon, 2007), p. 99.

C H A P T E R   1 1

MARRIAGE AND FAMILY

Businessmen in Clapham were generally successful financially, overwhelmingly Nonconformist, Whig and active in overseas trade. This chapter investigates their marriages and family structure based on details of 200 Clapham merchants and 135 of their marriages, a sample that is comparable in size to other research into seventeenth-century family structures and marriage relationships.[1] This allows the exploration of both the similarities and the differences arising between their random samples of merchants and one confined to Clapham.

Marriage was a serious business for merchant families of any kind. Nonconformist preaching emphasised rational rather than romantic love, control of feelings and constancy, and there was an emphasis on creating a spiritual household. The widespread opinion was that love came after the wedding, built on a companionate relationship. Godly men such as John Gould wanted to marry godly women, but preferably those from the right business background. Clapham may well have been viewed as a good place to find a wife who would have the right connections in the Nonconformist merchant community and be suitably devout. Such thoughts may have prompted the decision of the pious coal merchant Jonathan Shakespear, who did business with Arthur Shallett shipping coal from Newcastle to London, and also knew Michael Mitford. He recorded in his diary:

> *then it pleased God of his providence to direct me to*
> *Clapham where I took a wife out of Mr Arthur Shallett's*
> *family and was married at Clapham 26 April 1698 my*
> *wife Elizabeth being 19 years of age which God grant her*
> *and I long to live in his fear.*[2]

Some denominations, and particularly the Quakers, expected proposed marriages to be approved by the congregation. The record of Sarah Payne's marriage to John Barnard, a Quaker wine merchant who came to live in Clapham, was signed by the couple and the twenty-eight people present, as is the case for Quaker marriages today.

Nevertheless, some marriages were for love, or at least instigated by one or other of the couple, and Joseph Paice's diary records a love match with Mary Payne in 1683, when he was twenty-six, just after obtaining his freedom from his apprenticeship.[3] It is hard to judge how common this was, and the early death of Paice's father may have given him greater freedom to choose his wife. She died seventeen years later, but he married again after only six months. We have one other example where the couple's wishes determined the match. Sir Lawrence Bromfield had left his granddaughters £1,000 each when they came of age or married, but made it conditional on their having first obtained from their mother 'free and full consent under her hand and seal or declared before two or more credible witnesses'. He died only two years before one of them, Anne Corbett, did indeed marry before her twenty-first birthday.

Her husband was John Arthur, the son of the former rector of Clapham. He was both well-off, having inherited his father's extensive lands in Essex, and well-educated, having spent time at the Middle Temple and obtained a doctorate of medicine from Oxford. Anne sued the executors of her grandfather's will, who had refused to pay her the legacy; her mother's witness statement makes clear that she had been against the marriage at first, but 'when she saw her daughter's affections settled on him, she did not withstand the same, howbeit she was at first displeased.'[4] Both her parents agreed that Arthur was 'a person of good extraction and estate', and he had demonstrated an income of at least £160 a year, with another £200 when his mother died. Anne's father, Thomas, summed up:

Anne receives no disparagement nor diminution in
quality of estate by intermarriage with him, he well
meriting her and her portion especially when he shall
have settled the said jointure on her which he offers being
equivalent to her portion and estate.

To be on the safe side, he also commented that Arthur had indeed made the desired jointure and that he had several times heard his wife express consent before the marriage. As a result, the executors were able to pay the legacy, in an example of true love overcoming a hesitant if not antagonistic mother.

Without extensive letters, the only material that can shed light on the nature of a marriage are wills, in which the most common reference to a wife is 'loving' or 'dear', occasionally 'dear and loving' or even 'dearly beloved'. Even this may be an artefact of the style of the person helping to compose the will, since relations and friends were often also referred to as 'loving'. On the other hand, Michael Mitford is one of the few husbands not to refer to his 'loving' wife in his will, and she contested it, arguing that she had been done out of some of her rightful inheritance.

A number of wives asked to be buried 'as near as may be' to the graves of their husbands, or even in the same grave. Only two husbands made the same request, reflecting the fact that they tended to die first; one of these husbands, who had been married three times, left instructions that if he were to die near one town he should be buried next to the grave of his first wife, if near another town by the grave of his second wife, and otherwise in the churchyard where he now lived. Epitaphs might provide another clue, but there are few. One is for the wife of Martin Lister, Hannah, who was buried in Clapham in 1695:

Hannah Lister, Deare Wife! Died the 1st day of August
1695 and left six children in teares for a most indulgent
mother. She was daughter and Heir of Thomas Parkinson
of Carleton in Craven.

This was modelled on the one for Martin Lister's daughter Jane, who was buried in Westminster Abbey – at a time when the Dean and Chapter sold spaces for monuments rather than their being reserved for the great and the good. That reads: 'Jane Lister, dear

Childe died Oct. 7th, 1688', an inscription much loved by Victorian sentimentalists and even used as a text for a sermon by one dean of the Abbey. Lister died in 1712 and was buried in the grave of his first wife at Clapham.

The wedding itself was not always a big celebration. Although some of the merchants' families were married following the calling of banns, many avoided that because of the inevitable publicity. This led to more expense, because more people had to be asked to celebrate, but it could also lead to unseemly attention from the common people.[5] A slightly more expensive process was to obtain a licence from the Bishop of London or the Archbishop of Canterbury, thus avoiding the need for banns and the concomitant publicity. Many preferred this, and it may have been more appropriate for the start of a relationship based on commercial or family considerations rather than love. One such was the quiet marriage in Clapham between Anthony Lowther senior and Margaret Penn that Samuel Pepys describes as a 'private one, no friends, but two or three relations on his side and hers'.[6]

There are some implications that Clapham was a fashionable place for a Nonconformist merchant to get married. We have already seen this in the 1650s during the period of civil marriage, but it continued afterwards with the record of a number of marriages that involved people without obvious connection to the village. One such was the Lowther/Penn marriage; others were the marriage of the future alderman John Peake to Judith Hales, even though her family had already moved from Clapham to Beckenham; that of Henry Duncomb, aged seventeen and under the guardianship of a City lawyer, to the lawyer's daughter, aged sixteen; and the first occasion on which a member of the Denew family married outside the Huguenot community.

Marriage as business

While the couples' inclinations were certainly taken into account, marriage was often a means of building or securing a business. Of the 135 marriages of Clapham residents during this period for which we have complete information, 71 per cent are definitely among merchant families, and a further 8 per cent between merchant families and Nonconformist ministers or their daughters. It has not been possible to confirm that the remaining 21 per cent involved merchant families on both sides, but it is very likely that a fair proportion did so, a position that was encouraged by living at least part of the time in a village full of such families.

This is a much higher proportion of marriages within the merchant community than that found in other studies, although it is compatible with the observation that the richest merchants were the most likely to marry within their community.[7] The proportion of merchants' children from Clapham marrying landed gentry is vanishingly small, although some may have married minor gentry from the part of the country their family originally came from. It is only well into the eighteenth century that we find the first two Clapham children marrying into the aristocracy: Josiah Nicholson's daughter married one of the Verneys, with a portion of £60,000; and Sir John Barnard's daughter married the younger son of the first Viscount Palmerston, and was the grandmother of the third Viscount and prime minister.

Marriage could strengthen business arrangements in a number of ways. Apprentices might marry their master's daughter or other relation, such as Richard Salway and Ann Waring, Anthony Stephens and Hannah Hughes, John Brett and Martha Mainwaring, and Andrew Stone and Anne Holbrooke. This was a good way for a master to pass on his business to someone one he knew and trusted, in the absence of a male heir. Having married the niece of his banking master, Stone was made a partner in the bank shortly afterwards. Stone being faced with three sons all under ten years old, Richard Smith used his will to offer Stone the opportunity to buy his share of the bank for £9,000. The banker Abraham Atkins gave his daughter a dowry of £10,000 to marry his partner.

The negotiations involved in these marriages are illustrated by a letter from John Arthur to a Robert Doughty, a member of the local Norfolk landed gentry and prospective husband for his daughter. Arthur had offered a dowry of £500 or £600 with another £100 a year after his death for her life and then for her children. Doughty had asked for £1,000 and the transfer of the estate(s) worth that amount. This was too much for Arthur, although he was prepared to increase his offer by £100 or so and indicated that there would be more 'if the Lord do bless me with a better estate'.[8] He specifically refused to pass over the freehold to a son-in-law, writing: 'I will not do her so much wrong as to give away her fee simple for a jointure for in case you die her estate is clearly gone from the issue of her body that she hath by a second husband.' He also refuted any suggestion that his daughter had any other possible suitors in tow: 'believe me she would not give way to any offer if they have never so greater an estate.'

In this correspondence, Arthur is acting as a man of substantial means used to doing business (which he was, with many land holdings in Essex), rather than as a minister of religion. It shows that the details of the marriage deal were thought through very carefully according to the very natural desire to keep the money in the family, and his letter was cast in legal language to make clear how the money would be dealt with in the case a variety of order of deaths. None of the subsequent correspondence remains, but the negotiations must have failed, since both halves of the couple married someone else.

Marriage settlements involved significant financial transactions with commitments on both sides. The wealthier the families, the more likely they were to have a formal legal settlement setting out the relative contributions and responsibilities. When John Gould married his first wife, Elizabeth Thorold, the daughter of one of the major merchants of his day and sister of his business partner Charles Thorold, there was a £4,000 marriage portion and a dowry of £6,000 worth of land, but it was coupled with a bond of £10,000 from Gould in favour of his future father-in-law, to ensure that he maintained the covenants he had undertaken in the settlement to provide for his wife. In any case, the interests of widows and children of freemen of the City of London were protected by the Custom of the City, which set out how the freeman's estate should be divided.

A bride's family generally gave her a marriage portion, whether in cash or in land, which was designed to assist with – or even cover – the cost of maintaining her and the children. The husband had the use of it during his lifetime, and it could make a major contribution to his business. When he died it reverted to his wife, and, if there were no children, it was returned to her family after her death. In some cases a man had used the portion to help finance his business, rather than buying property to secure his widow's income; in such cases, the widow had the choice of taking the third of the estate guaranteed her under the Custom or insisting on the portion. Her response would be determined by the amount of money in the estate and the likelihood of the executor (which might be her) sorting things out within a reasonable time. Edmund White junior's will enjoins 'his loving son in law [Thomas Hunt] to purchase what land is necessary to be sold [from my estate] and settle it on my daughter and heirs since there was no settlement made at marriage'. This had the advantage of keeping the property in the family, and one presumes that there was already an understanding about how large the settlement should be. White left the rest of his estate to his daughter and felt it necessary to say 'I bequeath no other legacy to any other relation.'

Another example involved Edward Lambert, a Goldsmith, who had married Anne, the daughter of Jean Dumaistre, at the church in Tooting. He died only a year later, before he had been able to invest his wife's portion. His will makes clear that the portion was £2,000, with which he was expected to buy an estate worth £100 a year, returning the capital sum to her after his death. He solved this problem by creating a trust worth £3,500, administered by his father and brother, to purchase an estate within 120 miles of London, approved by his father-in-law, and which would generate an income of £175. This would go to Anne after his death while she lived and then to any children of the marriage. If there were no children it would revert to his brother's children, not to her family. However, if she challenged the will the legacy would be reduced to the portion of £2,000, and he appointed his father-in-law and his partner Nathaniel Woolfreys as executors. The matter was resolved by Anne's marrying Woolfreys and their coming to live in Clapham in what had been her father's house.

Not all cases ended so satisfactorily. Margaret Mitford sued the executors of her husband's estate to get a better deal.[9] She had brought a portion of £1,200 but, claiming he could no longer find a copy of the agreement, he left her the lease of his house in Clapham and its contents, an income of £100 a year and some other legacies. However, he made clear that if she objected to the will or challenged it in court she should lose all the legacies he had made to her. She objected to the division, claiming that the original marriage agreement had entitled her to half of his estate, and was prepared to give up her rights under the will in order to receive this. The court upheld her position, even though it might prevent the payment of other legacies.

Complications could also arise if a marriage had taken place abroad. William Brooke senior had lived in Lisbon and there married Catherine Crofford, the sister of another English merchant in Lisbon. They had entered into a legal agreement under Portuguese law that, giving up all rights under any other system, she should have one sixth of her husband's estate if he died first, but in case of remarriage only the interest or income from that share. This was a less good deal than the Custom of the City, and Brooke pleaded in his will:

> *It having pleased God to bless us with a plentiful fortune*
> *and to permit me to return and settle in my own country*
> *and plant my family under the Laws and Government of*
> *this Realm, now it is my earnest desire that they will in this*
> *respect as well as others conform themselves to the Laws*
> *and usage of this Realm and not insist on the said Marriage*
> *Agreement but wholly waive the same on all sides.*

Giving effect to the will could be a major task, one that required not just dealing with the various properties but also unwinding or transferring the existing business with the various debtors and creditors. In the cases of John Doggett and Henry Powell, for example, that ran to over £10,000. This made the choice of executor a very important decision. Although many merchants appointed their wives executrix, this was often jointly with either their partner or a son or son-in-law. Of those cases in which the wife was still alive, about one third appointed her sole executrix, one third joint (whether with sons or 'overseers') and one third chose a son and/or son-in-law. Two who died young chose their mothers as executrix. Women, chiefly widows, normally chose their sons, but occasionally daughters and even grandsons.

Where there was no obvious family executor, whether because of death or disagreement, the choice became all the more important. Mitford chose his executors carefully: his partner Thomas Nisbet; George Mertins the Goldsmith and future Lord Mayor, who had married his cousin John Mitford's daughter; and another relation, William Mitford, a lawyer. Elizabeth Wiggsell, the landlady of the White Hart, chose the affluent Thomas Juxon and David Polhill.

The work involved in settling some estates was so great that some testators left a legacy to their executors, and Thomas Joliffe gave the banker Henry Hankey £1,000 for this purpose.

Age at marriage

Apprentices were required to remain unmarried, so it is not surprising that merchants tended to marry relatively late in their twenties or even their early thirties, as demonstrated in Figure 3. Few had the financial wherewithal to marry earlier; those who did were all children of affluent merchants who may well have obtained their freedom by patrimony rather than by serving with a master, and so were already established.

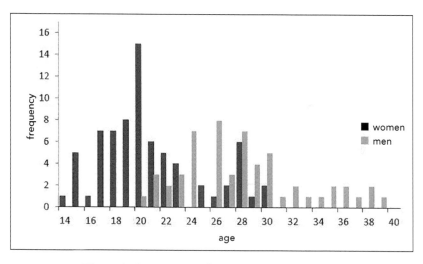

Figure 3. Age at men's first marriage 1640-1720

The average age of marriage for men is 28.2, with 28 being the median, while for women marrying bachelors the average age is 20.5 with a median of 20. Both are very close to the data found in other studies.[10] A relatively large number of women married at the age of fifteen, and one, from the Huguenot community, even at fourteen, although all their spouses tend to be relatively young and from rich families. The graph also shows a second peak for women in the late twenties, largely explained by the number of widows marrying bachelors.

The average age difference between spouses was 8.2 years and the median is 8, but there was a wide range, as shown in Figure 4.

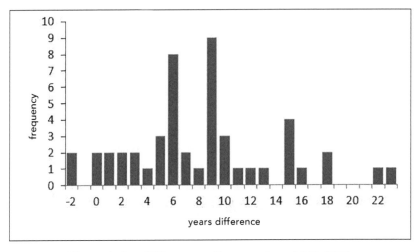

Figure 4. Age difference at first marriage 1640-1720

Widowers were often further from their wives in age, particularly when they married spinsters; Hugh Forth was thirty-four years older than Amy Gurdon when he took her as his third wife; Henry Knight was twenty-seven years older than his second wife, Mary Tichborne; and Gabriel Carpenter thirty-one years older than Ann Harris, although this appears to have been a first marriage. In all three cases the widow lived for at least twenty years afterwards.

Second marriages

With shorter life expectancy, widowhood was common. Widowers were more likely to marry again than widows, at least if there were no female relations to live with them and manage the household. Samuel Moyer married two of Thomas Thorold's daughters, first Margaret and, after her death, her younger sister Rebecca, a fact that may have saved the Thorolds a second dowry. Remarriage of older husbands was often to a younger woman, particularly if she were a younger child and the widower was not so dependent on her bringing a substantial portion with her. There are good examples of this in the Gurdon family. John Gurdon was a prominent Puritan lawyer, an MP and a member of the Council of State in 1649/50. He had eleven children, the last four of whom were girls. Judith Gurdon first married John Doddridge, whose third marriage it was and who must have been at least thirty years older than her. He died after only eighteen months and she then married John Gould, again as his third wife, outliving him by twenty-five years. Her sister Anne married, relatively late, a first husband about her own age; she subsequently married John Joliffe, who was thirty years her senior, and survived him by thirty years. The third sister, Amy, married Hugh Forth, who was thirty-seven years her senior, and then Rev. Thomas Jacombe, a distinguished Puritan minister, who was twenty years older than her. She survived him by almost forty years.

A few widowers, such as John Gould, Hugh Forth and Lawrence Brinley, had as many as three marriages as their wives died, but the record is surely held by Sir Owen Buckingham, who managed to have six wives: four rich widows and two major heiresses. Three of them died within eighteen months of marrying him; the last widow, whom he married within ten months of his previous wife's death, was reputed to be 'an apothecary's widow in King Street, Cheapside, with whom he had £180,000 fortune.'[11]

Many widows lived on in Clapham for twenty or thirty years after their husband's death, often with unmarried daughters or other female relations, and there is no obvious change in their propensity to do so later in the century. Abigail Crisp married, aged twenty-nine, the widower George Macey, who was more than twenty years her senior and deputy to Sir Isaac Newton as Warden of the Mint. Macey died two years later, leaving Abigail a widow in Clapham for another forty years.

On the other hand, some young widows married other Clapham residents quickly, as did Susanna Wood (née Arthur) Thomas Rodbard and Winifred Burrows (née Daniel) Thomas Powell. A number of Clapham widows were quickly picked up by prominent merchants within two years of being widowed and moving to Clapham; Hannah Browne married Thomas Aldworth, Hannah Curtis married Owen Buckingham, and Elizabeth Scott married George Juyce. Juyce must have known many Clapham residents well, since he was clerk to the governors of St Thomas' Hospital and had also been a witness to the will of William Daniel, a colleague on the hospital's governing board.

Second marriages could be particularly important if there had been no children or especially no son. Henry Tatham, who moved to Clapham in the early 1660s, had four children by his first wife. Elizabeth survived, but the other three all died shortly after birth or as very young children (all were girls, all called Mary). His wife died in the 1670s and Henry married again, this time Ann Beck, a seventeen-year-old. She gave him five children, including another Henry, born posthumously, for whom Henry senior added a codicil to his will to ensure that he got his share of the inheritance. Ann was only twenty-one when her husband died, and she subsequently married Edward Grace shortly after he arrived in 1691 as the new minister of the congregational church in Clapham. He was only a few years older than her.

Not all husbands were keen that their widows should remarry or that, if they did so, they or their new husbands should continue to benefit from the estate. William Brooke senior was careful that the legacies to his wife applied only during her widowhood, and while he left her all his plate, this was reduced to a third of it if she married again, when she would also cease to be an executor of his will. Roger Hughes left a house to his wife, but only for one year after her widowhood ended if she should marry again. John Hanscomb, the builder, was even more explicit, and his legacies to his wife continued only 'provided she remained unmarried'. Even the godly and good Joseph Paice asked his executors to allow his 'dear and loving wife' to remain in his house after his death with use of all the contents, but only 'so long as she continue a widow'. Women could take the same position, and Susanna Cooke left her widowed daughter-in-law £8 a year 'while she remains a widow'.

It is often commented on that there were very few non-nuclear families in early modern England, but this was not so in Clapham. The evidence comes from a number of sources. In their wills, women often described themselves as 'of Clapham' but were not recorded as a ratepayer; legacies went explicitly to the people or servants with whom they were sharing a house; rate books showed occupiers over the years; and lists of Clapham subscribers to good causes included their names, sometimes specifically characterising them as lodgers. Many women continued living in Clapham as the head of household after they had been widowed, and it was relatively common for them to live with relations who were also widowed, such as Judith Gould and her two sisters. Equally, widows sometimes lived with their married children or with their married sisters or brothers, or even more distant relatives. Mary Wright, 'widow of Clapham', who made her will less than three months before she died, left forty shillings 'to be distributed in the family where I shall die'. She was related to two families in Clapham; her aunt was Ann Hughes and her cousin the daughter of the elder Edmund White. Mary's executor, Anthony Stephens, had married Ann Hughes' daughter, and they had moved into Ann's Clapham house with her only two years previously. Unmarried women often lived with their brothers-in-law, as Susan Marshall did with Thomas Langham or Grace Thomason with William Stonestreet. There are also cases of grandparents looking after grandchildren when both parents had died.

Family relationships

Of all the family and business connections within Clapham, the Daniel family's are the most extensive, and they are illustrated in Figure 5.

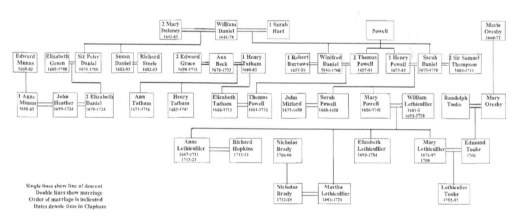

Figure 5. Daniel genealogy

Source: Parish registers and rate assessments

William Daniel moved to Clapham in 1641 and stayed there until his death in 1678. He was a beavermaker and possibly had dealings with James Sherley, who had sole rights on the beaver skins imported from the *Mayflower* community. Daniel went to the same City church (All Hallows Lombard Street) as three other Clapham residents.

He was one of eight Clapham residents who was Common Councilman for the Bridge Within ward, and one of three who paid a fine rather than become alderman for Farringdon Within.

One of Daniel's daughters by his first wife married a Clapham resident, Richard Burrows, who died shortly afterwards. She then married Thomas Powell, a good friend of his and brother of her sister's husband, Henry. Both Powell brothers had houses in Clapham. Henry was a factor for the East India Company at Kazimbar, and he, William Daniel and Daniel's son Peter all had extensive dealings in its shares, often acting together. Henry Powell's daughters both married Clapham merchants: Sarah married John Mitford and Mary William Lethieullier. Three of the latter couple's children had houses in Clapham for at least part of their married life. One of them married the grandson of another Clapham resident, and their son (a great-great-grandson of William Daniel) had a house in Clapham in the 1750s. Thomas Powell's son married the daughter of another Clapham resident, Henry Tatham senior.

It was William's second wife, Mary, who lived with him in Clapham. Their only son, Peter, did not live in Clapham himself but was the only merchant to carry out extensive development in the village. He built at least eight houses, one of which was lived in by his widow. He was unusual in that he was a Tory in a Whig family. His daughter married another Clapham merchant. One of William's daughters by Mary moved into the family house with her husband after Mary's death. The husband of another was made responsible by Henry Powell for the education of his son. All four brothers-in-law did business together. The family ties to Clapham can be judged by the fact that four of the surviving Daniel children lived in Clapham after their marriage, five of their grandchildren, and at least four of their great-grandchildren.

Marriage of children

Children were expected to gain their parent's approval for marriage, and this was of course essential if there were to be a marriage settlement or if the marriage were designed to strengthen commercial links. Thomas Lye, a widower, was concerned about leaving his two daughters without any advice on marriage, and required his younger daughter, Mary – who was still underage – to take the advice of her elder sister, Sarah, 'in all things especially as to the disposal of herself in marriage'. To be on the safe side, he appointed two more overseers to the will, requiring both daughters 'to observe [their] advice and counsel on their disposal of themselves in marriage'.

Wills often contained the constraint that legacies to daughters would be withdrawn if their marriage was not approved by the widowed mother or whoever was left as guardian, as in the court case involving Anne Corbett and John Arthur. Wills also withheld legacies because the son had already married without consent. Ann Warner left her son John the interest on £550 to be paid weekly; after his death, the capital was to go to the children, if any, that he might have by a second wife, because 'he had married without our consent and against our will and express command of his deceased father and myself'. However, even this income was withheld until he had children by a second wife, except for two shillings and sixpence a week for such clothes and other necessaries that her son-in-law Charles Perkins and Arthur Shallett (a neighbour and active Nonconformist) might deem convenient.

On the other hand, shortly before his death in Clapham, Samuel Pepys made a codicil to his will expressly withdrawing his generous legacy to his nephew Samuel Jackson:

> *whereas since the time of writing my will ... my nephew Samuel Jackson has thought it fit to dispose of himself in marriage against my positive advice and injunctions and to his irreparable prejudice and dishonour I do think myself obliged to express the resentments due to such an act of disrespect and imprudence and therefore I the said Samuel Pepys (in consideration whereof) do by these presents revoke retract and make null and void the said devise.*

A similar approach was taken by the apothecary James Whitchurch. He had left his daughter Sarah £1,800, payable when she came of age or married, but a few weeks after she married Hamon L'Estrange 'without the consent of me or her friends', her father added a codicil to his will. This withdrew the legacy and left it instead in trust to his brother with instructions to give her and then her children the money as he saw fit, but to ensure that her husband could not make use of it. Whitchurch was a strong Nonconformist and may have objected to his daughter marrying the nephew of Sir Roger L'Estrange, who, as Licenser of the Press, was responsible for rooting out Dissenting writing. Brothers, too, could take a firm line. Shallett's son Joseph bequeathed his sister Mary, whom he noted was of age, £310 'in case she does not marry Robert Cole or Thomas Summerhayes and in case she does I only give her one shilling'.

Samuel Crisp also restricted what he left to his eldest son, Pheasant, to his house in London and his farm in Merton, leaving the residue to his other sons. Pheasant had married 'without my knowledge or consent although her positively hardhearted father will not believe me', and Crisp ended his will by saying that he gives 'but little to my son Pheasant because God has greatly blessed him as to this world'.

Not all marriages went well or were accepted by the family, and one such involved Samuel, the son of John and Judith Gould. He had been left £2,500 and an eighth part of Rowlyes plantation in Barbados by his father in 1679, when he was only ten, but he must have lost it. According to his mother's will in 1704, he had gone to live in Barbados at some stage and had subsequently made the property over to her. Her will returned it to him with an addition bringing his share up to a seventh. She appointed trustees to spend £1,000 for the sole benefit of her son and his children on a 'house in a good street in London or on land within twenty miles of London'. It was to be settled solely on Samuel and with the benefit of 'counsel learned in the law' in accordance with written instructions that she had set out on 'a certain piece of paper under my hand and seal'. While she left him many books, including those that had belonged to his father, and a stone cabinet, she left him no money directly, in contrast to her other sons.

The problem seems to have got worse, since Thomas Joliffe's will in 1722 is much more explicit about his cousin Samuel Gould. It asked that his executors, his half-brother Sir William Joliffe and cousin Daniel Gould, by then a merchant in Livorno,

> *should be kind to my cousin Samuel Gould and that each*
> *of them would allow him five shillings per week only*
> *paying it into his own hand for the term of his natural*
> *life, my meaning is that it should not be paid to his wife*
> *or children nor to any other person besides himself well*
> *knowing what his wife was before he married her.*

Daniel Gould's will in 1732 makes no mention of his elder brother, but does leave the residue of his estate to two of Samuel's children. Samuel had married a Catherine Hicks in Plymouth, where his family came from originally, and two of his children were buried in Clapham, but records do not allow us to look behind this story to understand what actually happened.

Some wills suggest that relations within families were not always perfect. Elizabeth Fulker, the widow of the Clapham smith and innkeeper, wrote in her will 'and lastly I do exhort all my [five] children to live in love and unity one with another', a request that is surely unlikely to have been made unless necessary. John Sole, a yeoman who died in 1650, requested that his wife should continue to live with his son after his death 'so long as they can lovingly agree together', but prudently made explicit provision for the division of the property if they could not.

Some testators also envisaged there being arguments over legacies. Penelope Blake left her daughter her gold striking watch and gold chain and all the trinkets with a diamond hood belonging to it on condition that she give her brother the gold watch and chain that she already had; if she should refuse to do so, her brother should have the striking watch and the other things belonging to it, but not the hood. This was in 1715, when watches were still luxury items and much sought after.

On the other hand, Joseph Paice wrote in his will:

> It is my dying request that my sons Joseph and Nathaniel
> do continue in their present partnership as long as
> they live and that my grandson Joseph may be brought
> up under them in the same business and they take all
> necessary care to continue the business in the family as
> long as there is a male in it unless they shall see it to be
> more all their interests and good to do otherwise.

This did indeed happen and, although Joseph the son died fairly young, the grandson continued the business and gave early employment to the essayist Charles Lamb. Paice also asked his sons to preserve his journal and accounts in order to instruct future members of the family business. He explained: 'I have kept [them] from the first day of my beginning to trade to this day and shall continue to do until the last with the greatest care and exactness possible in the true Italian method.'

Another such example was Susanna Lillington, who took the opportunity of her will to thank her daughter for looking after her and her husband, who had died not long before. She wrote: 'And also to my dear daughter Caswell for her great love tender regard and dutiful affection which she has always shown to her father and myself in all our long sicknesses and infirmities.'

Relations with children

Legacies to children were relatively straightforward, although stepchildren were not usually included because they would have legacies from their natural father. The Court of Orphans oversaw the estates of freemen of the City of London who died intestate or leaving children underage. The Orphans' funds were increasingly deposited with the Chamberlain of the City, so providing a very useful source of ready money for the City Corporation. The temptation to use them proved irresistible, but the City did not arrange any segregation, and so in the mid-1690s it was found that there was no longer sufficient funds to pay the orphans what they were owed. Although the accounts were eventually restructured, much of the money was lost to those who should have received it. This lay behind Thomas Manning's comment in his will of 1707: 'I do request that my said executors would not interest any part of my estate in the Chamber of the City of London by whom the poor orphans have heretofore been greatly oppressed.'

Many of the financial transfers to children effectively took place while the father was still alive, whether as a marriage portion for a daughter or paying for the son to take up an apprenticeship or to finance his starting in business. A number of testators went to great pains to explain in their will what they had done for their various children, to avoid their distribution being overturned by the Court. Henry Powell said: 'the large wedding portions that I have provided for my daughters Sarah Mitford and Mary Lethieullier are to be in full satisfaction and discharge of what they may or might claim or pretend to out of my estate by the Customs of the City or otherwise.' Thomas Tanner wrote in 1710:

I do declare that I have fully advanced all my children except my son Thomas by several sums of money by me heretofore given unto them which amounts to more than their proportions out of my personal estate and therefore I dispose of the estate I now have as follows.

Some went further. Henry Tatham threatened that the legacies would be made void if the children sought to contest the will at the Court of Orphans. A similar approach was adopted by John Mitford, Henry Markinfield, Hugh Bellamy and Sutton Sharp. Sharp spent his last years living in Clapham near his daughter Sarah and her husband, Humphrey Bell. Sharp appears to have thought that his son might challenge the will, since he added a codicil two years later stating clearly that his legacy to his son was 'in full satisfaction of all claims and demands that my said son William may make or pretend to have ... by virtue of the Custom of the City of London or otherwise'. Quite a lot was at stake, since among other things Sharp owned an estate 'in Grub Street called Hanover Square', which was just then being rebuilt as a fashionable area.

Even after the role of the Court of Orphans had been virtually removed, testators continued to try to prevent law cases, and William Lethieullier made it clear that 'if any of his said children or the husbands of the said daughters shall at any time bring any action or commence any suit or otherwise disturb my executrix ... in the execution of this my will', all their legacies were to be made null and void and shared between the others.

However, the most dramatic complaint about authority is found in the will of Daniel Gould, albeit about lawyers generally:

I have been during the course of my whole life an enemy to law suits that what little I leave may not be squandered away on the Gentlemen of the long Robe for whom all the veneration I have is at a distance wishing there was more justice and less law in the world as also that my executor may not be troubled or molested in the execution hereof my will and pleasure is that my said residuary legatees be obliged to stand to the accounts he shall give.

Devices had to be used if real property were to be left to a married daughter, since it was otherwise automatically controlled by her husband. One way was to create a trust managed by a friend in favour of the married daughter. Mary Daniel made it clear that the trustee she named in her will, Thomas Langham, was to act 'without any intermeddling of her [daughter's] husband'. Elizabeth Babington made the same restriction in leaving money to her daughter Elizabeth Cooke. Despite making her son-in-law John Cooke her executor and residual legatee, her will included, on more than one occasion, a rubric of the kind:

> To the intent and purpose that neither the said John
> Cooke ... or any husband which my said daughter
> shall or may herself have or take in any manner or wise
> intermeddle in all or any part of the aforesaid sum of
> one thousand pounds or of the gains interest or profits or
> proceeds thereof.

In some cases it was the widow's children who were warned off, and Philip Tilbury left the residue of his estate to his wife 'for her own proper use to have and to hold till the time of her demise without any let or molestation from any of my surviving children or any other person whatsoever'.

Another example concerned Elizabeth Fowke, who was sued by her grandchildren for not passing on the legacies of property specified in her husband's will. She argued successfully up to the House of Lords that because none of her own children were living at the time of her husband's death, different rules of the Custom of the City applied. In particular, the grandchildren were not automatically guaranteed all that would have gone to the children, and she was entitled to more than the standard third.[12]

Contrary to some suggestions, grandchildren were regularly mentioned in wills.[13] Indeed, given that many merchants married in their late twenties and their daughters married at eighteen, it was quite possible to be a grandparent before fifty, an age that was commonly reached by those who had survived to adulthood. William Daniel and Rebecca Atkins even gave legacies to great-grandchildren. Not all references to grandchildren were good, however. Mary Wilson discovered that her grandson Tobias Crisp had opened and read her will, 'contrary to modesty and ingenuity', and as a result she revoked 'my legacy to him of part of a pearl necklace and [gave] his part to my daughter'.

Many men died while their children were still young, and this caused some to give their spouses guidance for their education. This was mostly the concern of the dedicated Puritan, who expected them to be brought up in the fear of God, without extravagance and expecting to work for their living. As perhaps might be expected, such sentiments were strongest during the Cromwellian period, and – at least on the limited evidence available for Clapham residents – the strictures became weaker later in the century. Daniel Taylor was chiefly concerned in 1655 that his children were instructed to wear 'plain apparel' and forbidden to wear gaudy clothes or learn dancing. His daughters were not to be placed in boarding schools, which had previously catered for young gentlewomen. Charles Harvey in 1672 asked that his children 'be brought up in virtuous education true religion and the fear of God'; John Gould in 1679 asked that they be 'well educated and be brought up with as much thrift as may be unwilling that any one should have a maintenance above forty pounds per annum'; while Henry Tatham in 1682 required that his son 'be maintained educated and brought up soberly in the fear and dread of the Almighty God'.

As far as work was concerned, Taylor made clear that his son was to be brought up as a merchant or 'in some other honest calling so that he might not live like a drone but be serviceable to his God and country', while Harvey said that 'my said son Charles Harvey [should] be put either to one of the Universities or to some laudable trade or calling which shall best suit his Genius.' This care could extend to grandchildren. William Molins left £100 to one of his grandsons, also William, to be delivered to him after he had started his apprenticeship 'in some good trade'. However, possibly not trusting his widowed daughter-in-law, he desired that 'the child may have breeding and education from his grandmother until he be of age to be put apprentice.'

A more unusual bequest, specifying work for a married daughter, is that of Mary Foster, who was not a poor widow and whose husband had described himself as a 'Gent' in his will. She left her daughter, who was widowed with three small children, £30, but on condition that

> *she learn the art of a midwife with the sum to be*
> *administered by her executor to pay the midwife*
> *instructing her and for her maintenance but if she*
> *neglects or declines learning said art of a midwife within*
> *the terms of two years of my decease she wholly omitting*
> *and not fully endeavouring to be instructed therein she ...*
> *shall forfeit all her claims to the said thirty pounds,*

which would then pass with the rest of her estate to her grandchildren.

Henry Powell changed his will after his wife, Sarah, appointed James Hussey as her chaplain. Hussey was a virulently anti-Catholic Nonconformist, and his approach was apparently unattractive to Powell. The latter had appointed his 'loving wife' and his brother-in-law William Meade joint executors, including custody of his son. A few days after he had written his will, in December 1681, however, he added a codicil, which – while it left Sarah joint executor for all the financial part of the will – gave Meade sole control of the more religious aspects, including both his funeral and the bringing up of his son. Thus:

> *I hereby order will and appoint that my said executor*
> *William Meade shall have the sole care tuition and*
> *government of my sonne John Powell ... until he shall*
> *have attained his full age of one and twenty years to*
> *the intent that he my said sonne may ... be maintained*
> *educated and brought up soberly in the feare and dread*
> *of the Almighty God until the accomplishment of his said*
> *age of one and twenty years in such manner and by such*
> *persons as in and by the judgement and discretion of my*
> *executor William Mead shall from time to time be thought*
> *most fitting and convenient for that end and purpose.*

This provision was not successful, however: Henry Sampson tells this story in his day book of 1693, the only example we have of riotous behaviour in Clapham during this period:

> *My wife tells me from Clapham of a great debauchee who*
> *when young lived there, the son of India Powell as he was*
> *called and he has forsaken his mother's family (viz my Lady*
> *Thompson) for the greater opportunity of lewdness. He*
> *is much at a Parkkeepers, who has sold his wife to young*
> *Powell to be at his command and pleasure for a guinea,*

*she had a brother a fit blousing companion for him, who
last New Year's day morning (having sat up all night) was
very sick and had like to have dropped away and died. But
recovering himself a little, 'Give me another glass,' said
he 'The dival had like to have had a New Year's gift this
morning but he has missed it'. But no sooner had he drunk
his glass but he sank down and died. These are the effects
of profuse drinking, and profane jesting, yet all this has no
effect upon this young man and thereof he is likely sooner
to come to poverty than to repentance with word. Nay he
would not be warned tho one should rise from the dead.
That might affright rather than convert him.*[14]

One can speculate whether the unmarried Henry Tatham, the
posthumous son of the senior Henry Tatham, had indulged in the
same way. His will left his estate to 'the young gentlewoman who
lives with me who is commonly called or known by the name of Mrs
Mary Tatham whom I have bred up from her infancy.'

Wills and other material show that responsibility was felt for the
wider family. Many wills wrote off loans to nephews or grandchildren;
unmarried daughters and widowed mothers or mothers-in-law
were taken into the family house; nephews or cousins were given
apprenticeships. Thomas Rodbard senior's will attempted to ensure
that his nephew remained working in the cheesemonger's shop with
his son by giving him a third of the profits. Michael Mitford also took
his responsibilities to both friends and relations seriously. One of his
letters records that he had assisted the husband of Sarah Goldfinch

*with money and clothes. He came from France without
either and is now endeavouring by the first opportunity
to come for Dantzig. He is pretty well recovered of his
health and was with me the other day at Clapham.*[15]

Another letter records that Mitford had willingly given 'his best
advice' to a young man recommended by his mother.[16] And one, to
his kinsman Sir John Delaval, who had been an MP at the same time
as Mitford, reported apparent neglect of the children of another
Michael Mitford, and sought Delaval's intervention with the child's
grandfather:

But such was my affections and tenderness to his children when
I found two of them (Michael and Ralph) in such a deplorable

condition that they had not six pence to buy them a dinner and I may be bold to say if I had not taken care of them they must of necessity have taken ill ... All that I desire is he'll [the grandfather] in a special manner take care of the education of his grandchild and my godson Michael Mitford[;] pray press him to promise it to you[,] for although the father might have offended him yet the innocent child is in noe ways to blame.[17]

Mitford looked after his niece Mary Harrison while she was at school in London, an establishment that was presumably thought better for her than the schools in Newcastle, where her parents lived and where her stepfather did business with Mitford. She started at a school in Kensington, where she was a half boarder, but then moved 'for some reason best known to my wife and Mary' to be a full boarder with a Madam Mountfort at Stepney.[18] This was more expensive, and Mitford wrote to his sister:

Your daughter Mary has removed to school at Stepney for some reason that my wife had that she should not be continued at Kensington. I now pay £20 a year for her diet besides all other extraordinaries. ... Her Aunt hath already had £45-2-6 of me since she came to London and makes Mally keep an account of every particular thing thats laid out for her, for if that were not done she might forget hereafter her uncle and aunt if she did not keep an account herself of every penny. But she is a very good girl and I hope will answer expectation.[19]

The final problem was how to continue the family name if there were no children. When Mitford died childless he left £4,000 in his will to purchase an estate in 'some northern county within sixty miles of Newcastle on Tyne where I was borne' that would bring £200 a year, and promised it to his niece Mary (or another of his nieces) if she married 'any person who by his family shall be a gentleman and of the name of Mitford or Midford', and also specified that her first son by such marriage should be called Michael. As we have seen, his widow was less keen on this and challenged the will. Mitford was not the only person who sought to continue his name in this way. William Hewer, who was unmarried, left his estate, reported in the newspaper as worth over £100,000, to his nephew Hewer Edgely on condition that he take the surname Hewer. This he did, becoming Hewer Edgely Hewer.[20]

Conclusion

Family was an important influence on the seventeenth-century merchant. It was the source of advice, even control, but could also provide access to funds and a network of people who could be trusted. While marriage increasingly allowed for the wishes of the couple, it was often used to reinforce commercial relationships, and the financial negotiations over portions and settlements could be hard fought. Legacies might be withheld if children married against the wishes of their parents, but there was an expectation that family would help orphaned children or those in difficulties. In all this, Nonconformist families were not radically different from other merchants, apart from an emphasis on finding a godly spouse and marrying children of Nonconformist ministers. As for rich merchants generally, there was a strong preference for marrying into other merchant families. Clapham provided a good marriage market for these, and many widows remarried there, although they and unmarried daughters or sisters often lived with other members of their family.

(Endnotes)

1. Richard Grassby, *Kinship and Capitalism* (Cambridge University Press, 2001); Peter Earle, *The Making of the English Middle Class* (Methuen, 1989); Lawrence Stone, *The Family, Sex and Marriage 1500–1800* (Harper and Row, 1977).

2. See http://freepages.genealogy.rootsweb.ancestry.com/~shakespeare/pedigrees/london/stepney/stepney_book.htm.

3. Anne Manning, *Family Pictures* (Arthur Hall, Virtue and Co., 1861), p. 8.

4. Arthur v Gillow and Rolfe, 1670, Arches A 8 2, Eee 4 ff. 253–54, 257–58, Lambeth Palace Library (and subsequent quotations).

5. Earle, *The Making of the English Middle Class*, p. 179.

6. Samuel Pepys, diary, 1 February 1667.

7. Richard Grassby, *The Business Community of Seventeenth-Century England* (Cambridge University Press, 1995), p. 303.

8. This and subsequent quotations from John Arthur, letter to Robert Doughty, 6 July 1655. Norfolk Record Office, AYL 535/4/9.

9. Chancery Reg. Lib., B 1707, fol. 352.

10. Grassby, *The Business Community*, pp. 59–63.

11. *Newdigate Newsletter*, 19 October 1704, quoted in Stuart Handley, 'Sir Owen Buckingham', History of Parliament online, www.historyofparliamentonline.org.

12. *Journal of the House of Lords*, vol. 16 (January 1697), p. 82.

13. Earle, *The Making of the English Middle Class*, p. 316.

14. Dr Henry Sampson, day book, British Library, Add Ms 4460.

15. Michael Mitford, letter to Mallabar and Lowther, 6 March 1705, Michael Mitford letterbook, London Metropolitan Archives.

16. Mitford, letter to his cousin Fell, 6 April 1704, ibid.

17. Mitford, letter to Sir John Delaval, 1 August 1704, ibid.

18. Mitford, letter to his mother, 30 May 1704; to his sister Webster, 27 July 1704, ibid.

19. Mitford, letter to his sister Webster, 1 August 1704, ibid.

20. *Daily Courant*, 7 December 1715.

CHAPTER 12

THE FUTURE OF CLAPHAM

W e leave Clapham in 1720 as a village of about 180 houses, over a third of which amounted to what Daniel Defoe described in 1724 as 'an innumerable number' of fine houses. Most of these were occupied by Whig Nonconformists, usually merchants or their widows but with an increasing number of bankers and lawyers. However strong their Nonconformism, they still supported the parish church, subscribing to the collections for additional lecturers who preached regularly, and to the various collections for the church silver or other improvements. This was in addition to maintaining the resident minister and assistant of the Clapham Nonconformist chapel, built when Judith Gould's death meant they no longer met in her house.

At first sight, it might appear that Nonconformism was an important factor in deciding who moved to Clapham, since a newcomer would know that he (or she) would be able to find the services and religious support he wanted, without encountering undue problems with the authorities. On the other hand, there were plenty of other villages with Puritan or, later, Nonconformist communities: Hackney and Stoke Newington, for example, were four or five times larger than Clapham. Clapham was the only village with a ready supply of retiring houses south of the river, and people needed a special reason to go there rather than to the more usual villages north and east of London.

While the vast majority of residents after 1660 were indeed Nonconformist, very few merchants moved to Clapham without having good contacts there already, whether family or business or both. Given the geographical convenience, these contacts were the determining factor in encouraging businessmen to move to Clapham. Coupled with the tendency to marry within the Nonconformist community and for Nonconformists to do business together, this had the effect of sustaining the village as a centre for Nonconformists. Two examples from slightly different periods illustrate this.

John Doggett had married Alice, who lived in Clapham in the 1630s with her father, John Beauchamp, a financier of the *Mayflower*. Doggett moved into the house of Robert Whitlock, a fellow Baltic trader, and did business in North America with the son-in-law of another neighbour, Edmund White junior. Doggett and White were both strong Puritans and later Nonconformists, and both paid a fine to avoid the post of churchwarden in 1671. Doggett also paid a fine to avoid taking the oath as alderman, while White was an active supporter of the missionary activities in New England. Doggett's daughters married merchants from the Dutch Reformed Church, Austin Friars, and both those men became elders of the church. Alice married David DeBarry and subsequently lived in Clapham. DeBarry had worked in Hamburg, where Doggett was born, and also did business with the Nonconformist merchant and Clapham resident Arthur Shallett. Elizabeth married Justus Otgher, who had started his business based in Doggett's London house. His brother Abraham was a witness to Doggett's will ten years before he too moved to Clapham.

Michael Mitford also had many contacts in Clapham before moving there. His cousin John Mitford had married a granddaughter of William Daniel and had a house there for twenty years; Mitford chose his cousin's son-in-law, the Goldsmith and banker George Mertins, as overseer of his will. Mitford moved into his cousin's house in 1701. Its availability might well have been reason enough for him to come to Clapham, but it would have been strengthened by the fact that Arthur Shallett, his friend and fellow coal trader from Newcastle, had already lived there for five years and his business associate Urban Hall for twelve years. His wife was cousin to the Otghers and DeBarrys; a lot of his financial arrangements were routed through an Amsterdam member of the Otgher family; and another Otgher was his apprentice. Other Clapham residents trading with Russia and the Baltic were Urban Hall, Peter Costin and Dormer

Sheppard, as well as John Cooke, who was also a long-time Assistant in the Court of the Russia Company. All this points to strong links to the village, making it a natural place for Mitford to look for a country place; he played his part in local affairs by being churchwarden in 1705 and 1706, but he had two Nonconformists as witnesses to his will, including the minister Edward Grace.

Although contacts were the determining factor for merchants moving to Clapham, this was not so true for the Nonconformist ministers. They naturally wanted a base from which they could fulfil their ministry, and ideally a means for providing their living. Clapham provided this, both by having a permanent minister and assistant and by providing positions as resident chaplain, for example in the households of Susan Powell and Judith Gould. Many of them preached at other Nonconformist chapels in London, and William Hughes was chaplain to St Thomas' Hospital. In addition, Clapham had a number of schools, which provided further employment as well as the opportunity to influence the young. Thomas Lye was a well-known educator and had thirty children living in his house; John Locke chose a Clapham school to educate the future third Earl of Shaftesbury; Thomas Doolittle, another Nonconformist minister and teacher, was in Clapham from 1683 to 1687, dispersing his pupils into a number of private houses there, after he was ejected from Islington, Wimbledon and then Battersea. Finally, two Nonconformist ministers who had become doctors, Henry Sampson and John Hutchinson, lived and practised in Clapham. This demonstrates that the village was indeed welcoming of Nonconformists and a place where they could live their lives relatively unimpeded.

None of this would have been enough, however, unless Clapham had been an attractive and convenient place to live. It was near enough to the City, at least for those working near London Bridge, for merchants and other businessmen to ride in every day if they wished, although the state of the roads was still complained about a hundred years later and there was always the danger of highwaymen. There were sufficient large houses to provide ample choice for short or long leases, including all necessary facilities such as stables, fish ponds, orchards and, increasingly, gardens. As Map 6 shows (see Chapter 6), most of the houses were well placed on a street away from the traffic of the two main roads. By the eighteenth century the village provided good facilities, including a livery stable, at least four inns and a coffee house, and good local company. The advertisement below, from 1728, demonstrates the range of social life there.

A fine Concert of MUSICK
Performed by Opera Hands at Clapham

A Mile behind Vauxhall at Mr Hanscomb's great House
Tomorrow the 10th Instant, at Five shillings a Ticket,
Concluding with a Ball. To begin at Six o'Clock

Most importantly, it was recognised as a healthy place to live, having good air, pure water and good views over to Hampstead. It was not just Samuel Pepys and his correspondents who commented on the air; two newspapers carried a sad story in the summer of 1722 that one Mr Partridge, 'a noted Brasier from Gracechurch Street[,] died in the necessary house of Mrs Hallam, where he had taken lodgings for the air'.[1] Defoe's description shows that Clapham's popularity was well established by the early 1720s, and a few years later the authors of *Magna Britannica* described Clapham as 'A pleasant village situate upon rising ground, full of good houses inhabited by rich gentlemen, and great merchants.'[2] This continued to be the case, and regular stagecoaches provided convenient transport between the village and the City.

It is perhaps difficult to imagine the views now, but we can get some idea from a print from 1795, drawn from a point a few hundred yards west of Clapham Common and giving a view of Chelsea and Battersea (see Illustration 19). The church of St Mary's, Battersea, rebuilt in 1776, and the nearby Fowlers' windmill, built in 1788, are shown at the right of the picture, with Chelsea on the opposite side of the river and the hills of Hampstead and Highgate behind. (The picture also shows the old Battersea Bridge, built in 1771, and, on the other side of the river, Old Chelsea Church, the cupola of which was removed as recently as 1815.)[3]

Illustration 19. J. Farington, *A View of Chelsea and Battersea from East Wandsworth*, 1795

There is a gap in the rate books between 1718 and 1745, with only one year (1733) extant, and so the same detailed analysis as in the rest of the book cannot be continued for that period. Nevertheless, some at least of the prominent families continued well into the second half of the century. The successful Nonconformist banker Abraham Atkins was succeeded by his son, who created a large trust in support of Baptist chapels, while Joseph Paice was succeeded by his son and grandson of the same name, the last of whom was renowned for his charity. Nathaniel Neal was a prominent Nonconformist layman. The other banking families also remained: the Hankeys were in Clapham for another hundred years, and Thomas Martin until his death in 1765; Henry Hoare built a house there in 1753, as did many other bankers, including four directors of the Bank of England. Rich Huguenots continued to live in Clapham, including members of the Dobree, de Visme, Loubier and Longuet families.

In Chapters 7 and 8 we saw that many Clapham merchants were members of the Russia Company, which covered trade with the Baltic from the ports of Newcastle and Hull. This continued for some long time, and may well have been an element in Henry Thornton's grandfather Robert moving to Clapham, although he may also have been attracted by the presence of three fellow directors of the Bank of

England or by his Hull colleague, a Mr Raikes, having a house there. Robert appears in the parish register for the first time in the mid-1730s and was the first of many Thorntons there; his brother Godfrey moved to Clapham in 1744; his son John and two daughters lived there after their marriages; and at least six grandchildren continued the tradition.

Clapham grew only slowly during the first half of the eighteenth century, and the construction of Westminster Bridge in 1750 with improved links to the West End had little effect on that growth. The composition of the village remained the same, with approximately one third of the houses occupied by the affluent, but there appears to have been a change in the approach to religion. Although there were undoubtedly some staunch Nonconformists, and the churches and chapels were well attended, the village as a whole seems to have lost any fervour, in keeping with the national trend. This is illustrated by the character of the priests and ministers in Clapham at that time.

The Nonconformist minister Moses Lowman, resident from 1710 until 1752, was later described as a poor preacher with the observation that 'His piety was rational, not superstitious; the effect of principle not enthusiasm.'[4] He was succeeded by Philip Furneaux, who had been viewed as heretical when attending his theological training and was described as 'not fully sensible of the importance of evangelical doctrine, and did not bring it forward with the frequency and fullness that the Gospel demands.'[5] His preaching, too, was criticised as having a disagreeable whine 'which would have disgraced a Scotch seceder'.[6] Nevertheless, Furneaux was among the most highly regarded figures within English Nonconformity, and played an important part in securing the decision by the House of Lords stopping the fining of Dissenters for declining offices in the City of London, a scheme the Corporation had designed to secure the funding for building the Mansion House.[7]

With one exception, the Anglicans were no different. The rector succeeding Nicholas Brady was Anthony Blackwall, a schoolmaster at Market Bosworth and tutor to one of the Atkins family. He was in his sixties and had to be ordained to become rector, being succeeded shortly afterwards by John Goodwin (then vicar of Market Bosworth), who had married Dame Rebecca Atkins' granddaughter. He was succeeded in turn by Sir John Stonhouse, brother-in-law of Dame Rebecca's great-grandson and an absentee rector for forty years. Clapham had to make do with curates or lecturers during that time.

The one Anglican priest who was different was Henry Venn, who was appointed curate to run the parish when Stonhouse became absentee rector in 1753. Venn was an early evangelical, having experienced his conversion after ordination and only a year or two before moving to Clapham. Evangelical conversion was based on recognition of the total depravity of mankind, and that eternal damnation was avoidable only through utter repentance and absolute trust in Christ as atonement for those sins.[8] After experiencing conversion, believers embraced a vital, emotional and passionate Christianity that they expressed fully in every part of their lives. Worldly pleasures were shunned, seriousness was a virtue to be cultivated, and good works were evidence of their conversion.

Not many in Clapham in the middle of the eighteenth century were ready for this. After one sermon, a woman took Venn's wife aside and asked her 'to repress the disgusting earnestness of her husband'.[9] For his part, Venn described the village as 'where many London merchants having acquired fortunes, chose their country seats, desiring in general, only to enjoy themselves ... and the doctrine of the Gospel preached with zeal and boldness was very offensive to them.' Venn finally left in 1759, 'grieved at the obstinate rejection of the gospel during five years by almost all the rich (and there were but few poor in the place)'. The parish took no risks with his successor and appointed as lecturer John Acton, the rector of Walton-on-the-Hill fifteen miles away. He continued to live there, although he finally took a house in Clapham for the last year of his appointment.

Not long after Venn left Clapham, the parish took steps to prevent another Nonconformist place of worship being created there, was was reported in a pamphlet by the pastor of the Congregational church at Shad Thames in Bermondsey.[10] He was asked to come back to Clapham to preach, and had converted a stable for that purpose, but his second sermon there was forcibly broken up. Attempts to get a warrant to prevent this happening again failed, largely because the banker Sir Thomas Hankey was the instigator, and another service was violently disrupted by rioters claiming, 'we fear nobody. We are employed by a gentleman on the other side of the common, and he will stand by us.'[11]

By the second half of the century Clapham was no longer known for its Nonconformity, although there was a thriving Nonconformist congregation whose move to new and larger premises in 1762 was overseen by Furneaux. The congregation was described by the *Gentleman's Magazine* as 'one of the most opulent and considerable among the protestant dissenters'.[12] Equally, after Venn's departure, Clapham's parish church no longer provided a centre for evangelicals. This was despite the efforts of John Thornton, Henry Thornton's father, who had undergone conversion at about the same time as Venn and remained an active evangelical for the rest of his life, giving enormous sums of money to the cause as well as to a range of charities.

We can observe the lack of evangelical enthusiasm in Clapham in the journal of John Thornton for two separate years, 1768 and 1779.[13] Among other things, they record his reflections on many of the evangelical sermons he heard, which concentrate on preachers away from Clapham. These include the famous George Whitfield in Tottenham Court Road and William Romaine near Blackfriars, as well as two incumbents whom he had appointed himself, Roger Bentley at Camberwell and his son-in-law Richard Conyers at Deptford. He used to hear all these men in their churches, going by carriage after dinner on Sunday afternoon. During the whole of 1768, he mentions only one name that could possibly have been at Clapham, a Mr Wise, although his position is not clear as he does not appear in any records. When John Acton came to Thornton to resign his position as lecturer, he made clear that 'many of the gentlemen disliked Mr Wise very much,' and Thornton's diary records that he decided 'to decline the lectureship to Mr Wise'.[14] Lecturers were usually appointed by decision of the congregation as a whole, or at least a substantial part of it, and Thornton clearly thought better of pushing unsuccessfully for an evangelical. This may have been one element in his purchasing the advowson for Clapham that would allow him (or his heirs) sole discretion on the eventual appointment of the rector in succession to Stonhouse.

The opening of Blackfriars Bridge in 1769 allowed convenient access to Clapham from more of the City and produced a slow and steady increase in houses in the village. By then it was already known as a home for businessmen, as shown by a satirical cartoon published in 1771 (see Illustration 20).[15]

A COMMON COUNCIL MAN of CANDLESTICK WARD, and his WIFE on a visit to M.ʳ DEPUTY at his Modern Built Villa near CLAPHAM

Illustration 20. *A Common Councilman of Candlestick ward and his wife on a visit to Mr Deputy at his new built house near Clapham*, 1771
Courtesy of the Lewis Walpole Library, Yale University

Clapham grew more rapidly after the Common was drained and beautified by public subscription in 1772 and, just as importantly, the highwaymen between Clapham and the City came under greater control.[16] The houses in Clapham had originally clustered around the medieval church, which was some distance from the then untamed Common. However, the original church became too small and in 1776 over sixty trustees and subscribers secured an Act of Parliament enabling them to build a new, larger church on Clapham Common itself. These supporters included John Thornton and such prominent Nonconformists as Abraham Atkins and the Russia merchant James Brogden, who had both supported the building of the larger Nonconformist chapel fifteen years before. The presence of the new church encouraged further new houses, enlarging the village by at least a third again. By the beginning of the nineteenth century, there were seventy-five houses around the Common, spreading to the west side, where Henry Thornton had bought his house. It, like Wilberforce's house next door, was actually in the neighbouring parish of Battersea.

The demand for this expansion was not driven by Nonconformist or evangelical faith. As before, the businessmen came because Clapham was convenient, with good air and water, and they already had contacts there, whether merchant, banking or family. Sir Richard Colt Hoare explained that his banker grandfather had built a house in Clapham 'that he might be enabled, with greater convenience, to attend to business in London, without being obliged to sleep within its smoky atmosphere'.[17] Daniel Defoe's comments on Clapham in 1724, that 'this glorious show of wealth and plenty is really a view of the luxuriant age which we live in, and of the overflowing riches of the citizens', still applied.[18] As the religious zeal of the inhabitants declined, it is hardly surprising that this was also true of the friends and contacts who followed them there.

Some have argued that Clapham at the end of the eighteenth century was the first 'modern' suburb,[19] reflecting the evangelical view that 'God made the country and man made the town', an idea expressed by William Cowper but that went back to ancient Rome.[20] On this basis, the detached but interconnected houses around the Common allowed Henry Thornton to attract first William Wilberforce and then others to live, together with their families, away from the iniquities of the city and to establish a base from which they could exercise their influence more widely and to great effect. Lampooned in their own time as the 'Clapham Saints', they acquired the label 'Clapham Sect' only later in the nineteenth century, following an article by the civil servant Sir James Stephen, the son of one of the members.[21]

Evangelical thinking certainly lay behind Henry Thornton, Wilberforce and their friends living together in Clapham in what Thornton called his 'chummery',[22] and he had great intentions for it, writing later in his diary: 'God grant that Clapham may more and more become the theatre on which elevated piety is exhibited without affectation and without extravagance.'[23] However, those members of the Clapham Sect who lived in Clapham (and not all did) were only a small proportion of the affluent residents, and evangelical thinking was far from universal there. While the large majority of the affluent went to church and/or chapel regularly, and provided financial support when it was needed, their opinions were exactly those that Wilberforce objected to when he wrote

*It seems in our days to be the commonly received
opinion, that provided a man admit in general terms
the truth of Christianity, though he neither know of nor
consider much concerning the particulars of the system;
and if be not habitually guilty of any of the vices against
his fellow creatures, we have no great reason to be
dissatisfied with him, or to question the validity of his
claim to the name and privileges of a Christian.*[24]

When Stonhouse died, John Thornton's will required the appointment of an evangelical rector, and John Venn, the son of Henry, took up the post in 1792. He had been in two minds about accepting, and described in a letter his worries about the consequences of having 'to direct those whose pride and wealth renders them jealous of religious authority; to dwell amongst some of the most determined enemies of Christ and the Church of England'.[25] He knew that the large congregation was hostile to his evangelical approach, and told old friends that his initial sermons were cautious as a result. Although he recognised that the rich Clapham residents were exemplary as far as the 'outside of religion' was concerned, he told a friend, 'alas here they rest, and I fear that it will be very hard to convince them that the power of religion must be felt in the heart, as well as the form of it kept up in their lives.'[26]

Evangelicals disapproved of the indulgent ways some parishioners spent their time. John Venn wrote an address to the inhabitants of Clapham urging them to set an example to 'the lower orders' by avoiding such 'improper pursuits' on the Sabbath as 'travelling, visiting, diversions, reading secular books, writing letters or settling accounts'.[27] Dancing, theatres, cards and novels were of course eschewed on any day.[28] One young man, a minister's son from Scotland and future Lord Chancellor, was profoundly unsatisfied by the very liberal and unserious world of the West Indies merchants in Clapham, where he was acting as a tutor. He found it 'very irksome and it became more and more unbearable ... The company frequenting the house consisted chiefly of West India merchants and East India captains, and the conversation turned on the price of sugars, the rate of freights, and the trifling gossip of the day.'[29]

The more liberal reciprocated this disapproval, seeing religious enthusiasm as naturally leading to Jacobinism and the French

Revolution. Members of a card club that met in a local inn on Sunday evenings objected to Venn starting a Sunday evening lecture in the church, seeing it as likely 'to spread amongst the lowest orders of society a factious, zealous spirit'.[30] In this case the vestry accepted the proposal, but only after a three-hour meeting from which Venn had absented himself.

In some cases there was a much wider divergence of opinion, since not everyone shared the Sect's views on the slave trade; George Hibbert, a leader of the later Parliamentary opposition to Wilberforce, lived close by in Clapham; William Vassall, who owned plantations in Jamaica and had been expelled from Boston after American Independence, lived virtually next door to Wilberforce for five years. His letters contain many references to Wilberforce's attempts to ban the slave trade, and he continually assured his correspondents in the 1790s that 'Most people that I converse with think that the trade will not be abolished.'[31] At an early stage, however, he gave instructions 'to buy more negroes now' as a precaution.[32]

Despite the Clapham Sect, the late eighteenth-century village as a whole was not evangelical, nor did the vast majority of the affluent population come there for reasons associated with religion.[33] Clapham had also changed radically since the early part of the seventeenth century. Then, there was a high proportion of merchant's houses, and as late as 1750 Henry Venn claimed that there were few poor there. By the end of the century the population had more than trebled and was much more mixed; John Venn commented that 'the poor are numerous here and extremely dissolute.'[34]

Late eighteenth-century Clapham does not correspond to an idealised first suburb peopled solely or chiefly by the religious affluent, living their lives in the purity of the country. That may have been true for the Clapham Sect themselves, but they were a small proportion of the population of the village. Many of those other residents who were sympathetic to their political ends, such as William Smith and the two Robert Barclays, were in fundamental disagreement with their religious views.

By the end of the eighteenth century the new bridges across the Thames had made Clapham more accessible to many in the City of London, and increased population and wealth meant that more could afford a retiring house there. The village grew and correspondingly became less homogeneous. While the pattern was still for people to look for a retiring house in places with good air and water, the choice of village was, as it always had been, determined by family or business connections. In the 1630s this meant Puritan merchants, and from 1660 to 1720 Nonconformist merchants, but the religious element became less important in the second half of the eighteenth century and there was a greater diversity of both religious belief and income.

Those identifying eighteenth-century Clapham as the first modern London suburb focus on that small part lived in by Henry Thornton, Wilberforce and their nearby colleagues, where they chose the 'right' rector and lived out the evangelical life with their families. But that was different from Clapham as a whole. A better example of the first such suburb is seventeenth-century Clapham, where from 1630 onwards, well before the Plague and the Great Fire, businessmen and their families took retiring houses to be neighbours of people they already had contact with or knew well. These Puritan merchants were very active politically and can well be described as the First Clapham Saints, making later Clapham a well-known centre of Nonconformity, which then declined in the same way as religiosity in the nation as a whole.

(Endnotes)

1. *London Journal, Weekly Journal*, 21 July 1722.

2. Thomas Cox, Anthony Hall and Robert Morden, *Magna Britannica* (1738), p. 346.

3. Drawn by J. Farington, engraved by J.C. Stadler, published by J. and J. Boydell.

4. *Protestant Dissenter's Magazine* (1794), pp. 465–69.

5. David Bogue and James Bennett, *The History of Dissenters, from the Revolution to the Year 1808*, vol. 4 (1812).

6. Ibid.

7. Alan Ruston, 'Philip Furneaux', in *Oxford Dictionary of National Biography*.

8. Ian Bradley, *A Call to Seriousness* (Cox and Wyman, 1976), p. 22.

9. Henry Venn, 'Sketch of the Life of Eling Venn' (1767), MS, Venn Family Papers, University of Birmingham Special Collections Department (and subsequent quotations).

10. John Dolman, *An Account of the Riots Which Were Made at a Dissenting Meeting-house at Clapham in Surry, on Thursday, December 27, 1759, and the Thursday Following, etc.* (1760).

11. Eric Smith, in Clapham Antiquarian Occasional Sheet, February 1968.

12. *Gentleman's Magazine* (1783), p. 1,063.

13. John Thornton, journal, London Metropolitan Archives ACC/2360/001–3.

14. Ibid., 2 and 27 October 1768.

15. The cartoon displays the City businessman and wife with a fashionable black servant but falling out of the carriage because they are unused to travelling in one. The Clapham house demonstrates poor taste by being a mishmash of styles. 'Mr Deputy' was the Common Councilman appointed to be deputy to the Alderman of the ward.

16. Timothy Walker, *Twixt the Commons: The Development of a South London Suburb* (Timothy Walker, 2010); *Survey of London*, vol. 50: *Battersea* (Yale University Press, 2013), pp. 362–84.

17. Sir Richard Colt Hoare, *Book of the Hoare Family* (1819).

18. Daniel Defoe, *A Tour through the Whole Island of Great Britain* (1724), pp. 125–26.

19. Robert Fishman, *Bourgeois Utopias* (Basic Books, 1987), pp. 51–62; Justin Wilford, *Sacred Subdivisions: The Postsuburban Transformation of American Evangelicalism* (New York University Press, 2012), p. 57.

20. William Cowper, *The Task* (1785), I, 40; Varro, *De Re Rustica* (37 BC), III, i.

21. Sir James Stephen, *Edinburgh Review*, vol. 80 (July–October 1844), p. 269.

22. Anne Stott, *Wilberforce: Family and Friends* (Oxford University Press, 2012), p. 52.

23. Henry Thornton, diary, 6 November 1814.

24. William Wilberforce, *A Practical View of the Prevailing Religious System of Professed Christians in the Higher and Middle Classes ... Contrasted with Real Christianity* (1797), p. 91.

25. John Venn, letter to Mrs Elliott, 4 August 1792, Venn Family Papers, University of Birmingham Special Collections Department GB 150 CMS/ACC81.

26. Venn, letter, 1793, ibid.

27. John Venn, *Christian Observer* (July 1805), pp. 402–4.

28. Michael Hennell, *John Venn and the Clapham Sect* (Lutterworth Press, 1958), p. 159.

29. Mrs Hardcastle (ed.), *Life of John, Lord Campbell* (Murray, 1881), p. 32.

30. Venn, letter to Edward Edwards, 3 January 1795, Venn Family Papers.

31. William Vassall, letter to James Wedderburn esq. in Jamaica, 3 April 1793, Sheffield City Library.

32. Ibid., 4 April 1792.

33. Stephen Tomkins, *The Clapham Sect* (Lion, 2010); Milton Klein, *An Amazing Grace* (University Press of the South, 2004); Standish Meacham, *Henry Thornton of Clapham* (Harvard University Press, 1964); Stott, *Wilberforce*.

34. Venn, letter to Edward Edwards, 24 May 1793, Venn Family Papers.

APPENDIX   1

THE SOURCES

T he principal sources are those of the parish itself – the parish registers giving baptisms, marriages and burials; and churchwarden's records, including vestry, accounts and the rates collected for expenditure on either the poor law or church and other spending.[1] The parish register is fairly complete from 1553, although there are some gaps at the end of the seventeenth century. The rate assessments start in 1638, with almost a complete set through to the eighteenth century and later, albeit with larger gaps around 1657–63 and from 1718 to 1745; the accounts and minutes are not always preserved.[2]

The rate assessment contains a list of the occupier of each house (the head of household) with what they owe. A measure of their social status is given by their description as Esq., Mr (or Mrs) or some other title such as Sir, Doctor, Judge, Sheriff or widow. No street names are mentioned, if indeed there were any. These documents are necessarily a better account for the well-off, since the low rateable assessments are not always included, perhaps because they were hard to collect in practice. The rates give an indication of the size of the house and lands, although not whether the value comes from the house or from the land. Even so, there are apparent inconsistencies, most probably reflecting improvements or farmers adjusting their landholding according to their financial position. In practice, discounts were applied for empty houses and sometimes for widows.

Before the Restoration, the rates were constructed to produce a round sum of no more than £10, and the calculations were done very roughly, producing simple sums to collect. There is no strict consistency between what was charged to one property in different years, or even for different calls in the same year. Often all those of the same status were charged the same, whatever their house or land. By the late 1690s there is much more consistency from one year to the next, and the rate was set at a specific poundage, for example at sixpence in the pound on the rateable value. This information can be supplemented by material from maps, deeds, marriage settlements and associated litigation. The seventeenth-century buildings have largely been demolished, but a few prints still exist.

Information from the rates can be backed up by other tax returns, including those in the City of London parishes where Clapham residents had houses, and the poll taxes of the 1690s. One of the most important of these is the Hearth Tax, which was calculated on the number of hearths in a house, a proxy for size. Records survive for Clapham for 1662, 1664 and 1674 and give the name of the occupier as well as the number of hearths. Records also exist for Surrey, Middlesex and the City of London, and have been edited to produce returns for 1666 for the City of London and Middlesex, and 1664 for Surrey.[3]

Without detailed family records or information from parish registers, the main way of elucidating family structures is through the surviving wills and associated litigation. All wills started with the testator's name, occupation or livery company, status and place of residence. A high proportion of wills were made a few weeks or months before death, perhaps whenever a person became seriously ill. Even so, some died intestate.

As now, the wills had to go through a probate process, which was then provided by the Church.[4] These documents were dealt with by the appropriate diocesan court, which in Clapham's case was the diocese of Winchester. Where the testator owned property worth more than £5 or in more than one diocese, the wills were dealt with by the court of the Archbishop of Canterbury.[5] This applies to the Clapham merchants and is also true of many of the village's yeomen, carpenters, gardeners, innkeepers and so on. There are 234 Canterbury wills in total, and another 45 are from the diocese of

Winchester.[6] A substantial fraction of these are the wills of women: 69 from Canterbury and 15 from Winchester.

Some inventories of testators' property exist. One source is the Court of Orphans, which ensured that underage children of a freeman of the City were properly looked after, as well as the widow and anyone else specified in the will. The inventories cover the detailed contents of every room in the house, together with a valuation, as well as details of all outstanding creditors and debtors. Nine of these still exist in more or less detail for Clapham residents.[7] Disputes over wills could also give rise to inventories relating to lawsuits, and a further eight of these exist associated with Clapham residents.[8]

The residents of Clapham were active in business, politics and religion, and this is captured in many documents. They appear in lists of merchants, members of City livery companies, shareholders or officials of various corporate entities, holders of political office and those matriculating at university; they are recorded as signatories of petitions and they appear in a variety of Parliamentary and state papers as well as litigation. Some were well enough known to have ballads written about them or to be praised or damned in pamphlets of the time. The more important are covered in a range of history books.

Nonconformists were discriminated against, if not persecuted, for decades after the Restoration. There was a long tradition of writing about the lives of those involved, both ministers and prominent laymen. Since many of these lived in Clapham, such writing is a major source of material. While a multitude of doctrinal differences are covered, there is much about their lives and personal characteristics, and some funeral sermons give information about the deceased. There are also strong links to the Puritans who went to North America, and they have stimulated an enormous literature, including family histories.

There are a few sources of a personal nature. A letter book of the merchant Michael Mitford is useful, but naturally concentrates on the business side of life;[9] there are extracts from the diary of Joseph Paice,[10] part of a day book by the Nonconformist doctor Henry Sampson[11] and a memoir of his sister by Samuel Crisp.[12] Other diarists record matters of interest about Clapham, most notably Samuel Pepys, who went to live there almost forty years after he had first visited the village,[13] but also John Evelyn,[14] Thomas Juxon,[15] William Nicolson[16] and others. Detailed biographies are rare, but, apart from that of Pepys,[17] include those of Edward Winslow,[18] Joseph Paice[19] and John Loveday.[20] Some letters survive, and the newspapers that appeared towards the end of the seventeenth century include references to Clapham. A few portraits still exist, particularly of Nonconformist ministers.

(Endnotes)

1. London Metropolitan Archives, series P95/TRI1.

2. Ibid.

3. For City/Middlesex, see Matthew P. Davies et al. (eds), *London and Middlesex Hearth Tax*, British Record Society Hearth Tax Series 9 (British Record Society, 2014); for Surrey, see Hearth Tax online, www.hearthtax.org.uk.

4. Tom Arkell et al. (eds), *When Death Do Us Part: Understanding and Interpreting the Probate Records of Early Modern England* (Leopard's Head Press, 2000), passim.

5. National Archives, series PROB 11.

6. London Metropolitan Archives, series DW/PA.05.

7. Ibid., series CLA/002/02/01.

8. National Archives, series PROB 3–5, 16, 22.

9. Michael Mitford, letterbook, London Metropolitan Archives, CLC/521/MS11892A.

10. Anne Manning, *Family Pictures* (Arthur Hall, Virtue and Co., 1861).

11. British Library, Add Ms 4460.

12. Bodleian Library, Rawlinson D 106, ff. 33b, 34.

13. Samuel Pepys, *The Diary of Samuel Pepys*, ed. Robert Latham and William Matthews (University of California Press, 1970–83).

14. John Evelyn, Diaries and Correspondence of John Evelyn, ed. William Bray (H. Colburn, 1882).

15. Keith Lindley and David Scott (eds), *The Journal of Thomas Juxon, 1644–1647* (Royal Historical Society, 1999).

16. Clyve Jones and Geoffrey Holmes (eds), *The London Diaries of William Nicolson, Bishop of Carlisle, 1702–1718* (Oxford University Press, 1985).

17. Claire Tomalin, *Samuel Pepys: The Unequalled Self* (Viking, 2002).

18. Jeremy Bangs, *Pilgrim Edward Winslow: New England's First International Diplomat: A Documentary Biography* (New England Historical and Genealogical Society, 2004).

19. Manning, *Family Pictures*.

20. Sarah Markham, *John Loveday of Caversham, 1711–1789: The Life and Tours of an Eighteenth-century Onlooker* (M. Russell, 1984).

APPENDIX 2

CHRONOLOGY

England		Clapham
		1580 Benjamin Clerke moves to Manor House
London has 200,000 inhabitants	1600	
		1615 Francis Taylor becomes rector of Clapham
		1616 Henry Atkins buys Manor House
Voyage of *Mayflower*	1620	
		1624 Sir Robert Heath leases Manor House
Charles I becomes king	1625	
Massachusetts Bay Company formed	1628	
		1631 Francis Bridges moves to Clapham
		1633 James Sherley and John Beauchamp move to Clapham
Outbreak of Plague in London	1636	1636 Plague in Clapham
		1640 William Courten moves to Clapham
Additional Sea Adventure to Ireland	1642	1642 Fourteen Clapham residents subscribe to Irish Adventure
First Civil War	1642	1642 Taylor succeeded as rector by John Arthur
Solemn League and Covenant signed	1643	
Ordinance for demolishing monuments	1644	1644 Parish signs Covenant
		1645 Font, raised altar and Communion rails removed
Charles I captured	1647	1647 Lawrence Bromfield sent to Tower
Putney debates	1647	
Pride's Purge and Rump Parliament	1648	1648 School built
Second Civil War	1648	

Charles I executed	1649	1649	Edward Winslow comes to Clapham
Commonwealth	1649	1649	Churchwardens abolished in Clapham
Society for the Propagation of the Gospel to Indians	1649	1649	Clapham raises £90 for Society
		1650	Moyer, Molins and Winslow on Compounding Commission
Battle of Worcester	1651		
First Dutch war	1652–54	1652	Richard Salwey Commissioner for the Navy
End of Rump Parliament	1653	1653	Extension of church and Frost chapel
Barebones Parliament	1653	Secular weddings in Clapham	1653–57
Death of Oliver Cromwell	1658		
Return of Rump Parliament	1659		
Restoration of Monarchy	1660	1660	Salwey and William Sydenham sent to Tower
		1660	Dennis Gauden becomes Victualler to the Navy
Corporation Act	1661		
Uniformity Act (ejection of Nonconformists)	1662	1662	Samuel Moyer sent to Tower
		1663	Salwey sent to Tower
		1663	Arthur succeeded as rector by John Gurgany
Conventicle Act	1664	1664	Gauden rebuilds Clapham Place
The Plague	1665	1665	East India Company meets at Clapham
Five Mile Act	1665		
Great Fire	1666		
First Test Act	1673		
		1675	Gurgany succeeded as rector by John Savill
		1677	William Hewer buys Clapham Place
		1677	Philip Lamb arrives as Nonconformist minister
Popish Plot	1679		
Exclusion Crisis	1679–82		
		1680	First daily stagecoach to Clapham
		1684	Roger L'Estrange describes Clapham as 'Whig Warren'
Accession of James II	1685		
Monmouth rebellion	1685		
Glorious Revolution	1688	1688	Death of Gauden
Toleration Act	1689	1689	Samuel Pepys and Hewer arrested
		1689	Lamb succeeded as rector by Edward Grace

		1689 Samuel Crisp publishes his father's sermons
Nonconformist common fund formed	1691	1691 Dame Rebecca Atkins installs memorials in church
		1693 William Lethieullier moves into Peter Daniel's Great House
Bank of England created	1694	
Nonconformist Fund splits into two	1695	1695 Arthur Shallett treasurer of Congregational fund
London has 575,000 inhabitants	1700	1700 Argument over appointment of schoolmaster
		1701 Pepys moves to Clapham Place
		1703 Death of Pepys
		1706 First terraced houses
		1706 Savill succeeded as rector by Nicholas Brady
		1714–20 Terrace of twenty houses built
		1715 Death of Hewer
		1715 Grace succeeded by Moses Lowman

APPENDIX 3

BIBLIOGRAPHY

Allen, Paul, *A Christian Rosenkreutz Anthology* (Virginia, 2007)

Anderson, Robert, *The Great Migration: Immigrants to New England, 1634–1635*, (Boston, 1996–2011)

Andrews, Kenneth, *Ships, Money, and Politics* (Cambridge, 1991)

Anon., *A Pair of Spectacles for the City*, 4 December 1647, British Library, E.419/9

——, *A Case for the City Spectacles*, 6 January 1648, British Library, E.422/7

——, *Advice to the Liverymen of London in their Choice of a Lord Mayor* (1692), British Library, 74/L.R.404.n.5

Archer, John, *Architecture and Suburbia* (Minnesota, 2005)

Arkell, Tom, et al. (eds), *When Death Do Us Part: Understanding and Interpreting the Probate Records of Early Modern England* (London, 2000)

Astrom, Sven Erik, *From Cloth to Iron* (Helsingfors, 1963)

Aylmer, G.E., *Essays in the Economic and Social History of Tudor and Stuart England*, ed. E.J. Fisher (London, 1961)

——, *The State's Servants* (London, 1973)

Babington, Abraham, *An Answer to a Discourse intituled, Truth it's manifest, &* (London, 1648)

Baker, T. F. T., (ed.), Victoria County History. Middlesex: Volume 10: Hackney (London, 1995)

——, and Elrington, C. R., (eds.), Victoria County History Middlesex Vol. 6 (London, 1980)

Bangs, Jeremy, *Pilgrim Edward Winslow* (Boston, 2004)

Beier, A.L., and R. Finlay (eds.), *The Making of the Metropolis* (London, 1986)

Bell, W.G., *The Great Fire of London in 1666* (London, 1923)

Birken, William, 'The Dissenting Tradition in English Medicine of the Seventeenth and Eighteenth Centuries', *Medical History*, vol. 39, no. 2 (April 1995), p. 198

Bland, John, 'The Humble Remonstrance of John Bland of London Merchant', *Virginia Magazine of History and Biography*, vol. 1 (1894), p. 144

Bogue, David, and James Bennett, *The History of Dissenters, from the Revolution to the Year 1808* (1812)

Boulton, Jeremy, *Neighbourhood and Society* (Cambridge, 1987)

——, 'London 1540–1700', in P. Clark (ed.), *Cambridge History of Britain*, vol. 2 (Cambridge, 2000)

Bowett, Adam, *English Furniture* (London, 1988)

Bradford, William, *Of Plymouth Plantation*, ed. Samuel Morison (New York, 1952)

Bradley, Ian, *A Call to Seriousness* (London, 1976)

Brenner, Robert, *Merchants and Revolution* (London, 2003)

Brown, John, *The English Puritans* (London, 1998)

Bunker, Nick, *Making Haste from Babylon* (London, 2011)

Burnet, Gilbert, *Burnet's History of My Own Time*, ed. M.J. Routh (Oxford, 1823)

Calamy, Edward, et al., *A Compleat Collection of Farewell Sermons* (London, 1663)

Capp, Bernard, *Cromwell's Navy* (London, 1992)

——, *England's Culture Wars* (Oxford, 2012)

Cherry, Bridget, and Nikolaus Pevsner, *London 2: South* (London, 1983)

Cleal, Edward, *History of Congregationalism in Surrey* (London, 1909)

Coates, Ben, *The Impact of the English Civil War on the Economy of London 1642–50* (London, 2004)

Cowper, William, *Retirement* (London, 1782)

——, *The Task* (1785)

Cox, Thomas, Anthony Hall and Robert Morden, *Magna Britannica* (1738)

Dale, Rev. T.C., *Clapham and the Clapham Sect* (London, 1927)

——, *History of Clapham* (London, 1927)

Davids, Rev. T.W., *Annals of Evangelical Nonconformity in Essex* (London, 1887)

Davies, K.G., *The Royal Africa Company* (London, 1957)

Davies, Matthew P., et al. (eds), *London and Middlesex Hearth Tax*, British Record Society Hearth Tax Series 9 (2014)

Davis, Lloyd, 'Women's Wills in Early Modern England', in Nancy Wright et al. (eds), *English Women and Property* (Toronto, 2004)

De Krey, Gary S., *London and the Restoration 1659–1683* (Cambridge, 2005)

——, *A Fractured Society* (Oxford, 1985)

Defoe, Daniel, *A Tour through the Whole Island of Great Britain* (London, 1724)

Delaune, Thomas, *The Present State of London: Or, Memorials Comprehending a Full and Succinct Account of the Ancient and Modern State Thereof* (London, 1681)

Durston, Christopher, *The Family in the English Revolution* (Oxford, 1989)

Earle, Peter, *The Making of the English Middle Class* (London, 1989)

Evelyn, John, *Fumifugium* (London, 1661)

——, *Diaries and Correspondence of John Evelyn*, ed. William Bray (London, 1882)

Finlay, R., A.P. Roger and Beatrice Robina Shearer, 'Population Growth and Suburban Expansion' in *London 1500–1700: The Making of the Metropolis* (London, 1986)

Fishman, Robert, *Bourgeois Utopias* (New York, 1987)

Galley, C., et al., *Infant Mortality: A Continuing Social Problem* (London, 2007)

Gauci, Perry, *The Politics of Trade* (Oxford 2001)

——, *Emporium of the World* (London, 2007)

Gentles, Ian, 'The Sale of Bishops' Lands in the English Revolution, 1646–1660', *English Historical Review*, vol. 95, no. 376 (July 1980), pp. 573–96

Gerhold, Dorian, *Putney and Roehampton in 1665*, Wandsworth Historical Society Occasional Paper 16 (2007)

——, 'London's Suburban Villas and Mansions 1660–1830', *London Journal*, vol. 34 (2009)

Glanville, Gordon, and Philippa Glanville, in Mireille Gallinou (ed.), *City Merchants and the Arts 1670–1720* (London, 2004)

Glass, Henry, *The Barbone Parliament* (London, 1899)

Gordon, Alexander, *Freedom after Ejection* (Manchester, 1917)

Granshaw, Lindsay, and Roy Porter (eds), *The Hospital in History* (London, 1989)

Grassby, Richard, *The Business Community of Seventeenth-Century England* (Cambridge, 1995)

——, *Kinship and Capitalism* (Cambridge, 2001)

Green, Michael, *Historic Clapham* (London 2008)

Grover, J.W., *Old Clapham* (London, 1887)

Hardcastle, Mrs (ed.), *Life of John, Lord Campbell* (London, 1881)

Harris, Tim, *Revolution* (London, 2006)

Hennell, Michael, *John Venn and the Clapham Sect* (London, 1958)

Hindle, Steve, in Alexandra Shepard and Philip Withington (eds), *Communities in Early Modern England* (Manchester, 2000)

——, *On the Parish?* (Oxford, 2004)

Hoare, Richard Colt, *Book of the Hoare Family* (London, 1819)

Hollond, John, *Two Discourses of the Navy* (1638 and 1659)

Hooke, Robert, *Philosophical Experiments and Observations* (London, 1726)

Hughes, Ann, *Gangraena and the Struggle for the English Revolution* (Oxford, 2004)

Hunter, J. (ed.), *Letters of Eminent Men* (London, 1832)

Jones, Clyve, and Geoffrey Holmes (eds), *The London Diaries of William Nicolson, Bishop of Carlisle, 1702–1718* (Oxford, 1985)

Keates, Jonathan, *Purcell* (New England, 1996)

Keene, Derek, in Lena Cowen Orlin (ed.), *Material London* (Philadelphia, 2000)

Kellaway, William, *The New England Company* (London, 1961)

Kippis, A., *Biographica Britannica* (London, 1778)

Klein, Milton, *An Amazing Grace* (New Orleans, 2004)

Knight, Caroline, *London's Country Houses* (London, 2009)

Knights, Mark, *Politics and Opinion in Crisis 1678–81* (Cambridge, 1994)

Lamb, Philip, *Funeral Sermon for Mrs Sarah Lye* (London, 1679)

Lander, S.J., *Sussex Archaeological Society Newsletter*, vol. 15 (1975), p. 68

Lang, R.G., 'The Greater Merchants of London in the Early Seventeenth Century' (D.Phil. diss., Oxford University, 1963)

Laslett, Peter, *The World We Have Lost* (London, 2005)

Launsbery, R.G., *British Fisheries at Newfoundland* (New Haven, 1934)

L'Estrange, Sir Roger, *The Observator* (London, 1684)

Levett, F. Reynolds, *History of Clapham Congregational Church* (London, 1912)

Lindley, Keith, and David Scott (eds), *The Journal of Thomas Juxon, 1644–1647* (London, 1999)

Lindley, Kenneth, *Popular Politics and Religion* (London, 1997)

Liu, Tai, *Puritan London* (London, 1986)

Loomes, Brian, in *Clocks Magazine* (August 2000), p. 26

Lovell, Percy, and William McBeath Marcham (eds), *Survey of London*, vol. 19: St Pancras (London, 1936)

Ludlow, Edward, *Memoirs* (London, 1698)

Lye, Thomas, *Funeral Sermon for Mr W. Hiett* (London, 1681)

Macaulay, Thomas, *History of England* (London, 1848)

McKellar, Elizabeth, *Landscapes of London* (Yale, 2013)

Malcolm, Corey, 'The Iron Bilboes of the *Henrietta Marie*', *The Navigator: Newsletter of the Mel Fisher Maritime Heritage Society*, vol. 13, no. 10 (October 1998)

Manning, Anne, *Family Pictures* (London, 1861)

Markham, Sarah, *John Loveday of Caversham* (London, 1984)

——, 'The Lethieullier Tomb at Clapham', *London and Middlesex Archaeology Transactions*, vol. 35 (1984), p. 135

Matthews, A.G., *Calamy Revised* (Oxford, 1934)

Meacham, Standish, *Henry Thornton of Clapham* (Harvard, 1964)

Moore, Susan, *Pilgrims: New World Settlers and the Call of Home* (Yale, 2007)

Moote, A. Lloyd, and Dorothy Moote, *The Great Plague* (London, 2004)

Morison, Samuel, *The Founding of Harvard College* (Harvard, 1963)

Murphy, Anne L., 'Learning the Business of Banking: The Management of the Bank of England's First Tellers', *Business History*, vol. 52, no. 1 (2010), p. 150

Newcome, Henry, *Autobiography* (Manchester, 1852)

Noonan, John Jr, *Bribes* (London, 1984)

North, Roger, *Of Building* (London, 1695)

Nourse, Timothy, *Campania Foelix* (London, 1700)

Ogilby, John, *Britannia* (London, 1675)

Oppenheim, M.A., *A History of the Administration of the Royal Navy* (London, 1896)

Oxford Dictionary of National Biography (Oxford, 2008)

Parker, Geoffrey, *Global Crisis: War, Climate Change and Catastrophe in the Seventeenth Century* (Yale, 2013)

Patrick, Symon, *Collected Works* (Oxford, 1858)

Penn, William, *Considerations Moving to a Toleration and Liberty of Conscience* (London, 1685)

Penny, Mrs Frank, *Fort St George, Madras* (London, 1900)

Pepys, Samuel, *The Diary of Samuel Pepys*, ed. Robert Latham and William Matthews (Berkeley, 1970–83)

——, *The Letters of Samuel Pepys, 1656–1703*, ed. Guy de la Bedoyere, (London, 2006)

Percy Society, *Early English Poetry, Ballads and Popular Literature of the Middle Ages*, vol. 4 (London, 1861)

Peter, Hugh, *Last Reports of English Wars* (London, 1646)

Pincus, Steve, *Protestantism and Patriotism* (Cambridge, 2002)

——, *1688: The First Modern Revolution* (New Haven, 2009)

Pinto, Vivian de Sola, *Peter Sterry: Platonist and Puritan* (Cambridge, 2013)

Prendergast, J.P., *The Cromwellian Settlement of Ireland* (New York, 1868)

Protestant Dissenter's Magazine (1794), pp. 465–69

Richardson, John, *Highgate: Its History since the Fifteenth Century* (London, 1983)

Roberts, Stephen K., 'Protecting the Rump', *History Today*, vol. 53, no. 5 (May 2003), p. 92

Rudolf, Robert de Montjoie, *Clapham before 1700* (London, 1904)

Rugg, Thomas, *The Diurnal 1659–61*, ed. W.L. Sachse (London, 1961)

Salwey, Thomas, *Occasional Poems: With a Memoir of the Author, and a Selection from Old Family Letters* (London, 1882)

Shaw, R.A., R.D. Gwynn and P. Thomas, *Huguenots in Wandsworth* (London, 1985)

Sheppard, Francis, *London: A History* (Oxford, 1998)

Smith, Eric, *Clapham Society Newsletters*

——, *Clapham* (Lambeth, 1976)

Smith, John, *Memoirs of Samuel Pepys* (Cambridge, 1828)

Spraggon, Julie, *Puritan Iconoclasm during the English Civil War* (London, 2004)

Stone, Lawrence, *The Family, Sex and Marriage 1500–1800* (London, 1977)

Stott, Anne, *Wilberforce* (Oxford, 2012)

Strype, John, *A Survey of the Cities of London and Westminster* (London, 1720)

Taylor, J.G., *Our Lady of Battersey* (London, 1925)

Thom, Colin (ed.), *Survey of London*, vol. 50: *Battersea* (London, 2013)

Thompson, F.M.L., *Hampstead* (London, 1974)

Tindall, Gillian, *The Fields Beneath* (London, 1977)

Tomalin, Claire, *Samuel Pepys: The Unequalled Self* (London, 2002)

Tomkins, Stephen, *The Clapham Sect* (London, 2010)

Toon, Peter, *Puritans and Calvanism: The Crispian Controversy* (Swengel, 1973)

Townshend, Dorothy, *The Life and Times of Endymion Porter* (London, 1897)

Underdown, David, *Pride's Purge* (Oxford, 1985)

Varro, *De Re Rustica* (37 BC)

Venn, John, *Christian Observer* (July 1805), pp. 402–4

Voitle, Robert, *The Third Earl of Shaftesbury* (Baton Rouge, 1984)

Wagner, Gillian, *Thomas Coram Gent, 1668–1751* (London, 2004)

Walker, Timothy, *Twixt the Commons: The Development of a South London Suburb* (London, 2010)

Walwyn, William, *Walwyn's Just Defence* (London, 1649)

Ward, Joseph, *Culture, Faith and Philanthropy* (London, 2014)

Warren, Ian, in Davies, *London and Middlesex Hearth Tax*

Waterhouse, Ellis, *Painting in Britain 1530–1790* (London, 1994)

Weyman, H.T., *Shropshire Archaeological and Natural History Society*, vol. 10 (1898), p. 48

Wilberforce, William, *A Practical View of the Prevailing Religious System of Professed Christians in the Higher and Middle Classes ... Contrasted with Real Christianity* (London, 1797)

Wilford, Justin, *Sacred Subdivisions: The Postsuburban Transformation of American Evangelicalism* (New York, 2012)

Wilks, Michael, *Gunpowder Mills Study Letter* (November 1990), pp. 10–11

Wilson, Alyson (ed.), *The Buildings of Clapham* (Clapham Society, 2000)

Winship, George, *The New England Company of 1649 and John Eliot* (Boston, 1920)

Wood, Alfred, *A History of the Levant Company* (London, 1964)

Wood, Anthony, *Athenae Oxonienses*, vol. 3 (London, 1691)

Wykes, David, '"The Minister's Calling": The Preparation and Qualification of Candidates for the Presbyterian Ministry in England, 1660–89', *Dutch Review of Church History*, vol. 83 (2002), p. 272

INDEX OF CLAPHAM RESIDENTS

Sometime Clapham residents before 1660

Clapham residents after 1660, before 1685

Residents after 1685, before 1720

Selected Clapham residents after 1720

INDEX